Communicable Diseases in Developing Countries

Communicable Diseases in Developing Countries

Stopping the Global Epidemics of HIV/AIDS, Tuberculosis, Malaria and Diarrhea

John Malcolm Dowling

and

Chin-Fang Yap

palgrave
macmillan

First published 2014 by
PALGRAVE MACMILLAN

Palgrave Macmillan in the UK is an imprint of Macmillan Publishers Limited, registered in England, company number 785998, of Houndmills, Basingstoke, Hampshire RG21 6XS.

Palgrave Macmillan in the US is a division of St Martin's Press LLC, 175 Fifth Avenue, New York, NY 10010.

Palgrave Macmillan is the global academic imprint of the above companies and has companies and representatives throughout the world.

Palgrave® and Macmillan® are registered trademarks in the United States, the United Kingdom, Europe and other countries.

ISBN 978–1–137–35477–8

This book is printed on paper suitable for recycling and made from fully managed and sustained forest sources. Logging, pulping and manufacturing processes are expected to conform to the environmental regulations of the country of origin.

A catalogue record for this book is available from the British Library.

Library of Congress Cataloging-in-Publication Data
Dowling, J. Malcolm (John Malcolm), author.
Communicable diseases in developing countries : stopping the global epidemics of HIV/AIDS, tuberculosis, malaria and diarrhea / John Malcolm Dowling, Chin-Fang Yap.
p. ; cm.
ISBN 978–1–137–35477–8
I. Yap, Chin-Fang, author. II. Title.
[DNLM: 1. Communicable Diseases. 2. Developing Countries.
3. Communicable Disease Control. 4. HIV Infections.
5. Malaria. 6. Tuberculosis. WC 100]
RA643
362.1969009172′4—dc23 2014024166

Transferred to Digital Printing in 2014

Contents

Figures and Tables

Figures

Tables

Acronyms

ACT	Artemisinin Combinational Therapy
AIDS	Acquired Immunodeficiency Syndrome
API	Annual Parasite Index
ARV	Antiretroviral
ART	Antiretroviral Therapy
BCG	Bacillus Calmette–Guérin
CDC	Center for Disease Control and Prevention
CPT	Co-trimoxazole Prophylaxis
DDT	Dichlorodiphenyltrichloroethane
DOT	Directly Observed Treatment
DOTS	Directly Observed Treatment Short-Course
EIR	Entomological Inoculation Rate
EMS	Electronic Medical record System
GDP	Gross Domestic Product
GEMS	Global Enteric Multicenter Study
GFATM	Global Fund to Fight AIDS, Tuberculosis and Malaria
GLS	Generalized Least Squares
GMAP	Global Malaria Action Plan
GNI	Gross National Income
HDI	Human Development Index
HIV	Human Immunodeficiency Virus
ICF	Intensified Case Finding
INH	Isoniazid
IPM	International Partnership for Microbicides
IPT	Isoniazid Preventive Treatment
IRS	Indoor Residential Spraying
MDA	Mass Drug Administration
MDG	Millennium Development Goals
MDR-TB	Multidrug-Resistant Tuberculosis
MSM	Men Who Have Sex With Other Men
ORT	Oral Rehydration Therapy
PEPFAR	President's Emergency Plan for AIDS Relief
PPP	Purchasing Power Parity
RDTs	Rapid Diagnostic Tests
SP	Sulfadoxine-Pyrimethamine

STD	Sexually Transmitted Disease
STIs	Sexually Transmitted Infections
TB	Tuberculosis
UN	United Nations
UNAIDS	Joint United Nations Programme on HIV/AIDS
UNDP	United Nations Development Programme
UNICEF	United Nations International Children's Emergency Fund
USAID	United States Agency for International Development
VC	Vectorial Capacity
VCT	Voluntary Counseling and Testing sites
WHO	World Health Organization
WHO-CMH	World Health Organization–Commission on Macroeconomics and Health
XDR-TB	Extensively Drug-Resistant Tuberculosis

1
Introduction

Health is the most significant determinant of well-being among developing country respondents in a recently published monograph by Dowling and Yap (2013). The book analyzes poverty and well-being in developing countries and reports a wide-ranging statistical analysis of the determinants of well-being in Africa, Asia and Latin America. The book draws on a database of surveys of respondents in these three regions conducted by the World Value Survey team over the past three decades. Drawing on this analysis, the current research explores the experience of developing countries in addressing the ongoing challenges of providing reliable and affordable healthcare. Particular reference is made to the contagious diseases of tuberculosis, malaria, Human Immunodeficiency Virus/Acquired Immunodeficiency Syndrome (HIV/AIDS) and cholera, and related intestinal maladies such as diarrhea. In 2001, these four diseases accounted for the bulk of the disease burden facing developing countries, resulting in over 7.2 million fatalities each year (2.5 million from HIV/AIDS, 1.8 million from diarrheal diseases, 1.6 million from tuberculosis and 1.2 million from malaria) and countless years of suffering (Lopez et al., 2006). With the exception of HIV, the bulk of deaths were among infants and children under five years of age. By 2011, despite the recent advancements in healthcare, the fatalities faced were still close to five million each year in developing countries (out of which 1.6 million deaths were from HIV/AIDS, 1.8 million from diarrheal diseases, 0.8 million from tuberculosis and 0.6 million from malaria). According to the baseline scenario forecast for 2030, World Health Organisation (WHO) predicted that fatalities in developing countries due to HIV/AIDS and diarrheal diseases would remain around 1.7 and 1.5 million, respectively. There is a possibility of a decline in deaths from tuberculosis and malaria – to

0.5 and 0.3 million, respectively. It is to be noted that WHO has revised upward its 2030 estimates of total deaths from its original 2008 study, particularly that of fatalities due to diarrheal diseases.

A number of markers have been suggested to measure the progress that has been made in addressing the performance of health systems in countries around the world. Life expectancy, infant mortality and more aggregative measures such as the human development index of the United Nations (UN) have all been used as performance yardsticks. Other, more specific measures, such as the incidence of TB, malaria and HIV, have been developed to track more specific aspects of healthcare systems. Using life expectancy in years, global health has been tracked by economic historians and other researchers going back to the Middle Ages and even earlier.

Data from antiquity and through the Middle Ages suggest that life expectancy did not increase with time, remaining at around 40 years of age or so through the Middle Ages. This was primarily because many died as infants or children. If one survived to become an adult, life expectancy was longer at about 50 years of age in the 15th and 16th centuries, and this didn't change much until the late 18th and 19th centuries. With the advent of the industrial revolution, discoveries in medicine and technological developments, life expectancy began to increase in Europe during the 18th and 19th centuries. By the dawn of the 21st century, life expectancy in Northern Europe and Japan approached 80 years and the rest of the industrial world was not far behind. Jamison et al. (2006) calculated that from around 1840 the maximum life expectancy increased by about two and a half years per decade for 160 years. Table 1.1 adopted from Jamison et al. shows that life expectancy continued to accelerate at a rate of four to nine years per decade, with China posting a whopping 11 years per decade between 1960 and 1990. However, not all countries and regions shared in this sustained increase in life expectancy. After World War II, the spread of diseases in Africa and Asia slowed the increase in life expectancy and introduced further roadblocks in raising health performance.

Progress in the developing regions of Latin America (four years per decade), South Asia (4.7 years per decade) and Sub-Saharan Africa (3.3 years per decade) was slower. In the following decade (1990–2002), the growth in life expectancy slowed further and even fell in Sub-Saharan Africa as a result of the spread of HIV/AIDS. Internal differentials in the delivery of health services within countries have also probably widened, although data are spotty. The hill tribe peoples in Southeast Asia and the poorer provinces in sections of India and inland China have been

Table 1.1 Levels and changes in life expectancy, 1960–2011

Region	Life expectancy in years				Rate of change in years per decade		
	1960	1990	2002	2011	1960–1990	1990–2002	2003–2011
East Asia and Pacific	39	67	70	75	9.3	2.5	2.0
China	36	69	71	75	11	1.7	2.0
Europe and Central Asia		69	69	76		0	3.4
Latin America and Caribbean	56	68	71	74	4	2.5	2.4
Middle East and North Africa	47	64	68	72	5.7	4.2	2.1
South Asia	44	58	63	66	4.7	4.2	3.2
India	44	59	64	66	5	4.6	3.3
Sub-Saharan Africa	40	50	46	56	3.3	−3.3	6.0
High income countries	69	76	78	79	2.3	1.7	2.8

Sources: Jamison et al. (2006, table 1.1) and World Bank (2013).

particularly affected, partly as a result of discrimination against minorities and also as a result of the continued concentration of medical personnel in urban areas. "Indigenous people everywhere probably lead far less healthy lives than do others in their respective countries." (Jamison et al., p. 6). During 2003–2011, there were improvements in life expectancy, particularly in Sub-Saharan Africa. However, life expectancy for Sub-Saharan Africa still remains lowest among all the regions.

This is not to say that some of the less affluent countries have been unable to increase life expectancy and other health indicators to a level nearly comparable with countries that have very high levels of income. The 1985 Rockefeller Foundation published the study "Good Health at Low Cost" and presented the experiences of countries such as China, Sri Lanka, Costa Rica and the Indian State of Kerala as shining examples of how countries with fairly low income levels could achieve relative good health performance compared to their high income counterparts. Despite modest levels of per capita income and health spending as a percentage of Gross Domestic Product (GDP) (Cuba and Costa Rica being exceptions with regard to health spending), they have attained life expectancy of 70 years and higher, literacy of over 90% as well as low levels of infant mortality and incidence of HIV and TB. Recently, a revisit of the same theme by Balabanova et al. (2013) provided five new country examples, namely, Bangladesh, Ethiopia, Kyrgyzstan, Thailand and the Indian state of Tamil Nadu, which had achieved substantial improvements in health or access to services or implemented innovative health approaches (see Table 1.2 for selected indicators for these countries).

These are by no means isolated historical accidents. In Europe, life expectancy and health outcomes improved rapidly without any sustained upward push in per capita income (see Easterlin, 1996 and Easterlin and Angelescu, 2012). One of the lessons to be learned from these case studies and the European experience is that similar strides can be taken by countries in the developing world by adopting the policies and practices suggested by the "best practice" experiences of China, Costa Rica, Sri Lanka and Cuba. Furthermore, there are a variety of powerful low-cost options available that can improve health and raise life expectancy, which make for a quality life with less pain and suffering. We will delve into greater details of such country experiences and the lessons that can be learnt in subsequent chapters.

It should also be noted that there are a number of measurable economic benefits of better health outcomes. The first of these is the impact on the growth of per capita income. The direct benefits of better health

Table 1.2 Selected indicators for China, Cuba, Sri Lanka, Costa Rica, Kerala (India), Tamil Nadu (India), Bangladesh, Ethiopia, Kyrgyzstan and Thailand

Country/Region	GDP per capita (PPP), 2012	Health spending as % of GDP 2011	Infant mortality 2012	Life expectancy 2011	HDI rank (level) 2012	Adult literacy rate 2011	Prevalence of HIV, total (% of population ages 15–49) 2012	Incidence of TB cases (per 100,000 pop) 2012
China	7958	5.2	12.1	75.0	101 (0.699)	95.1 (2010)	0.1	73
Cuba	9900	10.0	4.3	78.9	59 (0.78)	99.8	0.1	9.3
Sri Lanka	5384	3.4	8.3	73.9	92 (0.715)	91.2 (2010)	0.1	66
Costa Rica	11156	10.9	8.6	79.5	62 (0.773)	96.3	0.3	11
Kerala (India)	4500 (est)	na	12.0	74.0 (2006–2010)	na	94.0	0.26	275 (2005–2006)
Tamil Nadu (India)	3522 (2010)	4.0 (2006–2010)	21.0	66.2 (2006–2010)	na	80.1	0.34 (2005–2006)	508 (2005–2006)
Bangladesh	1622	3.7	33.1	69.9	146 (0.515)	57.7	0.1	225
Ethiopia	971	4.7	46.5	62.3	173 (0.396)	39.0 (2007)	1.3	247
Kyrgyzstan	2077	6.5	23.6	69.6	125 (0.622)	99.2 (2009)	0.3	141
Thailand	8463	4.1	11.4	74.0	103 (0.69)	93.5 (2005)	1.1	119

Sources: World Bank (2013), WHO (2013), UNDP (2013) and Government of India (2013).

are evident in higher productivity of healthy versus unhealthy workers. Also, healthy workers contribute to tax revenues and help expand desirable government programs including healthcare. So there is a powerful virtuous cycle of better health and higher incomes at work. Conversely, those who are ill are not so productive and make fewer contributions to the public purse. Rather they draw down revenue by requiring more health benefits.

There are also subtle benefits of better health, particularly on infant mortality and the impact on demography. As birth rates adjust to increased survival rate that goes with increased life expectancy and lower infant mortality, a rapid demographic transition occurs from high birth and death rates to much lower birth and death rates. In this transition, the death rate falls more rapidly than the birth rate, resulting in rapid population growth and shifts in the age distribution of populations. There are more entrants into the labor force as the population surges and before family size adjusts to a larger and slowly aging population. The baby boom that occurs during this demographic transition to low population growth and a lower death rate (longer life expectancy) creates a hump in the age distribution. There are now more workers relative to the young and the elderly. This results in a temporary boost in aggregate supply and demand and perhaps more rapid growth as aggregate spending increases relative saving. As life expectancy increases and people can rely more on living longer, opportunities to plan for retirement arise along with saving for children's education. These new savings help to fund investment opportunities that arise as incomes grow further.

There are quantitative estimates of how an increase in life expectancy makes its way through these various channels to impact living standards. Bloom, Canning and Sevilla (2004) estimate that one year of extra life expectancy raises GDP per person by 4% in the long run, while Jamison, Lau and Wang (2005) estimate that reductions in adult mortality explain 10–15% of global economic growth that occurred between 1960 and 1990. Furthermore, there is some evidence that better health matters more for poor countries compared with richer countries (see Bhargava et al., 2001). Putting all of these evidences together suggests that health and income growth are positively related over time, with some lags in adjustment and the possibility that causation runs in both directions.

Consider also the impact of poor health and the ebb and flow of epidemics on well-being and economic activity. From an analysis of historical trends, it is clear that epidemics resulted in economic, social and psychological devastation. The bubonic plague wiped out an estimated 30–60% of the population in Europe in the 14th century and over 25% of the world's population. An estimated 100 million or more lives were lost as global population fell from an estimated 350–250 million. Because the plague killed such a large proportion of the working population, some economic historians believe that the rise in wages that resulted from a shortage of healthy workers was a stimulus to economic development. However, the agriculture sector had difficulties as cultivation and harvesting became difficult. The economies of the world took many generations to regain the standard of living and vibrancy that was lost as a result of the Black Death.

Smallpox killed an estimated 400,000 people in Europe during the last part of the 18th century and, of those infected, between 20% and 60% died. Moreover, the fatality rate was an estimated 80% among children. In total, between 300 and 500 million people died in the 20th century.

Returning to the subject of economic growth, over five decades ago Robert Solow (1956) demonstrated that increases in labor and capital alone are not sufficient to explain the increase in total output. He called what is left out as technical progress. It turns out that there can be two kinds of technical progress. The first is that which is embodied within the factors of production manifesting as better educated and skilled workers and more efficient capital. The second is the way in which the factors of production are combined to create new products through innovative management of the factors of production.

And technical progress has also taken place in health. The germ theory of disease played a central role in developing sanitary conditions that reduced mortality and morbidity while a variety of developments in medicine resulted in vaccines that have eliminated many diseases that were often fatal in the past. Practical implementation of these developments in medicine and health do not depend solely on the level of income of the country. Vaccines are available globally as are medications that have been developed to treat a variety of diseases. This is why the high health performers displayed in Table 1.2 were able to develop such effective health systems. In these countries the emphasis has been on prevention rather than cure. This is achieved by developing health infrastructure that is able to receive and treat large numbers of patients in a widespread and accessible system of healthcare locations. The advantage of building up a system of diagnostic and treatment centers is its flexibility in dealing with a wide variety of diseases. Such a system can be dynamic and responsive to changing patterns of disease, new treatment protocols and an ability to keep track of the flow of patients and treatments.

Children's health is an important example of how an efficiently run health delivery system can address a variety of issues with this focus. Stillbirths and neonatal deaths account for about half of deaths of children under five. Tetanus, pneumonia, diarrhea and asphyxia are major causes of death, all of which are easy to control in a favorable treatment environment. Low birth weight is more difficult to deal with, but is still manageable within a sterile environment. Care of the newborn, including cleaning, drying and warming and exclusive breast-feeding in the early days (assuming mother does not have HIV) along with appropriate nutrition for the mother are also important. Prevention of malaria is also critical in high infestation intensity environments. Diarrhea, malaria and HIV are addressed in more detail in later chapters. The key takeaway is that China, Cuba, Sri Lanka, Costa Rica, Thailand and Kerala (noted in Table 1.2) have low infant mortality rates, suggesting that their health systems are efficiently run with emphasis on prevention of diseases.

The subject of infant and under-five mortality highlights an issue that has been discussed by development economists and health professions. Some highlight the importance for greater health funding and a focused effort on reducing infant mortality. This is the approach adopted by Jeffrey Sachs and his colleagues at World Health Organization-Commission on Macroeconomics and Health (WHO-CMH). The other approach stresses the importance of the capacity and organization of the healthcare system itself. This latter approach seems to be what has been working for the countries and states highlighted in Table 1.2 for their relatively better health outcomes. Budgets are modest in relation to GDP, per capita incomes are not high and yet they have done a superb job in delivering health services that might well be the envy of countries with much higher levels of per capita income.

We will come back to this issue in our discussions on communicable diseases in chapters to follow. In the meantime, consider which of the four diseases has the biggest mortality impact and where is it? The answer is that for three of the four diseases, excluding HIV, the impact is primarily on the young. About 60% of those who die from malaria are under five years old. For cholera and diarrhea, the percentage of child deaths is even higher and from TB, over half, and perhaps more. Once deaths from transmission from mother to child are eliminated, most deaths in other age groups will result from HIV.

What factors are most responsible for progress in increasing life expectancy in the 21st century? And what factors are holding back progress? To explore these questions, we developed a statistical model with life expectancy as the dependent variable and a variety of explanatory variables relating to health and income. The model is based on results for 187 countries from 1995 to 2012 totaling over 2200 observations, and the results highlight the importance of infant mortality, gross national income per capita and AIDS mortality. In this study, we utilized generalized least squared regression method. The usual ordinary least squares method tends to assign equal weight or importance to each observation, and it does not make use of the "information" contained in the unequal variability of the dependent variable. Members of the pool may be of different sizes and different economic development. There is considerable variability in the variables of different countries. Hence, we make use of the generalized least squares method (GLS) pooled regressions so that observations that come from populations with greater variability are given less weight than those coming from populations with smaller variability. Thus, it is capable of producing estimators that are best linear unbiased estimators. Equation 1.1 shows our basic model.

$$Y_{it} = \alpha + Xit'\beta it + \delta i + \gamma_t + \varepsilon_{it} \tag{1.1}$$

where Y_{it} is the dependent variable, and Xit' is a k-vector of regressors, and ε_{it} are the error terms for $i = 1, 2, \ldots, M$ cross-sectional units observed for dated periods $t = 1, 2, \ldots, T$. The parameter represents the overall constant in the model, while δi and γ_t represent cross-section or period-specific effects (random or fixed). We utilized life expectancy as the dependent variable and the regressors as health expenditure, infant mortality rate, gross national income per capita, AIDS mortality rate, TB mortality rate and a dummy variable for countries with low Human Development Index (HDI).

The major findings in Table 1.3 are that life expectancy is positively affected by the extent of health expenditure and gross national per capita income. The higher the extent of health expenditure and GNI per capita, the higher the life expectancy in countries in general. The *t* statistics are significant and of positive sign. Next, if we were to look into the impact of infant mortality, AIDS death rate and TB mortality rate, these variables are negative and significantly related to life expectancy. Life expectancy is highly negatively influenced by infant mortality (*t* statistical value of −118), AIDS mortality rate (*t* statistical value of −35) and TB mortality rates (*t* statistical value of −11).

A dummy variable inserted to reflect the status of the countries with low ranking in the UN's human development index (refer to Table 1.3)

Table 1.3 Determinants of life expectancy model

Constant	74.561750*
	(0.094665)
HEALTHEXP	0.153632*
	(0.012096)
INFANTM	−0.227156*
	(0.001924)
GNIPC	0.000119*
	(0.000003)
AIDS	−0.000041*
	(0.000001)
TBM	−0.015798*
	(0.001373)
HDI dummy variable	−2.383984*
	(0.113142)
R^2	0.99048
No of observations	2288

Note: The method used generalized least squares regression, with standard errors in parentheses. Data are available for a total of 187 countries. * denotes statistical significance at the 5% level.
Life expectancy: Life expectancy at birth, total (years).
HEALTHEXP: Health expenditure, total (% of GDP).
INFANTM: Mortality rate, infant (per 1000 live births).
GNIPC: Gross National Income (GNI) per capita, PPP (current international $).
AIDS: AIDS estimated deaths (UNAIDS estimates).
TBM: Deaths due to tuberculosis among HIV-negative people (per 100,000 population).
HDI dummy variable: 1: countries with low HDI and 0 as others.

was also statistically significant. This suggests that, other things equal, the countries with low HDI had an even lower life expectancy than other countries in the sample.

These results generally suggest that health factors, such as infant mortality, were extremely important, followed closely by income and AIDS death rate in affecting life expectancy. The poorest countries have an additional disadvantage in terms of living a long life. Infant mortality likely is a place holder for infant deaths as a result of poor health and nutrition of the mother and infant as well as the lack of clean water and high incidence of diarrheal disease. This suspicion is confirmed by another regression where infant mortality was found to be closely related to sewage and sanitation spending, which are good indicators of community health (see Table 1.4). In the subsequent chapters, we will further explore the determinants that affect the mortality rates of

Table 1.4 Determinants of infant mortality model

Constant	127.259*
	(0.592)
Sanitation	−0.452*
	(0.006)
Safe water	−0.776*
	(0.011)
R^2	0.993
No of observations	2821

Note: The method used generalized least squares regression, with standard errors in parentheses on a total of 214 countries. *denotes statistical significance at the 5% level.
INFANTM: Mortality rate, infant (per 1000 live births).
Access to safe water: Improved water source (% of population with access).
Access to sanitation: Improved sanitation facilities (% of population with access).

communicable diseases such as HIV/AIDS, tuberculosis, malaria as well as diarrhea.

By looking at the countries that had the highest levels of HIV, malaria and tuberculosis, it is evident that these diseases are most likely to occur in a similar set of countries, primarily in Africa. Referring to Table 1.5, six of the top ten countries reporting confirmed malaria cases are also in the top categories for HIV and tuberculosis while nine of the 20 countries with the highest tuberculosis incidence are also countries with high HIV incidence. Furthermore, those countries with the lowest rankings in the human development index are more likely to have lower life expectancy outcomes.

The conclusion that we can draw from this analysis is that the economies in Africa that have a high incidence of the three communicable diseases of malaria, TB and HIV also have low incomes, poor health support systems, lower life expectancy and a low level of human development.

Aside from the inference that Africa presents a whole host of health and human development challenges, it seems as if some of the common health features present possible opportunities of developing a holistic approach to health and the treatment of communicable diseases in these countries. Rather than treat each disease separately with specialists in health centers trained to address the diagnosis and treatment of a specific disease, health professionals could be trained to deal with a range of communicable diseases.

Table 1.5 Tuberculosis cases, HIV cases and malaria deaths over time

	TB prevalence per 100,000	**TB prevalence per 100,000**	**HIV prevalence over 15% in TB**	**Number of cases in 2007**	**Malaria deaths 2010**	**Top 10 malaria deaths**
Country	1990	2004	Cases 2007	1000*s*		
India	586	311		1962		
China	327	220		1306		
Indonesia	443	274		528		
Nigeria	282	573	x	460	4238	x
South Africa	769	676	x	461	83	
Bangladesh	639	444		353		
Ethiopia	323	613	x	314	1581	x
Pakistan	430	333		297		
Philippines	799	534		255		
Congo	209	477		245	23,476	x
Russia	69	136	x	157		
Vietnam	365	226		150		
Kenya	125	410	x	132	26,017	x
Brazil	124	63		92		
Tanzania			x	120	15,819	x
Uganda	206	472	x	102	8431	x
Zimbabwe	409	652	x	104	256	
Thailand	336	188		91		
Mozambique	287	567	x	92	3354	x
Myanmar	411	168		83		
Cambodia	928	696		72		

Sources: WHO (2013) and World Bank (2013).

Some efforts in this direction are already being made in some African countries through the treatment of HIV and tuberculosis together in the same clinic. This facilitates the sharing of diagnostic, treatment facilities and medications. It also encourages diagnostic tools for one illness to be used to promote diagnosis for others. For example, those diagnosed with TB should also be tested for HIV. Similar efforts are also being made with respect to coinfection of malaria and HIV.

Within the geographic and sociological context of these diseases, the overall health and sanitation environment is an important component of the overall healthcare apparatus. A cleaner environment helps to reduce the spread of diarrheal diseases and TB where crowded and unsanitary conditions are widespread as well as contributing to the reduction in the incidence of malaria through cleaning up of stagnant water and other places where mosquitoes breed. The fact that infant mortality is related to sewage, availability of toilets and latrines as well as clean water is also an indication of the importance of environmental factors.

These arguments gather more force when we consider which countries around the globe are the poorest performers in terms of life expectancy, infant mortality and the human development index. Looking at the global rankings for each of these indicators, almost all countries at the bottom are in Africa. For example, of the top 50 countries with highest infant mortality rankings, all but nine are in Africa (UNICEF, 2013). For the human development index, all but a few were in the bottom 40 out of 186 countries surveyed, and a similar conclusion is true for life expectancy (see Table 1.6). It stands to reason that the need in Africa

Table 1.6 Under-five mortality, human development and life expectancy ranks for selected African countries

Country	Under-five mortality rate (per 1000 infants) 2011 value	Under-five mortality rate (per 1000 infants) 2011 rank	HDI index rank[1] 2012	Life expectancy rank (of 198 countries) 2012
Sierra Leone	185	1	177	198
Somalia	180	2	...	185
Mali	176	3	182	184
Chad	169	4	184	190
Democratic Republic of the Congo	168	5	186	195
Central African Republic	164	6	180	192
Guinea-Bissau	161	7	176	197
Angola	158	8	148	186
Burkina Faso	146	9	183	173

Table 1.6 (Continued)

Country	Under-five mortality rate (per 1000 infants) 2011 value	Under-five mortality rate (per 1000 infants) 2011 rank	HDI index rank[1] 2012	Life expectancy rank (of 198 countries) 2012
Burundi	139	10	178	188
Cameroon	127	11	150	183
Guinea	126	12	178	177
Niger	125	13	186	175
Nigeria	124	14	153	182
South Sudan	121	15	...	...
Equatorial Guinea	118	16	136	187
Côte d'Ivoire	115	17	168	172
Mauritania	112	18	155	163
Togo	110	19	159	169
Benin	106	20		
Swaziland	104	21	166	171
Mozambique	103	22	185	189
Gambia	101	23	165	165
Congo	99	25	142	167
Djibouti	90	26	164	166
Uganda	90	26	161	178
Sao Tome and Principe	89	28	144	150
Lesotho	86	29	158	196
Sudan	86	29	171	159
Malawi	83	31	170	176

Note: [1]Low human development index is ranked from 142 to 186.
Sources: UNICEF (2013, p. 99) and UNDP (2013).

Table 1.7 Relative spending on public health (% of GDP and % of government budget, respectively)

Region	Health expenditure, public (% of GDP)		Health expenditure, public (% of government expenditure)	
	2002	2011	2002	2011
East Asia and Pacific	4.64	4.60	11.28	...
Europe and Central Asia	6.67	7.20	14.67	15.38
Latin America and Caribbean	3.08	3.76	8.97	...
Middle East and North Africa	2.82	2.85	...	8.66*
Sub-Saharan Africa	2.29	2.89	...	...
South Asia	1.04	1.18	5.98	7.47
Low and middle income countries	2.31	2.94	8.37	...
High income countries	6.43	7.36	15.85	16.97
World	5.72	6.00	15.12	...

Note: * Data for 2009.
Source: World Bank (2013).

is so much greater than in other regions that more resources should be devoted to problems facing these countries. Unfortunately this has not been the case. See Table 1.7 for data on relative spending on public health as a percentage of national incomes and government budgets by regions. In subsequent chapters we discuss the ways to address the challenges and policies required to tackle HIV/AIDS, tuberculosis, malaria and diarrheal diseases.

2
HIV/AIDS

Since the appearance of the HIV virus in the early 1980s in the United States, there have been reported AIDS cases in almost every country in the world. Each year more than 1.5 million people die of AIDS and there are now over 30 million people living with HIV today. By the end of 2012, there were about 30 million fatalities from AIDS around the world. More than 90% of all those infected with HIV live in developing countries, with the bulk of those in Africa. Despite nearly three decades of effort, vaccines to prevent infection with HIV are still in the trial stages[1] and there is no effective cure for those who have contracted HIV. However, there are now drugs available to treat patients who have HIV and many will be able to live for more years by taking the prescribed medication. There are also developments in the use of antivirals such as tenofovir to provide protection to HIV negative individuals from developing AIDS. If left untreated, an HIV prognosis eventually leads to AIDS, which is always fatal.

Ongoing pharmaceutical research and development of antiretroviral drugs that began in the late 1980s brings hope to those infected with HIV and suffering from AIDS. A wide array of antiretroviral (ARV) cocktails is now available for the treatment of HIV and has contributed to extending life for millions of patients. However, there are still large numbers of patients with HIV who are not on antiretroviral therapy (ART). The UNAIDS program estimates that in 2010 only around 63% of those who needed ART were getting it in Latin America, 50% in Sub-Saharan Africa, 56% in East and Central Africa, 30% in West and Central Africa, 39% in East and Southeast Asia, 23% in Europe and Central Asia and 13% in North Africa. Globally only 6.65 million infected individuals receive ART from an estimated infected population of over 14 million. This is a coverage rate of less than 50%. Those HIV-infected individuals who do not receive ART will eventually make the transition to full-blown AIDS.

There is new evidence from test trials conducted for a recently developed drug HPTN 052 that it reduces the risk of transmission of HIV to an uninfected partner by 96%. It is important that this new therapy be made available globally to all those infected with HIV as soon as possible.

In this connection much more needs to be done, even beyond the goal of nearly doubling coverage of HIV patients with ART. There are difficulties in meeting WHO goals of providing 15 million HIV-infected individuals with treatment by 2015. Despite the scale up in the coverage of ART in recent years, only 65% of the 15 million targeted (i.e. 9.7 million) people were receiving treatment as of end 2012. The rate of ART coverage for children younger than 15 years old has been growing, but the percentage increase was still smaller than for adults. WHO (2013a) also acknowledges the challenge of providing ART to all children eligible for treatment by end of 2015. There are cultural and logistics barriers in many countries along with the absorptive capacity of health systems to accommodate a doubling or tripling of the patient load in hospitals and treatment centers, which are already stretched beyond capacity. In Asia, Central Asia and North Africa there are considerable difficulties in getting ARV therapy to those who are in the greatest need and where the incidence of the disease is highest – men who have sex with men (MSM), sex workers and intravenous drug users. This is often due to stigma, discrimination and punitive laws which prevent the parties from receiving ART.

2.1 What happens to those who are not receiving ART therapy?

We don't know the status of HIV progression for those who are not receiving treatment. However, we can make some educated guesses about the progress of HIV over time based on averages of patients in clinical trials. Most analysis of the stage of HIV is based on CD4 cell counts. As the disease progresses the CD4 cell count declines. A healthy person without HIV would have a CD4 cell count between 600 and 1200 cells per cubic millimeter of blood. If the cell count dips below 500, it is an indication that something is amiss with the immune system. Someone with HIV who is not being treated will suffer a decline in the CD4 cell count over time. The rate of decline will depend upon a variety of factors and is subject to variation depending on race and age as well as personal genetics and general health. One clinical trial found a decline of 47.1 cells per cubic millimeter per annum for those with CD4 cell count greater than 500, 30.6 for those with CD4 count between 350 and 500 and 20 for those with CD4 count between 200 and 350. The rate of decline slackens with the decline in the cell count. When the cell count reaches 200, the person has made the transition from HIV to AIDS and is more likely to die soon.

One study found that nonwhites have slower declines than whites and older patients have more rapid declines. Keep in mind that these figures are benchmarks based on samples of patients in specific locations. Nevertheless, the longer those with HIV remain untreated, the likelihood of contracting an opportunistic infection such as TB is greater and their chances of contracting AIDS and dying are higher. Those at the high end of the cell count, who are not yet receiving any therapy, will have a greater chance of survival once they do receive ART, hopefully within a few years. Those at the low end need it right away. Many who have HIV don't know they are ill and have not been tested. In many cases they will only go for testing only when they feel sick, often with symptoms of tuberculosis, a common opportunistic infection. This is more likely to occur where their CD4 cell count falls below 350.

When should ART therapy be started? The US Department of Health now suggests that ART should begin as soon as HIV is diagnosed no matter the level of the cell count. WHO has also revised its guidelines in 2013 to recommend earlier initiation of ART and immediate ART in certain circumstances. The new guidelines recommend initiating ART earlier – at CD4 count less than 500 cells/mm^3 – and immediately initiating ART for serodiscordant couples, pregnant women living with HIV, people with TB and HIV, people with HIV and hepatitis B and children living with HIV who are younger than five years, irrespective of CD4 cell count. If fully implemented, the new guidelines are predicted to avert an additional three million deaths as compared with continuing under the 2010 guidelines. The number of people eligible for ART in low- and middle-income countries globally would increase from 16.7 to 25.9 million (WHO, 2013a). Thus, there is an urgent need for the guidelines to be applied globally and implemented immediately.

This is not the case in many locations. For example, in many African countries the threshold needed for ART is sometimes lower than a cell count of 500 and even as low as 350. The situation can be more dire in low-income countries, where about one in four people initiate ART late – when CD4 count is less than 100 cells/mm^3 (WHO, 2013a). This is not a good starting point both from the viewpoint of providing protection against further deterioration in health and also for the cost-effectiveness of treatment. Fortunately, health officials are beginning to realize that the burden of care and drugs required will be higher the lower the CD4 cell count when treatment starts. This is why it is critical that as many HIV patients as possible are placed on ART as quickly as the health systems can absorb new patients. It is really a life and death struggle and resources need to be found to treat maximum patients as soon as possible. Without an all-out global effort it is possible that the recent optimistic outlook for conquering HIV presented at the latest HIV conference in Washington, DC will fail to be realized.

2.2 Identifying those at risk

2.2.1 Geographic distribution of HIV incidence

The geographic distribution of HIV incidence is displayed in Table 2.1. Of the 34 million people living with HIV globally, 23.5 million are in Sub-Sahara Africa and 4.8 million in Asia. The rest are spread between North America and Europe (3.7 million) and the rest of the world.

2.2.2 Identified parties at risk

Historical records suggest that those most at risk to contract HIV are in one of several high-risk categories – sex workers,[2] both male and female, intravenous drug users, truck drivers who move from location to location over the course of a few weeks or more, men in the military, migrant workers and other men who are away from home for prolonged periods of time. These groups have and will continue to be the subject of

Table 2.1 Global distribution of HIV/AIDS, 2011

Region	Number of cases
Oceania	53,000
North America	1,400,000
Caribbean	230,000
West and Central Europe	900,000
Sub-Saharan Africa	23,500,000
East Europe and Central Asia	1,400,000
East Asia	830,000
Middle East and West Asia	300,000
South and Southeast Asia	4,000,000
Latin America	1,400,000

Source: UNAIDS (2012, p. 14).

intensive media campaigns to make them more aware of risks and the importance of taking preventative measures. However, in many cases those at risk are trying to hide their sexual practices, making it difficult to identify and treat them. Furthermore, recent analysis of those in these risky groups suggests that current practices need to be further modified.

Those with more well-established family relations were thought to be in less-risky categories. However, because people are almost never forthcoming about their sexual practices, the pigeon holing of people into different groups is still subject to error. Recently, however, Steve Bellan of the University of Texas and his colleagues have developed a model that predicts the spread of HIV. Relying on a survey of 22,000 married and co-habiting couples in 18 African countries, they were able to establish a range of probabilities that one or both members were being unfaithful. The survey looked at who in the couple was infected, how long the couple had lived together and the age at which each member of the couple became sexually active. They had the intuition that most people don't lie about these questions, except perhaps age at first sexual encounter, even though they will lie about whether they are cheating on their partner. They also were able to show that even that estimate could be wrong by a year or so without affecting the results. Bellan's mathematical model took account of prevalence of HIV in the country and how long the citizens can live once they have been infected. These facts allowed their model to estimate the proportion of HIV infections that had resulted from one or the other partner becoming infected before the couple got together, whether it occurred as a result of either partner being unfaithful or whether they were infected by their partner. Bellan et al. (2013) estimated that extra-couple transmission accounted for 27–61% of all HIV infections in men and 21–51% of all those in women. The range reflects differences between different countries. They estimated that in 2011, extra-couple transmission accounted for 32–65% of new incident HIV infections in men in cohabiting couples, and 10–47% of new infections in women in such couples. Their findings suggest that transmission of HIV within couples occurs largely from men to women. Because of the large contribution of extra-couple transmission to new HIV infections, Bellan et al. suggest that interventions for HIV prevention should target the general sexually active population as well as groups at high risk.

Further information on the spread of HIV among men who have sex with men was obtained from a meta-analysis of studies of transgender women (men who pose as women to have sexual encounters) in the United States, six Asian–Pacific countries, five Latin American countries and three European countries, and is reported in the *Lancet*. The selected countries include the United States, Spain, Singapore, Israel, the Netherlands, Brazil, Belgium, Indonesia, Australia, Thailand, Uruguay, India and Italy. The study by Baral et al. (2013) found that transgender women were, on average, four times more likely to have HIV than female sex workers. This is an extremely high burden compared to female sex workers and is probably because of the high incidence of unprotected anal intercourse and anal intercourse which is much more likely to spread HIV than penile to vaginal intercourse. Furthermore, 73% of transgender women who tested HIV positive were unaware of their status and continued to be at risk for spreading HIV to their clients.

All countries in the study have predominant HIV epidemics in men, and most have high rates of injecting drug use and also high rates of HIV infection in gay, bisexual and other MSM. There also appears to be a gender gap in access to antiretroviral therapy (WHO, 2013a). Men appear less likely than women to be accessing ART, especially in the African region. Out of 109 countries surveyed in 2011, the male–female ratio for people receiving ART stands at 41–59%. In the African region, men accounted for 44% of people eligible for ART, but only 36% were receiving it. When accessing treatment, men tend to have lower CD4 cell counts than women.

It is important that members of these high-risk groups be identified and specifically targeted for media campaigns and also brought for tests and eventual treatment.

2.3 Transmission

HIV is transmitted predominantly in three ways – *sexual transmission, exposure to infected blood or blood products and perinatal transmission including breast-feeding*. On a global scale sexual transmission is the predominant mode of transmission and accounts for about 80% of all transmissions. Some know they have HIV and yet continue to practice unprotected sex. The risk of sexual transmission is determined by several factors including behavior, which influences the risk of exposure to individuals who are infected with HIV and by infectivity in the case of exposure. There are many factors involved in infectivity, and the actual chance of becoming infected will be influenced by these factors. Of course, infectivity in individual cases will depend on chance as well.

Intercourse Generally, anal intercourse has a higher transmission probability than penile–vaginal intercourse and male to female transmission is more likely than female to male transmission. Untreated sexually transmitted diseases (STD) can increase the risk of transmission several fold. Vaginal infections including trichomonas also increase the risk of transmission. Circumcision also affects the chance of transmission. Men who have been circumcised have a significantly lower chance of becoming infected, about half the rate of those men who have not been circumcised and perhaps even more in particular cases. Infectivity also depends on the stage of the disease of the patient and whether they are currently undergoing therapy for the HIV infection. People are more infectious right after they become infected and again during the later stages of the disease. ART significantly reduces the level of the virus, often to the point where HIV tests cannot detect the virus in the patient's blood. Studies in Africa suggest that the risk of sexual transmission between couples was strongly correlated with the viral load (strength of the virus in the bloodstream) in the infected partner. If the viral load is high the chances of transmission are increased. The use of contraceptive devices reduces the risk of exposure dramatically. Male condoms are the most common contraceptive device. Recently a vaginal ring has been found to be effective and should be available in more countries in the future. The ring has to be changed once a month. It is medicated with an antiviral and lasts for a month.

Injection HIV has been introduced where there is needle sharing among intravenous drug users. Sharing of injection equipment and the frequency of injection are both correlated with the spread of HIV. Sharing needles with anonymous injecting partners and where there are many partners raises the risk of transmission dramatically.

Blood transfusions Blood that is contaminated is virtually guaranteed to transmit HIV and the recipient may develop AIDS almost immediately because of the size of the viral load in a transfusion. WHO estimated that between 5% and 10% of HIV infections worldwide are the result of transfusions with contaminated blood. Maintenance of an uncontaminated blood supply will virtually eliminate HIV transmission through transfusions.

Mother-to-child transmission Mother-to-child transmission can occur during pregnancy, labor and delivery or breast-feeding. Without treatment, around 15% to 30% of babies born to HIV-infected women will become infected with HIV during pregnancy and delivery. A further 5–20% will become infected through breast-feeding. The higher the viral load of the mother, the greater is the probability that a newborn will be infected with HIV. It is important to reduce the risk of this mode of transmission by ART for the mother before delivery. Also the mother must continue with ART following delivery and for the rest of her life.

The appropriate drugs should be determined by doctors and healthcare workers familiar with ART that are appropriate for the mother, given her viral load. Aspects of ART will be discussed further in a later section. A recent case in Mississippi suggests that early treatment with ART (AZT and two other anti-HIV drugs) 31 hours after birth resulted in the baby becoming free of the HIV virus after a month and all treatment was stopped after 18 months (see ScienceNOW article by Jon Cohen, 3 March 2013). If this result can be replicated with any other transmission from mother to child, it would be a breakthrough that would save many lives and eliminate the need for ART for thousands of children around the world. The 2013 WHO guidelines currently recommends initiating ART immediately for all children younger than five years of age diagnosed with HIV, irrespective of CD4 count.

Breast-feeding There have been a number of studies on the transmission of HIV through the breast milk of the mother. The chances of transmission increase over the time the infant is breast-fed. There is also evidence that mixed feeding with formula increases the likelihood of transmission. If the mother is under ART, the chances of transmission are reduced. In general, however, mothers with HIV are advised not to breast-feed whenever the use of breast milk substitute (formula) is acceptable, feasible, affordable, sustainable and safe. However, if the mother cannot be sure the water is safe, then she may choose to breast-feed, since the risk of life-threatening conditions from formula feeding may be higher than the risk from breast-feeding. An HIV-positive mother should be counseled on the risks and benefits of different infant feeding options and should be helped to select the most suitable option for her situation. Furthermore, in cases where breast-feeding is the norm, a woman who chooses not to breast-feed may draw suspicion, isolation and other forms of discrimination or reprisal from family and community. This would draw attention to her possible HIV status and further difficulties including abandonment by her family. As a final note, the contraceptive effect of breast-feeding is significant and will lengthen the interval between pregnancies since nursing mothers cannot generally conceive.

2.3.1 Progress of HIV to AIDS

The progress of HIV to AIDS is sometimes gradual and sometimes swift. However, without treatment it is always fatal. The immune system becomes further compromised as it is depleted and the patient is subject to a growing number of opportunistic infections. Figure 2.1 depicts the path of infections and cancers that develop as the immune system is

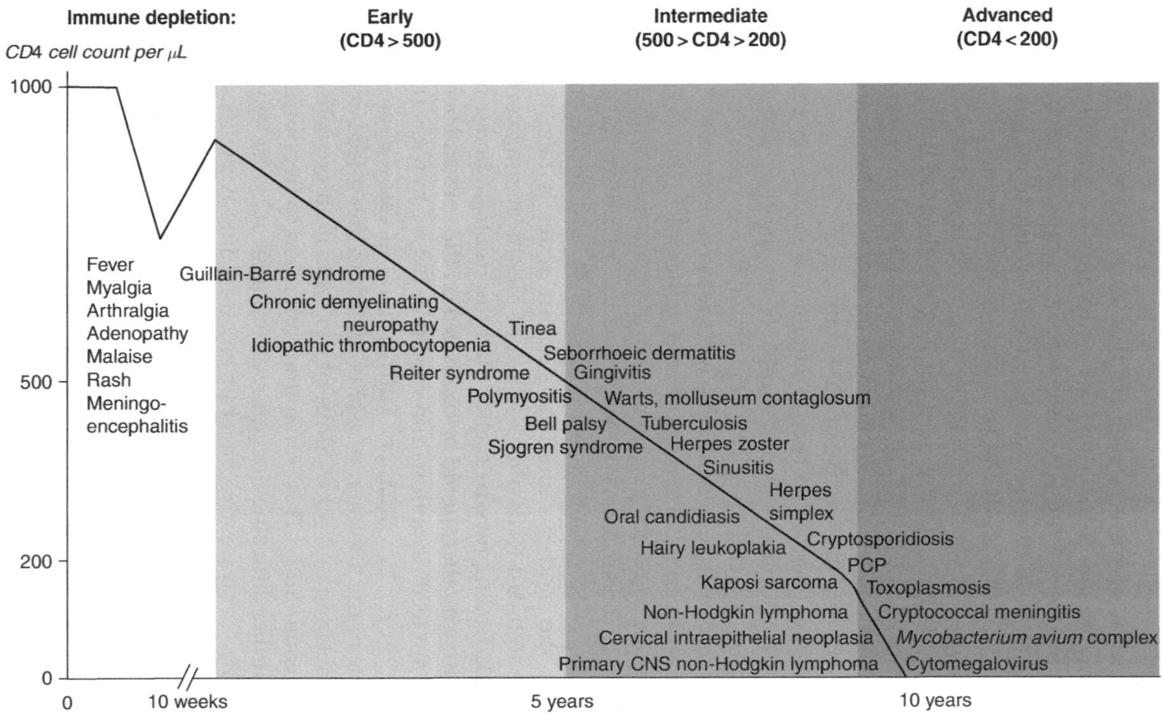

Figure 2.1 Cascade of infections and cancers that develop as immune function is depleted
Source: Jamison et al. (2006, Figure 18.1, p. 353).

compromised over time. The horizontal axis shows the number of weeks and years from the onset of the disease while the vertical axis depicts the path of the CD4 cell count per milliliter of fluid from healthy levels of 1000 per ml to until the CD4 cell count falls below 200 and the early stages when the HIV can be treated and the patient is still AIDS free. People living with HIV may appear and feel healthy for several years. However, even if they feel healthy, HIV is still affecting their bodies.

All people with HIV should be examined on a regular basis by a healthcare provider experienced in treating HIV infection. Many people with HIV, including those who feel healthy, can benefit greatly from current medications used to treat HIV infection. These medications can limit or slow down the destruction of the immune system, improve the health of people living with HIV and may reduce their ability to transmit HIV. Untreated early HIV infection is also associated with many diseases including cardiovascular disease, kidney disease, liver disease and cancer. Support services are also available to many people with HIV. These services can help people cope with their diagnosis, reduce risky behavior and find needed services. People with HIV are in zones two and three of Figure 2.1 with CD4 cell counts above 200. However, those patients with counts close to 200 would be more likely to have other diseases. TB is particularly prevalent in HIV patients in Africa and Asia.

AIDS is the late stage of HIV infection – when a person's immune system is severely damaged and has difficulty fighting diseases and certain cancers. The Mayo Clinic says that people infected with HIV progress to AIDS when their CD4 count falls below 200 or they experience an AIDS-defining complication, such as:

> Pneumocystis pneumonia, Cytomegalovirus, Tuberculosis, Toxoplasmosis, Cryptosporidiosis

Before the development of any medications, people with HIV could progress to AIDS in just a few years. Currently, people can live much longer – even decades – with HIV before they develop AIDS.

In the United States estimates of the survival for HIV patients with access to current treatments is 24 additional years of life according to Schackman et al. (2006). This is because of "highly active" combinations of medications that were introduced in the mid-1990s. There are a number of intervening factors that have an impact on the path of the disease including diet, living conditions, regularity of visits to health facilities and the availability of antiretroviral therapy. The estimate of median survival time for patient with HIV for a more diverse population including developing countries is between 7 and 13 years of additional life (Williams and Dye, 2003). All cases are different and anyone who suspects that he or she has been exposed to HIV should contact a health professional immediately. Sometimes symptoms do not appear for months or even years even though the virus is present. However, a conventional blood test will be able to detect the presence of the virus and the health professional will be able to suggest a treatment regime based on individual symptoms and patient profile.

The critical point to recognize in all of this discussion is that we now have a medication treatment and care toolkit to extend life of HIV patients for a long time. Yet, globally at least half and perhaps more of those with HIV are not receiving ARV therapy. Without it they will all eventually make the transition to AIDS and die shortly thereafter. As the AIDS Task Force Interim Report says

> Only treatment can substantially prolong the lives of 40 million people who already carry the HIV virus. In the highest prevalence countries, only urgent expansion of treatment will forestall continued catastrophic rates of illness and death and the attendant social and economic devastation. Moreover, the current situation in which access to life saving treatment is determined by ability to pay or country of residence is fundamentally unjust.

By making ART available to everyone with HIV, who would benefit from it, millions of lives will be saved. The push to treat all of these new patients will require a number of support services.

2.3.2 Coinfection with tuberculosis

The coinfection of HIV and tuberculosis has increased dramatically in the last decade or so. In Chapter 3 we shall note that HIV patients are highly susceptible to contracting TB, perhaps as much as 20 times more likely than others in the community and this has led to a rapid increase in coinfection and the rate of TB infection has risen dramatically. In countries where there are high rates of both HIV and tuberculosis, Williams and Dye (2003) suggest strengthening TB control programs and to treat HIV and TB at the same time. By treating TB patients with ARV therapy immediately along with the ongoing therapy for TB, the chances of long-term success in reducing the mortality rate and raising life expectancy can be increased. Such activities include providing ART during TB treatment, co-trimoxazole prophylaxis during TB treatment, isoniazid preventive therapy for people living with HIV and diagnosing

TB early by systematically screening people living with HIV. Evidences have shown that the risk of active TB can be reduced by a six-month (or longer) course of isoniazid preventive therapy. Isoniazid preventive therapy is therefore recommended as a key intervention in HIV care settings.

One reason for doing this two-pronged approach is that most of new TB patients have CD4 cell counts between 150 and 300 per ml and this is the range where ARV therapy can work effectively. Chapter 3 will discuss the DOTS protocol for TB in detail. For a patient with HIV and TB, neither anti-TB drugs nor ARV alone is likely to increase life expectancy. However, the two therapies used in tandem should provide a strong protocol for treating both diseases. Furthermore, it is not recommended to delay the treatment of HIV until TB treatment has ended.

Trials by Dr. S.A Karim have yielded strong results that the two should be treated together. The work with his colleagues found that patients waiting to complete TB treatment before beginning HIV therapy were 50% more likely to die than patients being treated for both diseases simultaneously. Visit http://www.voanews.com/articleprintview/401302.html. He cautions not to wait for them to finish their TB treatment.[3]

2.4 Resources needed to achieve universal access to ART

2.4.1 Trained staff

There is a shortage of trained and skilled healthcare workers everywhere in the developing world. On average there are nearly 20 times the numbers of doctors in the United States than in Africa. When treating HIV and AID patients, healthcare workers are often subjected to the risk of infection and the possibility of death. Seventeen percent of healthcare workers in Botswana died of AIDS between 1999 and 2005 (see UNAIDS, 2006). Skill levels need to be upgraded and current staff have to be used more effectively. Lay people have to be trained and more resources devoted to training additional healthcare professionals to take care of the increased patient load. Qualified health workers can also be trained to perform some of the work that previously were the responsibility of doctors or nurses. Care must be taken to ensure that the quality of care is not compromised. See a report of such an experience in Uganda in Lutalo et al. (2009). There have been many successful programs that can be replicated to bring about a rapid rise in the number of competent health professionals working in this field. For example, successful programs have been implemented in Zambia since 2004 (AVERT, 2013) and in South Africa since 2010 (AVERT, 2013a).

2.4.2 Reliable supply chains

Accurate systems of forecasting drug inventory requirements need to be implemented to keep adequate, but not excessive supplies of drugs on hand to meet expected patient needs. This could prove difficult if there are interruptions in supplies or there is an unexpected uptake of in-patient admissions which could take place if new diagnostic or treatment protocols are introduced. Furthermore, secure storage facilities have to be made available as the demand for drugs increases. WHO estimates that only 20–30% of costs related to treatment are direct drug-related, and the rest are associated with delivery and storage costs. Suppliers who managed its supply chain received the most money from the U.S. President's Emergency Plan for AIDS Relief (PEPFAR) according to UNAIDS report.

2.4.3 Maintaining effective drugs

Introducing new drugs and treatment plans and phasing out other drugs is an ongoing task which sometimes does not receive enough attention at the local or even the country level. The phasing out of a particular antiretroviral drug *stavudine* is a case in point. Many countries have been phasing it out, as recommended by WHO while others have been slower to respond. (See AVERT 2013b, Universal Access to AIDS Treatment: Targets and Challenges, section on effective drugs and equipment.) Many of the developing countries would like to develop non-stavudine medications but patents and pharmaceutical firms' influences can deter ARV generic development. While monitoring of the effectiveness of treatment and toxicity of drugs has been an important routine to follow in the past, recent research indicates that money could be channeled into providing more antiretroviral drugs to patients rather than extensive laboratory monitoring. The trade-off favors treating patients in a timely manner rather than slowing treatment because of further testing.

2.4.4 Cost of HIV treatment

Universal access will require additional budgetary resources to fund the drugs, physical and human resources required to ramp up both detection and treatment facilities around the world. There are three major funding sources – the US government through its PEPFAR program; the Global Fund to Treat TB, HIV and Malaria and the resources of individual countries that are involved in the fight against HIV and AIDS.

The global economic downturn which began in 2008 has hampered efforts to raise the resources to meet the target of achieving universal access by 2015. Estimates made in 2012 suggest that there is a shortfall of around $10 billion. Based on its 2010 report, UNAIDS estimates that an investment of US$25 billion was required for the global AIDS response in 2010 for low- and middle-income countries. This compares with around $15 billion currently budgeted from all sources. The investment need was based on the country-defined targets to reach universal access to HIV prevention, treatment care and support by 2010. International lenders would supply $17 billion with the rest coming from local sources. This means that universal access will be postponed further into the future. The budget shortfall also means that treatment expansion will be particularly difficult in lower-income countries where there are epidemics of HIV and TB. These include Uganda, Tanzania and Zambia and South Africa to a lesser extent. These countries depend heavily on foreign funding for their health programs. Eastern Europe and Central Asia are also vulnerable and only about 25% of those needing treatment are receiving it. Health expenditures have also fallen as aggregate economic activity has remained sluggish. There have been civil disturbances in Russia, protesting the lack of drugs to treat HIV. Hopefully, more resources will become available as the global economy recovers. Regional antiretroviral therapy coverage is already much below levels required to approach universal coverage. Table 2.2 gives details of ART coverage at the regional and global level as of 2011.

As a component of the efforts to reach universal coverage, new budgetary resources will be required to build new treatment facilities and laboratories as well as computerization to handle the increased paper burden. Approximately one-third of the total is earmarked for bringing about social changes that will facilitate the treatment of those who have been outside the normal channels for diagnosis and treatment such as men who have sex with men, sex workers and intravenous drug users.

Whether this budget includes treatment of the remainder of those not covered is unclear, although it does seem to, since the term "universal coverage" is used. While these targets seemed reasonable at the time the report was drafted, the global recession had an impact on budgets of all countries and universal coverage was not achieved.

In a perfect world how much more money is required to achieve universal coverage with ART along with all the support envisioned? As noted earlier, the answer is about $10 billion a year as a continuing additional commitment for all countries with HIV budget shortfalls. This is taking into account the current funding levels from both local

Table 2.2 Regional antiretroviral coverage as of 2011

Region	Antiretroviral coverage (ART) in %	Estimated number of people receiving ART coverage (millions)	Estimated number of people needing ART (millions)
Sub-Saharan Africa	49	5.1	10.4
Eastern and Southern Africa	56	4.2	7.6
Western and Central Africa	30	0.8	2.8
Latin America and Caribbean	63	0.5	0.8
East, South and South East Asia	39	0.9	2.3
Europe and Central Asia	23	0.1	0.6
North Africa and the Middle East	10	0.01	0.1
Total	47	11.6	24.5

Source: WHO (2013).

and international sources, all of which is projected to continue at current levels. What level of goods and services does $10 billion buy in today's market? It costs 1.3 billion to run the US government for one day and an aircraft carrier costs around $5 billion. So, about two aircraft carriers or eight days of running the federal government. The overall US federal budget is $3834 billion. To put the $10 billion required in perspective look at the reaction to such a number in Washington. As one congressman is rumored to say – programs like this are so small they fall in the category of "rounding error."

Put this up against the number of lives that would be saved, patients whose dignity would be preserved, the children that would survive to become adults, the mothers who would not lose their babies. Sounds like a good trade-off? Despite the rhetoric and good intentions of health professionals working in the field, it isn't likely to happen. The poor, sick and neglected in developing countries don't have enough sway with governments in industrial countries to call forth more assistance; at least not yet. It is up to donors in the industrial world to continue to carry the burden.

2.5 Better treatment

In 2010 UNAIDS and WHO launched a new program called Treatment 2.0, a program to make ARV more affordable and accessible and also to achieve and sustain universal access. Aside from universal access, Treatment 2.0 has five areas of focus, which are discussed next.

Optimizing treatment regimens To achieve better and more effective treatment requires a combination of activities to give the patient the most effective combination of drugs available at the lowest cost. This can be achieved by developing the most up-to-date therapies combined with easy to use methods of delivery and maintenance in view of the need to maintain drug intakes for months and even years to come. This involves active engagement with trade agencies to sustain the importation of the most effective drugs at least cost. There is also a need to be cognizant of the possible ramifications of other diseases including TB and hepatitis and the special needs of children and pregnant women.

Diagnostics that can be used at home are also important and can lead to a higher rate of diagnosis. Such a point of care test is now available and is now sold at pharmacies in the United States (see Branson (2003) and Arnold (2012)). There are issues of how those who are tested HIV positive should proceed and what referrals are available, both in person with a health professional and via Internet counseling. The home test now costs $40 and is too expensive for widespread distribution in other countries, where facilities would also have to be made available to handle inquiries and new patients who would come to health clinics as a result of finding a positive result. However, it is critical that the test be made available in developing countries, particularly where HIV is already present in epic proportions.

Now, much of the work in identifying HIV-positive patients is through coinfection with TB. Early diagnosis while patients are still in good health will increase life expectancy and reduce morbidity and mortality, without relying on the presence of another disease, which also has to be reckoned with. Export of the test should first go to high-risk countries where the stigma of HIV still keeps people from testing, and who continue to spread the disease to their partners. The use of point of care tests in Africa has enabled clinics to process and treat many more patients than was previously possible in voluntary counseling and testing sites (VCT). More patients get their results and are counseled for appropriate action to take. Fewer patients fall out of the system. In Kenya, for example, the number of VCT sites has increased from 3 to 70 and in Malawi patients processed has jumped from 5000 to 40,000 in a short period of time. Some of these sites may be using tests that have not been approved in the United States or by the UN.[4] Nevertheless, many more patients are moving through the system and more people are being diagnosed and treated. This accounts partially for the sharp drop in HIV infections.

More work globally needs to be done to track testing procedures and analyze patient data. This also calls for a more systematic approach to data processing, retrieval and analysis with computers as suggested later in the chapter.

Simplifying diagnostics HIV diagnosis is a difficult and challenging task and it often keeps programs from being more effective. Because the symptoms of HIV can be slow to develop, it is important that everyone who could be infected is tested. If the test is positive, it is equally important to get the patient started on a treatment program as soon as possible and also keep patients from leaving treatment programs in between. It is estimated that as many as seven million people in developing countries are HIV positive but do not know it. They are at risk and risk is also for those who they may come in contact with for sex and/or use of needles for injecting drugs. Integrating HIV testing into routine health services has helped to increase the effectiveness of the diagnostic process. There are often lags between the test and the test results. In many cases the patient does not return to get the results. What is needed is a one stop protocol that combines testing with the diagnosis at the same time so that therapy can begin on the spot. Recently a point of care HIV test has been developed that requires no processing in a lab or any equipment such as a centrifuge or electricity. The procedures are very easy and involve a limited number of steps and do not require high precision or a good deal of training. The test can be carried out by staff with no formal laboratory training. Making widespread use of this new technology should increase the efficiency and accuracy of HIV testing and reduce the number of potential patients who do not keep appointment or follow up after testing. This alone will increase the effectiveness of diagnostic procedures and increase the ability of healthcare systems to treat more patients with HIV. Conventional testing requires a laboratory analysis and a test called ELISA (enzyme-linked immunosorbent assay). This test relies on microscopic examination of several sputum smears. Patients may have to return to a health center several times to get a confirmation of the diagnosis. The dropout rate can be as high as 40% when such a test is not available (see Kirwan and Gilman, 2013). There are now methods to diagnose TB in one day (see Kirwan and Gilman and also Chapter 3 on Tuberculosis in this book) and so for developing countries the diagnosis of an opportunistic infection such as tuberculosis is a simpler and more cost-effective way to also diagnose HIV. This approach has been highly successful and gives the added benefit of providing treatment for TB as well. Due to the high incidence of coinfection with TB, many high-risk countries are linking TB and HIV clinics together. This practice is also suggested in Chapter 3. For more information on coinfection, the reader is also referred to Harries, Maher and Graham (2004) TB/HIV Clinical Manual available at http://www.who.int/tb/publications/who_htm_tb_2004_329/en/index.html.

The need to catch patients early in the diagnostic/treatment cycle is important since people living with HIV may appear and feel healthy for several years. However, even if they feel healthy, HIV is still affecting their bodies and they can pass the virus on to others. Many people with HIV, including those who feel healthy, can benefit greatly from current medications used to treat HIV infection. As mentioned in Section 2.3.1, these medications can limit or slow down the destruction of the immune system, improve the health of people living with HIV and may reduce their ability to transmit HIV. Untreated early HIV infection is also associated with many diseases including TB, cardiovascular disease, kidney disease, liver disease and cancer. Support services are also available to many people with HIV. These services can help people cope with their diagnosis, reduce risk behavior and find needed services.

Rapid point of care tests (suggested earlier) and community-based approaches to testing may help to increase the ability of communities to identify who has HIV. When one member of a couple has HIV and the other does not, ARV therapy can be extremely effective in reducing the chances of the second person become infected so that treatment can become a component of a prevention strategy. Recently a point of contact test has been developed that gives patients the results in a matter of minutes and requires no elaborate equipment or time delays between the test and results (see Branson, 2003). Such point of care tests can provide immediate results especially when decisions needed to be made quickly such as whether to provide ART for the pregnant women going into labor or for the healthcare worker who have been accidentally exposed to blood or body fluids in his course of work. For the former, it is also the last chance to prevent mother-to-child HIV transmission (PMTCT), particularly in low-income developing countries where many rural women lack access to prior antenatal care. Given the general effectiveness of such tests, other considerations such as convenience, diagnosis time, shelf-life, and cost would affect the choice of the HIV test. Lately, newer 4th-generation, antigen-antibody combo rapid immunoassay (ARCHITECT) has been developed and allows for the detection of HIV infection prior to the emergence of HIV antibodies. However it will require greater validation and testing in diverse contexts before actual implementation.

Reducing costs The cost of ART has gone down substantially both as a result of lower cost of manufacture and greater subsidies by industrialized countries. There is now a wide variety of effective first-line drugs available to be taken alone or in combination. The choices may be bewildering to a layman and even to health professionals who are not keeping up with the latest developments in the field. In 2012, the average cost was about $10–$15 per month. Governments and health practitioners and providers should be aware of the various alternatives available and of the combination of drugs most powerful and cost-effective in a particular environment. Costs may continue to go down and adjustments will need to be made to take advantage of these developments. Health workers should also be aware of the possibility of some patients developing resistance to particular drugs or combination of drugs. Cost cutting can also be achieved by shifting some of the diagnostic and treatment burdens from doctors to other health personnel. This could also stretch budget resources so that more patients could be treated with the same resources. A recent study of such a program in South Africa was reported recently by Fairall et al. (2012), which aimed to assess the effects on mortality, viral suppression and other health outcomes and quality indicators of a program that provides educational outreach training of nurses to initiate and represcribe ART, and to decentralize care. The study compared results for an experimental group of over 8000 patients in several hospitals with a control group of over 7000 patients and found no statistically significant differences in the outcomes. The authors concluded that

> "Expansion of primary-care nurses' roles to include ART initiation and represcription can be done safely, and improve health outcomes and quality of care."

The importance of such a result cannot be overemphasized. By enlisting the support of nurses with no previous experience treating HIV programs can easily extend their reach to cover many more patients. It might also be possible to explore training lay people to handle some of the administrative and other activities associated with care for patients in large clinics and also as care providers in hospice and other care facilities.

Better diagnostic coverage Without improved diagnostic tools all the information and therapy in the world won't be effective in stopping the spread of HIV if coverage is not extended to more people who have

HIV. It is estimated by UNAIDS that globally only 40% of those living with HIV know their HIV status. There are many factors involved in the lack of knowledge, which is probably the most important single fact that people should know about their health. Without proper treatment it will eventually make the transition to AIDS, which is an irreversible death sentence. First, there is the stigma and discrimination attached to HIV and HIV testing. In many places those with the greatest chance of having HIV are most likely to be prohibited or discriminated against with regard to testing. In some cases they may even be denied of treatment. Second, those who should be tested are hard to reach and/or reluctant to be tested. Third, the young do not have a choice about being tested. Mothers who transmit HIV to their children are directly responsible for the health of their children. There is a growing body of evidence from several countries that demonstrates the beneficial impact of engagement with community service organizations has on increased HIV testing rates and increased treatment of HIV. Furthermore, those who have begun treatment within an umbrella of care and support are more likely to continue with treatment and are less stigmatized by the fact they have HIV. An important side benefit of timely entry into an HIV treatment program is that life expectancy is increased and the risk of acquiring other diseases is also reduced. For example, someone with HIV who has not sought treatment early in the course of the disease is much more likely to get tuberculosis.

Strengthen relationships within the community Communities with a strong base of support for those suffering from HIV and AIDS are highly effective in improving the ability of those high-risk populations (drug users, sex workers and men who have sex with men) to get treatment, to help others to get treatment and prevent new infections. They are also more likely to benefit from ART, since they are more likely to seek treatment before they become too sick. These conclusions were reached by analysis of community-based programs in Europe, Latin America and Southeast Asia, particularly when these programs were spearheaded by those who were living with HIV.

2.6 Public health and ART in developing countries

The HIV/AIDS epidemic has spread so quickly throughout the developing world that the usual public health networks have been unable to cope with the number of new patients, the care needs of existing patients and the complexity of antiretroviral therapy regimes. WHO has developed a program which integrates the management of all patients, whether they are young or adults, within a public health framework with particular reference to developing countries. This program is described more fully in a series of documents available from WHO and summarized by Gilks et al. (2006). The starting point was to develop a standardized treatment regime for treating HIV. There are a number of what are called first-line drugs, that is, drugs that are recommended when beginning HIV treatment. WHO recommends several packages of drugs that can be prescribed in a variety of circumstances. Because these are produced by several different manufacturers and they have more or less been standardized, competition has helped drive prices down to much more affordable levels. At the same time the process of checking for toxicity and switching to alternative drug cocktails has also been standardized and simplified combined with regular clinical assessment. Because HIV has a high mutation rate, drug resistance can occur frequently and this calls for some modification of the drug protocol. This requires constant monitoring and feedback among different treatment centers and these are channeled to WHO for changes in recommendations for various treatment centers around the world.

By developing a flexible and responsive public health approach to ART therapy, healthcare networks can provide a range of services for a full range of patient needs with diagnosis, treatment and care provided by teams headed by doctors and consisting of nurses, clinicians and lay people, either paid or volunteers as well as community health workers.

Aside from these general guidelines there are other factors that need to be considered in the development of a diagnosis and treatment program for specific countries. We consider some of these factors in the coming sections.

2.7 Interventions

General interventions The heading of general interventions is designed to cover a number of different ways to disseminate information about HIV and AIDS. It is hard to measure the effectiveness of these general interventions that are sometimes grouped under the heading of information, education and communication (IEC). It is important that the general public is informed about the various aspects of the disease and this will help to reduce the stigma that can be attached to being tested for HIV or discovering that the individual has HIV. Hopefully, a significant proportion of the general public might already know about the basics of how HIV is transmitted and prevented, and so the information campaign would be different than if a small percentage of the population had that awareness. The focus of the campaign will therefore depend upon the audience and also the chances that those in the audience could be infected. This is another reason to target those in high-risk groups.

Specific interventions A captive audience is one way to make sure that a segment of the population is being reached. We can start with high-risk groups, which are easy to contact and inform. These include sex workers in establishments, the military and police as well as truck drivers, prisoners, STD patients and IV users in treatment. Other high-risk groups would be harder to reach. These include freelance sex workers, IV drug users not in treatment, homosexuals and bisexuals. Those lower-risk groups would be easier to reach through schools, church groups, government workers and industrial work places. The message would be crafted to reach the most important information for each group. There is some evidence that interventions directed to individual groups have a beneficial impact on behavior, depending on the appropriateness and scope of the message. Abstinence – only education in schools is not effective according to several studies. However, when the message includes other sex aspects, including condoms, knowledge of HIV status of the partner as well as own status, these programs can be more effective. Peer education has been shown to be effective among sex workers in several countries including Chad and Thailand, particularly when pressure is put to adopt universal condom use. Where there is a high level of voluntary counseling and testing, the reduction in HIV can be quite dramatic. The trouble is that there are very few such programs and they tend to be most effective when HIV has reached epidemic proportions. This is when more people are likely to become more interested in their HIV status as well as that of others. This is particularly true now that ART is available to prolong life even if the individual has HIV. There is a good chance that HIV is no longer the death sentence it was a decade or two ago. Furthermore, if the individual unknowingly has HIV, the chances are high that he will die within a few years from AIDS. Once these facts are realized, people become more willing to be tested. As this knowledge filters down, more and more people are getting tested in developing countries.

Promotion of condom marketing, use and distribution Despite the experience of living with HIV worldwide for several decades now, there is surprisingly little evidence regarding the effectiveness of condom use in stopping the transmission of HIV. We know that used properly, modern condoms produced and distributed by reputable manufacturers are nearly 100% effective. Then why don't we have such evidence on the ground and in real-life experiments? The reason is that there are few experiments using control and experimental groups – the risks are too high. Therefore, we have to rely on anecdotes and the experience of couples that are known to be discordant – that is, one has HIV and the other does not. In these cases condoms are extraordinarily effective and also highly cost-effective. Even when both partners have HIV, condoms cut down the frequency of STDs and other diseases and reduce morbidity and mortality. In Thailand, the government and private foundations have promoted the distribution and use of condoms for sex workers and patrons of massage parlors with considerable success. There has been a significant reduction in the incidence of new HIV cases as well as the spread of STDs including syphilis and gonorrhea. Going beyond the Thailand's experience, much remains to be done including removing the stigma of HIV and providing equal access to all affected groups, particularly those in the highest-risk categories.

Preventing mother-to-child transmission The most effective way to prevent mother-to-child transmission is to have fewer babies and this can be achieved through better contraception practices. Taking drugs that inhibit the transmission of HIV to the fetus or newborn can cut the transmission rate by more than 95%, even when the mother is HIV positive (see Reynolds et al., 2004 and Sweat et al., 2004). This is a best case scenario. Other option is to include use of ART as an alternative to Sustiva. Currently, there is a need to increase the coverage of ART to pregnant women with HIV. Where there is an HIV epidemic, such as exists in many African countries, there is a need to extend ART therapy to more mothers. Presently, around 60% of HIV-positive mothers are receiving ART in Eastern and Southern Africa, a big boost from several years ago. However, in other regions of Africa and elsewhere in Asia and Latin America rates are much lower. In particular, ART coverage for pregnant women in Angola, Chad, and Democratic Republic of Congo is exceptionally low at 17% and less. See Table 2.3 for ART coverage of pregnant women in the top 21 African priority countries in the Global Plan.

As far as preventing transmission to the fetus, there are a variety of possible sources of transmission that increase with the level of infectivity of the mother. The risk to the newborn increases with the amount of maternal blood to which the newborn is exposed during labor and delivery. There can also be transmission from breast milk and this will depend upon the viral load of the milk which is measured by the CD4 cell counts. The risk of transmission increases with the time the

Table 2.3 ART coverage among eligible pregnant women in the 21 African priority countries in the Global Plan, 2011 and 2012[1]

	Antiretroviral coverage among pregnant women living with HIV, 2011	**Antiretroviral coverage among pregnant women living with HIV, 2012**	**Estimated number of pregnant women living with HIV needing antiretroviral medicines for PMTCT[2], 2012**
Botswana	>95%	>95%	13,000
Zambia	88%	95%	81,000
Ghana	80%	95%	9000
Namibia	94%	94%	8000
South Africa	95%	87%	268,000
Mozambique	53%	86%	94,000
Swaziland	87%	83%	12,000
Zimbabwe	52%	81%	69,000
United Republic of Tanzania	73%	77%	97,000
Côte d'Ivoire	53%	67%	20,000
Cameroon	55%	64%	27,000
Malawi	49%	60%	68,000
Lesotho	63%	57%	16,000
Kenya	66%	53%	86,000
Burundi	50%	53%	5000
Ethiopia	24%	41%	38,000
Nigeria	20%	17%	197,000
Angola	16%	16%	17,000
Chad	13%	14%	12,000
Democratic Republic of the Congo	6%	13%	32,000
Total	59%	65%	1,270,000

Source: WHO (2013a, Table 1.3).
Notes:
[1]Data is not available for Uganda, so the table only provides information for 20 African countries.
[2]PMTCT stands for Preventing-Mother-to-child Transmission.

child is breast-fed, although some studies suggest that the biggest risk is during the early months of breast-feeding. A breast infection could also increase the transmission from mother to child. The possible transmission of HIV from mother to child can be dramatically reduced by ART for the mother and ART prophylaxis for the child. However, coverage is still low. According to WHO, only a third of eligible children are receiving ART prophylaxis. One positive note is that a recent study shows that nearly all children infected with HIV (Thailand and Cambodia) were HIV-free following treatment with ART irrespective of whether they began ART therapy immediately or after some time delay (Puthanakit et al., 2012).

The Global Plan, launched in mid-2011, features two key targets: to reduce the number of children newly infected with HIV by 90% and reduce the number of mothers dying from AIDS-related causes by 50%. The Global Plan has 22 priority countries, all but one of which (India) are in the African region. The Global Plan priority countries are: Angola, Botswana, Burundi, Cameroon, Chad, Côte d'Ivoire, Democratic Republic of the Congo, Ethiopia, Ghana, India, Kenya, Lesotho, Malawi, Mozambique, Namibia, Nigeria, South Africa, Swaziland, Uganda, United Republic of Tanzania, Zambia and Zimbabwe.

As can be seen in Tables 2.3 and 2.4, Botswana and Namibia have already achieved universal access (with at least 80% of the children eligible for ART receiving it and over 90% of pregnant women living with HIV receiving ART). Other countries have also shown progress in their coverage of ART of needy recipients. However, the very low coverage in Angola, Cameroon, Côte d'Ivoire, the Democratic Republic of the Congo and Nigeria is of serious concern (see Table 2.4).

The effectiveness of ART will depend on how many women have HIV and the cost of finding them if they are not already in the healthcare system. There is a need to have stronger links between antenatal care, child health services, immunization clinics and HIV testing and care and treatment services for both mothers and their children.

Alternative allocation of funds for prevention and treatment Because the cost of HIV treatment over a lifetime is quite high, even in developing countries (estimated $500–$1000 per year per person in South Africa and other African countries for which data are available), a complementary strategy would be to keep citizens from getting infected. Cohen, Wu and Farley (2005) developed a procedure that suggests an allocation of funds across several interventions to prevent HIV infections in the United States.

This procedure is estimated to save about three times the number of lives saved by a number of interventions proposed by the Center of Disease Control and Prevention (CDC) in the United States. The CDC recommends that HIV testing be a routine in medical care, that new methods be developed to diagnose HIV outside of traditional medical settings, prevent new HIV infections by working with

Table 2.4 Children (0–14 years old) eligible for and receiving antiretroviral therapy, and antiretroviral therapy coverage in the 22 priority countries in the Global Plan, 2011 and 2012

	ART coverage among children, 2011	**ART coverage among children, 2012**	**Estimated number of children eligible for ART, 2012**
Botswana	>95%	>95%	10,000
Namibia	80%	87%	13,000
South Africa	71%	67%	210,000
Swaziland	48%	54%	14,000
Zimbabwe	35%	45%	100,000
India	28%	40%	86,000
Kenya	31%	38%	150,000
Zambia	32%	38%	90,000
Malawi	27%	36%	100,000
Chad	8%	29%	20,000
Uganda	[19–27%]	[27–42%]	[85,000–130,000]
Mozambique	22%	27%	100,000
United Republic of Tanzania	14%	26%	130,000
Ghana	16%	25%	14,000
Lesotho	27%	25%	22,000
Ethiopia	19%	23%	78,000
Burundi	18%	21%	9900
Côte d'Ivoire	14%	16%	35,000
Cameroon	13%	15%	33,000
Angola	11%	13%	23,000
Nigeria	14%	12%	260,000
Democratic Republic of the Congo	12%	9%	53,000
Total	29%	34%	1,660,000

Source: WHO (2013a).

HIV patients and their partners and continuing to decrease mother-to-child transmission. The new protocol suggested by Cohen et al. (2005) recommends an alternative approach that adopts a wide possibility of various interventions within the context of a mathematical model. A variety of possible interventions can be analyzed and evaluated. The model demonstrates that cost-effective interventions in the United States are those that target high-risk populations such as intravenous drug users, men who have sex with men (and sex workers in developing countries) and/or an inexpensive per person mass media campaign. A more detailed summary of possible interventions could be tailor-made to the disease profile of each country to be studied. While the specifics of each country model would depend upon various assumptions and parameter estimates of infection rates, size of population and other parameters of the general features can be spelled out as follows.

Target Focus intense interventions on high-risk groups such as intravenous drug users, sex workers, men who have sex with men, truck drivers, migrants, men who keep two homes (city and countryside) and those who are HIV positive to cut transmission.

Reduce serial transmission by reducing partner changes Studies have shown that high rates of transmission occur among those who have a variety of different sexual partners.

Testing of TB and malaria patients This is particularly important in countries that are in the high-risk category for these as well as HIV since coinfection rate is high.

Large-scale inexpensive interventions addressing low-prevalence populations These programs would stress importance of condoms, availability and cost of condoms and mass media on prevention of HIV transmission.

Other specific interventions Stress importance of circumcision to reduce probability of contracting and spreading HIV, reduce needle sharing, reduce STDs including screening and antibiotic treatments.

What doesn't work and is too costly Counseling and voluntary HIV testing are not effective in the United States and probably not effective elsewhere either.

New developments of a contraceptive for women that prevents HIV Two large clinical trials in Africa are ramping up to test the effectiveness of a vaginal ring that releases an HIV-fighting drug for a month or more, offering women at high risk a discreet way to protect them from the virus that causes AIDS.

The studies will test the effectiveness of a vaginal ring containing the antiretroviral drug dapivirine in thousands of women in several African countries to evaluate its ability to prevent new HIV infections. The studies will also assess its long-term safety.

According to the developer of the ring, Dr. Zeda Rosenberg chief executive officer of International Partnership for Microbicides (IPM), a nonprofit group founded by Dr. Rosenberg, the ring will add a long-acting device to the existing toolkit of HIV prevention options.

Because it only needs to be replaced by the woman once a month, the ring could relieve the necessity of women who have partners who refuse to use condoms, to stop relying on vaginal gels each time they have sex. Furthermore, there is growing evidence that vaginal gels may not be as effective as the new technology. In addition, irregular use is proposed to be the reason by a large study of the microbicidal gel containing the anti-HIV drug tenofovir as to why it failed to prevent infections in women in Sub-Saharan Africa.

Dapivirine, which is the medication used in these rings, is part of a class of antiretroviral drug that has long been used to treat HIV and prevent mother-to-child transmission of the virus. For further information on this new product and ongoing trials, see Fox News (25 July 2012).

2.8 New preventative measures

In 2012 Gilead Sciences Inc. was approved to sell a pill called Truvada, which can be taken by people who are at high risk of acquiring HIV through sexual activity. Those with an infected partner would be among the first candidates to use Truvada. It can also be used by high-risk groups such as sex workers and men who have sex with men. One study found that Truvada reduced infection transmission of HIV by 75% in heterosexual couples where one partner was infected and another study by 42% in healthy gay and bisexuals. While it is sold in the United States for around $480 per year, it has been sold for as little as $96 per year in developing countries. The cost of preventing HIV is still high even considering populations where HIV incidence is high. This is because the risk of getting infected is still low relative to the cost of the drug, which must be taken daily. Researchers estimate that it could cost over $10,000 to prevent one infection if half those high-risk individuals were given Truvada. Thirteen percent of infections would be averted over ten years (see Bloomberg, 17 July 2012). One research in Peru suggests that a drug like Truvada would be cost-effective in reducing the spread of HIV in populations with a high incidence of HIV. Further research also indicates that the effectiveness might not be compromised if patients don't comply fully with the one-a-day prescription. However, more work needs to be done to determine a recommended dosage profile. Certainly, a protocol that doesn't require daily use would cut costs and improve the economic efficiency of the drug and would make it very attractive for high-risk groups in developing countries.

Vaginal microbicides and vaginal rings are other new developments that would offer greater empowerment for women who are now more likely to contract HIV than men in Southern Africa. An intravaginal ring that could help prevent HIV infection could be ready for human trials sometime next year, according to researchers at the Population Council, an international nonprofit organization working on HIV and AIDS research. The ring would be nearly identical to contraceptive vaginal rings. Researchers say the ring would likely be used for 90 days at a time. Contraceptive rings are generally used for 21 days at a time. There is no date set when the ring might be available for distribution to the public.

2.9 Cost-effectiveness of prevention intervention

There are many challenges to efforts to establish the cost-effectiveness of different prevention intervention. There are overlapping and sometimes conflicting responsibilities and effectiveness of different interventions. Counseling, information dissemination, peer-based programs and education have aspects in common making it difficult to separate effectiveness of individual programs. Nevertheless, several studies have developed review procedures and estimates of the effectiveness of different interventions. Jamison et al. (2006, Chapter 18) provide a detailed analysis . We summarize the main components in what follows here.

Information, education and communication (IEC) Assessing the impact of various media on public awareness is difficult. What is recommended is a two-stage process. In the first stage a pilot questionnaire should be distributed to see the level of awareness of the ways HIV is spread, the chances of contracting HIV and methods of contraception that can be used and their effectiveness. In the second stage, an IEC program can be formulated and then implemented. If HIV has reached epidemic proportions, the program will be much more intense than if there are relatively few cases with targeting of key groups at risk. The specifics of these programs can follow the outlines suggested in the previous section on ***specific interventions*** outlined earlier.

School-based sex education The existing studies don't show much of an impact of school-based education on the incidence of HIV or STDs or condom use. Therefore, it is difficult to make any positive conclusions as to the general effect of these programs.

Voluntary counseling and testing (VCT) The evidence for the effectiveness of these programs depends on the context. In high-risk environments, there is more interest in establishing whether HIV is present and there is some evidence that VCT increases awareness and the status of HIV in populations at high risk. There is less evidence of the effectiveness of these interventions in less-risky environments.

Peer-based programs This intervention uses influential members of a targeted community to disseminate information or teach specific behaviors. In the United States, the work of the basketball player Ervin

"Magic" Johnson is a good example of a role model being used to influence those interested in sports. The peer role model does not necessarily have to be HIV positive but can be a well-known advocate of safe sex in the community such as Mechai Viravaidya in Thailand. Known affectionately as Mr. Condom, Mechai has been instrumental in getting sex workers to adopt condom use in Thailand and has promoted condoms in the country for many years. At the time he was the minister of tourism, information and AIDS, he was able to start a large and quite successful education campaign. He remains active in health affairs and support programs that aids in the control of HIV and AIDS. Work by Hutton, Wyss and N'Diekhor (2003) suggests that peer-based programs were highly cost-effective for sex workers, but less cost-effective for young people and high-risk men in Chad, a country where the incidence of HIV qualifies it as a high-risk environment (9% of adult population). These interventions were much less effective for young adults and high-risk men by 33- to 36-fold lower.

Preventing sexual transmission The promotion of condom marketing, use and distribution was discussed in the previous section. In this section, we address how cost-effective condoms are in preventing HIV. Surprisingly enough, as suggested earlier, there is not much evidence on this issue. There are no references to academic studies in the authoritative book by Jamison et al. (2006), although there is some anecdotal evidence that the use of condoms is probably effective in stopping the transmission of STDs. Without any direct evidence on the cost-effectiveness of condom use, we are left with only a general suggestion that people should use condoms!! They are cheap and do the job they were designed for. Recently a new device for women has been tested but has not been approved for general distribution in the United States. It plays the same role as the IUD does in preventing pregnancy. The HID ring, as it is called, can be used for a month and contains ARV ingredients that prevent the transmission of HIV. Hopefully it will be available shortly for distribution worldwide. It will provide women with an alternative method of preventing the spread of HIV without having to rely on their partner for protection.

Preventing mother-to-child transmission As noted earlier, the most effective method of preventing mother-to-child transmission is ARV and in particular when the HIV status of the woman is known. In cases where the status of the woman is unknown, additional costs are incurred to find whether the woman is HIV positive. The cost-effectiveness of ARV will be much lower in populations where HIV is not epidemic or rare. However, it may still be cost-effective if discovery of the woman's HIV status can be facilitated by a well-focused information campaign targeted to pregnant women. When the source of water is secure and health conditions are good and the income of parents is adequate to afford reliable substitute nutrition, it is not recommended that babies of HIV-positive mothers be breast-fed. However, in developing countries these conditions are not often met with a high probability, the question then becomes whether to breast-feed and for how long. There is evidence that prolonged breast-feeding may double the likelihood of mother-to-child transmission. Weaning is recommended at an early date and mixed feeding is not recommended. Research suggests that this probably increases the risk of transmission vis-à-vis reliance on breast-feeding and early weaning (see Jamison et al., 2006 p. 346). The solution as to whether to breast-feed or not will depend upon individual circumstances and the judgment of the health provider.

Blood-borne transmission A variety of programs have been implemented to reduce the incidence of HIV from tainted needles used by intravenous drug users. Given the high transmission rate of HIV through tainted blood and low cost of cleaning needles, needle exchange programs are very cost-effective. Blood safety is the other aspect of handling blood products to minimize the transmission of HIV. All donated blood should be screened for HIV, even though it is relatively costly. The risk of infected blood being used in hospitals and for other transfusions generally outweighs the cost. Evidence supports the WHO and UNAIDS recommendation that all countries, regardless of the nature of the HIV epidemic, should implement a safe blood program immediately. As an additional precaution anyone working with or around blood products should treat these products as potentially dangerous and exercise precaution in dealing with them, including gloves, gowns and goggles as well as normal safety precautions for syringes and disposal of waste products.

There is a large unmet need for safe blood in developing countries. Evidences from China and other countries suggest that there are extreme risks to transfusions of tainted blood (see for example Bad Blood, *Economist*, 8 September 2012). In Africa there is a desperate need for safe blood for seriously ill patients. The Safe Blood for Africa Foundation (http://www.safebloodforafrica.org/) says that approximately six million blood transfusions are administered to seriously ill patients in Sub-Saharan Africa each year. However, the estimated need for life-saving transfusion in Sub-Saharan Africa is triple that amount 18 million units of safe blood per year. At the same time WHO estimates that 5–10% of HIV/AIDS infections in Africa occur from unsafe blood transfusions.

Table 2.5 Prevalence of HIV, total (% of population ages 15–49) in Sub-Saharan Africa

Country name	1991	2001	2011
Botswana	8.4	27.0	23.4
Kenya	3.7	8.5	6.2
Lesotho	1.5	23.4	23.3
Malawi	8.9	13.8	10.0
Mozambique	0.7	9.7	11.3
Namibia	2.3	15.5	13.4
South Africa	0.8	15.9	17.3
Swaziland	4.0	22.2	26.0
Tanzania	6.0	7.2	5.8
Uganda	13.0	6.9	7.2
Zambia	14.4	14.4	12.5
Zimbabwe	15.9	25.0	14.9

Source: World Bank (2013).

Treatment in epidemics Earlier we discussed how high- and low-risk environments differ with regard to the focus of community action and finding HIV-positive members in the community. This section provides some additional specifics. It is more important to change the behavior and secure treatment for those at high risk of becoming infected with HIV. At the same time, protocols for environments where there is a generalized epidemic differ from those where only a few groups need to be targeted. What are important are the contact rate and the rate at which the infection can spread. In Chapter 18, Jamison et al. (2006) outline a series of preventive measures that are applicable for each of the four general categories of the epidemic. They are summarized as follows, starting with the most affected:

Generalized high-level epidemic In Sub-Sahara Africa (see Table 2.5) where there are 12 countries with HIV incidence greater than 5% and eight countries with incidence with 10% and above in 2011, a country-wide effort is needed in order to bring down the scourge of HIV. This includes the following immediate actions:

Establishing and maintaining surveillance of risk behaviors, incidence of sexually transmitted infections (STIs) and HIV for populations at risk.

Promote treatment throughout the country, including the offer of free HIV and STI testing.

Set up distribution network for free condom availability.
Voluntary counseling and testing for any couple planning to have children and also pregnant women regarding breast-feeding.
Using mass media to mobilize and inform society as well as changing social norms about HIV.

Use other opportunities to make information available about HIV including schools, work places, police stations, prisons, military camps, railroad stations and airports.

Formulate special programs for injecting drug abusers including therapy for those with addictions.

Generalized low-level epidemic Policies in these environments would be appropriate where the incidence is in less than 5% of the population and are similar in scope to policies for higher-level epidemics as follows and would apply mostly in the rest of Sub-Sahara Africa.

Establishing and maintaining surveillance of risk behaviors incidence of STIs and HIV for populations at risk with emphasis on young people.

Extending and intensifying mass media coverage.
Promoting STI and HIV testing through mass media for entire community.
Subsidizing condoms and promoting condom usage and providing universal access.
Offer HIV screening to all pregnant women.

Broaden coverage to information education and communication to everyone with high-risk behavior and high rates of STI.

Concentrated epidemics Some of the same policies that apply to generalized epidemics would apply including STI screening and treatment for key risk groups, drug programs and needle exchanges, peer-based programs for key populations at risk, HIV screening for pregnant women and distribution of condoms. In concentrated epidemics there can also be problems with harassment of some groups at risk including sex workers, gay men and women and intravenous drug users. There may also be stigma for some key subgroups.

HIV/AIDS in South Africa South Africa has the largest concentration of HIV/AIDS in the world. Out of an adult population of 32 million, about 17% are afflicted with HIV/AIDS or around 5.6 million people. While the historical record of HIV treatment has sometimes been characterized by neglect and lack of funding, the current political leaders are committed to a sound and wide-ranging program of identification, treatment and care. There are several features of the South African epidemic that can provide lessons for other countries with widespread epidemics. The number of deaths from AIDS has dropped dramatically as a result of this change in policy, a drop from 37,000 in 2001 to 27,0190 in 2011. Infant mortality also fell from 56.7 per 1000 births to 37.9 in 2011. There are more women with HIV than men, about 57% of the total. This has had a deleterious impact on families and has also resulted in a large increase in the number of orphans, currently estimated at nearly two million. The spread of HIV has created many expectant mothers with the disease and there has been a strategic move to increase the probability that HIV will not be transmitted from mother to child and this program has been quite successful as this rate has fallen dramatically.

The ART program has also been quite successful and it was estimated that by the end of 2012 there would be 80% compliance with a policy of having treatment for newly diagnosed cases of HIV. Recall that the PEPFAR estimation of new infections (350,000) to those in treatment (276,017) was 1.3% in 2011. Whether South Africa has reached its goal of treating all new infections is still a question. Nevertheless the government commitment is strong and consistent. This commitment is also backed up with a goal of targeting all those with CD4 cell count of 350 or less. This is a big step from a program where many patients did not receive treatment even with CD4 count below 200. These late initiation treatment programs are being phased out and it is also being recognized that some patients are denying to be treated because they still feel well. Further efforts have to be made to bring them into treatment programs immediately. It is also important to recognize that the case load of patients is increasing dramatically as ART treatments are being undertaken by more patients. As this happens it is critical that treatment protocols are not relaxed and that the patient gets his or her medications every day. There has been a rise in the dropout rate after three years, which is not a good sign. Drug shortages have also developed with the scale up in treatment. Renewed efforts have to be made to deliver required treatment in a timely manner.

Programs to raise awareness of HIV through a counseling campaign have not been as successful. While a survey showed that 90% of the population was aware of the HIV threat through one or more of several media campaigns, the level of accurate knowledge of HIV and AIDS is still poor, including widespread lack of knowledge of how HIV is spread and how to avoid becoming infected. The fact that having fewer sexual partners can also diminish the chances of contracting HIV was not widely recognized. On the other hand condom use has increased, particularly among the youth. A survey showed that married couples have a much lower condom use rate (15% for men and women) than those engaged in casual sex (75% of men and 56% of women). These rates need to go even higher, particularly when it is recognized that the incidence of HIV is particularly high for those working in the sex industry. Those in the risk groups (sex workers, gay men, intravenous drug users and so on) are often abused and discriminated against in South Africa, not only by their partners but also by the police.

We shall discuss the joint HIV and tuberculosis programs in Chapter 3. It is worthwhile here to reiterate the importance of integrating care of the two diseases in hospitals and clinics in order to increase efficiency and to take advantage of crossover treatment option. In some cases treatment of malaria patients can also be considered.

To conclude, one of the side benefits to a successful HIV and TB program is a happier and longer life. Life expectancy in South Africa increased by 10% between 2005 and 2010.

Case study of Uganda and Botswana Uganda is one of the poorest countries in the world and was riddled with a corrupt government for many years. When the HIV/AIDS epidemic began in the 1980s it had a limited health budget, few health professionals and a growing HIV epidemic. However, the regime was very open about the extent of the epidemic, that Uganda became known as the AIDS country. Uganda was one of the first African countries to investigate the transmission of HIV from mother to child and with the help of foreign doctors supported the publication of these findings in reputable medical journals. Openness in the society extended to the publicity about how HIV spreads. There were billboard displays showing how it can be contracted, where to purchase condoms and other facts about the disease. These messages were also translated into different dialects so that everyone in the country had the same information base. Soon after the information campaign was launched, a catchy phrase was spread to enable people to remember the basic facts about HIV and how to protect against it. It was called ABC. A was for abstinence from having sex before marriage, B stood for being faithful to your partner and C for using a condom. Uganda has had a long history of polygamy, since many men maintain two families – one in the city and one in their rural home. There was no mention of this practice but it was understood that the B implied faithfulness to both partners and with no fooling around on the side. The society was very open about the disease and how it spread and was also supportive of those who contracted it. There was some social stigma but not nearly as much as in more closed societies such as Botswana. There has also been a tradition of home care and many HIV patients are cared for by family and friends in a home environment. President Yoweri Museveni even went so far as to say that "HIV is a good disease". What he meant was that you could not catch it easily, like getting TB from someone coughing or by being bitten by a mosquito and getting malaria. One of the leading HIV support organization was founded by 16 people with HIV and is dedicated to helping care and support for HIV/AIDS patients. In 2003, the President's Emergency Plan for AIDS Relief (PEPFAR) was founded and began to put more emphasis on the A and B components of the ABC program with less emphasis on C. In any event, at an estimated 5.4% of the adult population infected Uganda has the lowest incidence of HIV/AIDS in Africa among the 21 high-risk countries.

Turning to Botswana, the environment is much different. Botswana is one of the richest and most rapidly growing countries in Africa. It has a strong and active government and a strong export sector led by diamond mining. It is among the world's most peaceful countries and achieved independence from Great Britain long before some other African nations. Despite all of these positive aspects Botswana is in denial when it comes to the HIV/AIDS epidemic. As noted by Helen Epstein in her book *The Invisible Cure*, no one talks about AIDS in public. There are few articles in the newspapers or on radio or television.

There are AIDS billboards on every major road and every schoolchild received education about the disease... (however) when patients went to hospitals for treatment, health workers informed them that they were suffering from tuberculosis or pneumonia and never gave them or their families the true diagnosis.

There was a change in 1999 when the new president, Festus Mogae, was elected and there was a push to create a more open environment. At that time Botswana had the highest HIV rate in the world and it is still ranked number two (only Swaziland is higher). Still, in 2003 in response to a question to a health worker about whether he or she talked to patients about AIDS, a representative from the Global Fund to Fight AIDS, TB and Malaria got the following answer:

No, a six-week counseling course had told him not to... I asked about the village chief – he does not feel qualified to talk about AIDS. I asked about the church, no one mentions it at funerals.

Epstein goes on to say that despite having a much richer economy than neighboring Uganda (per capita income $13,300 versus $1100 and health spending per capita of $1296 versus $118), it still has an HIV infection figure that is 4.4 times as high as Uganda's. One social scientist that Epstein talked to said a major reason was that in Botswana, AIDS is still considered a disease of the poor and marginalized. It had never been seen as EVERYONE'S problem. Without the conviction of the entire society that eradicating any disease is the responsibility of everyone, it is unlikely to happen. Despite shiny new facilities and very high per capita spending on health, Botswana has not made as much progress in dealing with HIV as has its poorer neighbor, Uganda. And, with the high rate of HIV has come coinfection with TB. In the 1980s TB was not much of a problem in Botswana. However, since 1989, Botswana has experienced a threefold increase in TB incidence. The increase has largely been attributed to the country's increasing HIV epidemic. It is estimated that 60–86% of TB patients in Botswana are currently HIV coinfected. By turning a blind eye toward HIV by the upper classes and by failing to grasp the importance of making HIV identification and treatment a priority for the entire society, HIV has continued to spread among the poor, despite having good treatment facilities. Furthermore, Botswana now also has a TB epidemic.

Western societies didn't get rid of smallpox or polio because a small group wanted to. It became public policy which everyone accepted, supported and financed. This is what is needed not only in Botswana but wherever there is a widespread epidemic. Greater progress is possible only when there is acceptance and recognition of the shared responsibility of diagnosing, treating and caring by all its citizens for all its citizens.

2.10 Treating the disadvantaged

To be realistic, ART will benefit those who can afford it first but continued efforts must be made to address the poor, those who are discriminated against and minorities who are hard to reach as well. Such groups include those with highest rates of infection in the riskiest categories mentioned earlier – sex workers, men who have sex with men, truck drivers, intravenous drug users, prisoners and the military and ethnic minorities who are hard to reach. Treatment cannot be denied to those who need it the most even though there are often strong motives for societies to withhold treatment from groups where there has been a long history of discrimination. Particular care should be taken to treat women and children under ten.

Vulnerable populations The list of those most at risk and who should receive the most initial attention were mentioned earlier. To these should be added a note that the epidemic should not be exacerbated by criminalizing and imprisoning drug users.

Integrate prevention and treatment HIV testing should be expanded and point of care diagnosis adopted whenever possible. Testing of potential patients can also be suggested in appropriate settings and in a highly vulnerable HIV environment. Diagnosis, treatment, care and counseling should be integrated so the patient feels supported and nurtured. STD diagnosis and treatment can also be part of the diagnosis and treatment regime. The cooperation of the community and an open environment to discuss and disseminate information is critical. Remember the different experiences of Uganda and Botswana.

Develop programs for women and girls Poverty, gender inequality, social disruption and discrimination are leading causes of HIV among girls and young women. Programs that support their health and education are critical to short circuiting the continuation of the HIV epidemic; particularly where women are objectified as sexual objects and prostitution is widespread. Better information and tools to prevent transmission of HIV are also important for young women to have a more informed view of their bodies and how to take care of them.

Orphans and other vulnerable children In many countries AIDS has created an entire generation of orphans for which there is no social safety net in place. UNICEF estimates that by 2010 as many as 20 million children in Africa have lost one or both parents since the epidemic began. New social structures have to be developed to keep these children safe as well as to house, clothe, feed and educate them. They are the innocent victims of the AIDS epidemic. Public support for the children is limited despite international commitments such as through United Nations General Assembly Special Session. More has to be done, for this is the next generation upon which these societies will depend for leadership and skill.

Provide more resources We have noted the shortfall in ART and the need to develop more comprehensive and expanded networks to provide a more vigorous environment to deal with the HIV/AIDS epidemic. The United Nations as well as all of its member governments has to play a role in this effort. Private resources will also play a role as they have in the past. But more needs to be done. The Global Fund now provides resources as do industrial countries. As noted earlier more resources are needed. The poor countries alone cannot defeat the epidemic and failure to do so will continue to exact a tremendous toll of death and suffering for countries that have already endured so much. The report also notes that the World Bank and other international financial organizations like the Latin American, African and Asian Development Banks sometimes impose restrictions on the use of their funds and also restrict hiring of locals in the health sector. There needs to be better coordination between these international financial organizations and local governments to achieve more efficient and effective use of resources to fight HIV. In this connection it is important that NGOs, the government health sectors along with international donors are partners in a coordinated HIV/AIDS program with clear guidelines and time lines to achieve specific objectives. These objectives should be reviewed periodically with a view to further improving the delivery of health services in the country.

2.10.1 Palliative care

For all HIV patients palliative care is important. This includes a wide range of activities including pain management, communication about the illness and prognosis with patient, family and friends, psychological, spiritual and social support and possible hospice or other support services. In many developing countries, where the burden of HIV is high there are additional constraints including the high patient load, racial and ethnic disparities in access to healthcare and limited access to drugs for pain management. In the latter instance, 90% of the global morphine supply is consumed by industrial countries. Some developing countries have adopted an integrated community-based home care system which features community caregivers as the centerpiece in a home-based setting. These programs need more funding and human resources particularly where the case loads have reached epidemic proportions. Further, the stigma of HIV is still strong and women still bear the bulk of the burden of care.

As Figure 2.1 demonstrates, patients with HIV can contract any number of other problems as a result of the immune system becoming weaker and weaker. This requires both pain and symptom management. Much of the pain management can be handled by drugs like morphine. ART can also help with pain and pain management can require some changes in dosage or in the recommended drug. WHO has a three-step approach to pain management (see www.who.int/cancer/palliative/painladder/en/). For most severe pains, medications should be administered around the clock. Other drugs, including antidepressants and muscle relaxants, may also be appropriate in selected circumstances.

Side effects and the development of opportunistic infections as a result of the compromise of the immune system will also present challenges for care givers and the medical community. Patients can also experience weight loss, nausea, anxiety or depression and coughs and fevers.

Since HIV and AIDS are life-threatening diseases that generally cause a shortened life expectancy, death is on the minds of those involved, both patients and family. In countries where the disease burden is heavy, everyone involved will be familiar with the course of the disease. Many will have witnessed the passing of relatives and friends. That it is familiar does not make it any easier. In any case it is useful to discuss the matter with patients. Legal considerations may also matter depending on the economic circumstances of those involved. Because HIV is so common in Sub-Saharan Africa, many of these issues will not be new. Nevertheless, there can be problems of trust and belief and possible discrimination. Whether ART is available or not can sometimes create tension, particularly if not all patients in a particular location are receiving it. When the time for transition to comfort from treatment is close, it is important to get both the patient and family ready for the eventual death of the patient. Following the passing away of the patient, burial and financial arrangements would need to be made. There may also be dependent children that have to be provided for.

2.10.2 Nutrition and food security issues

Those infected with HIV require greater caloric intake, particularly more protein. In high-risk environments there are already high fatality rates, fewer supportive family members and greater risks of continued food insecurity. Malnutrition increases the risk of opportunistic infections, increases the risk of transmission from mother to child and accelerates the progress of the infection. The World Food Program suggests food supplements and micronutrients for those with HIV. Realistically it may not be possible to provide these supplements in high-risk environments although these supplements could be provided to families in these environments, which could be shared with those with the greatest needs. These might include school feeding programs with special take home rations for families caring for orphans or those suffering from HIV. These programs have been shown to be highly cost-effective.

2.10.3 Treatment of opportunistic infections

Coinfection with TB has already been mentioned and in many cases is the first sign that a patient also has HIV. TB appears sometime between five and ten years after the onset of HIV. Without treatment the immune system continues to be compromised and eventually results in death. There are many scientific articles and medical discussions of the kinds of secondary infections. We will not go into them here aside from mentioning that around 90% of people with HIV suffer from some skin disorder and to note that ART is effective in reducing the onset of opportunistic infections. However, some patients who already have a lowered immunity will develop an illness which they believe to be a result of the antiretroviral therapy rather than HIV. These patients may be tempted to stop their medications. It requires a trained clinician to recognize and treat these opportunistic infections. In poor countries with limited treatment options, tuberculosis is the only opportunistic infection that is being systematically treated along with HIV. After five years, an estimated 40% of those with HIV with latent TB will have developed the active form of TB and require aggressive treatment.

2.10.4 Cost-effectiveness and other aspects of ART

Starting ART has been shown to benefit those with a CD4 count of fewer than 350 cells per cubic millimeter (see Palella et al., 2003). The benefits of starting earlier may be outweighed by the toxicities resulting from the treatment (see Mallal et al., 2000). In poorer countries treatment is often initiated when the patient is treated for an opportunistic infection such as TB. However, the science is generally not clear on the best time to begin ART. Realistically, in developing countries, it may be when TB is diagnosed.

2.11 Progress and prospects for the future

The latest report of the UNAIDS agency of the United Nations highlights the progress that was made in the decade from 2001 to 2011 with greater emphasis on the shorter period from 2005 to 2011. The outlook presents a sobering short-term future. There were 2.5 million new infections in 2011 and 1.7 million deaths. Thirty-four million people are infected with HIV, but sadly only an estimated half know their HIV status. Of those who know they have HIV – about 15 million would be eligible for treatment with ART but only eight million are now being treated. As for those 17 million who do not know their status, their health status will continue to deteriorate until they get treatment or die. They also present an ongoing risk as they could spread the virus to others.

Progress in cutting the rate of new infections is displayed in Table 2.6. The data show a rather dramatic decline of the impact of the disease – a sharp decline in the rate of infections as a result of better information, a change in habits and the wider use of prophylactic devices, and in mortality with the spread of antiretroviral therapy.

Table 2.6 PEPFAR report on country progress in reducing HIV infections and scaling up ART

Country	2011 New HIV infections	2011 Increase in new patients treated	Ratio of new infections to new patients treated
Botswana	8500	17,811	0.5
Côte d'Ivoire	13,000	6844	1.9
Congo	46,000	9375	4.9
Ethiopia	11,000	40,507	0.3
Kenya	91,000	93,912	1.0
Lesotho	22,000	5845	3.8
Mozambique	100,000	49,912	2.0
Namibia	80,000	14,539	5.7
Nigeria	270,000	56,789	4.8
Rwanda	8400	4083	2.1
South Africa	350,000	276,017	1.3
Swaziland	12,000	11,751	1.0
Tanzania	120,000	31,700	3.8
Uganda	120,000	60,014	2.0
Zambia	42,000	66,479	0.6
Zimbabwe	60,000	142,155	0.4

Source: Office of the United States global AIDS coordinator (2012, p. 7).

New patients beginning ART number around 1.4 million a year and should be much higher if the number of newly infected is to be reduced quickly. Those who are not on ART have a high probability of infecting others, whereas those on ART are extremely unlikely to infect others. As we have noted and suggested earlier, the report stresses the importance of targeting those at risk for contracting HIV. It also points out that some groups at risk – drug users and homosexuals – are often discriminated against and are much less likely to seek treatment. Every effort must be made to stop such discrimination and allow these parties the rights to access such life-saving treatments.

Realistically, science has provided a number of new tools to reduce the spread of HIV ever further. What is lacking is the political and financial will to do it. As more people who would have otherwise died are able to avail themselves of ART therapy, there will be more patients on a continuing medication regime putting further pressure on already stressed healthcare systems. As long as there are 17 million people with HIV engaging in risky behavior that can infect others, the threat of further spread of HIV will continue. More money is needed to reach these potential patients as well as to continue the progress that has been made in reducing the spread of HIV by adopting appropriate life style changes and further encouraging the involvement of all members of society in efforts to diagnose and treat those with HIV.

Policy makers have to struggle with the alternative strategies of prevention versus treatment. The balance will be determined by the relative strength of the pressure on policy makers and the healthcare systems in individual countries. Realistically, more people will become aware that they can easily and privately determine their HIV status and seek treatment if they are HIV positive. The general public will become aware that knowing your own HIV status is critically important for your current and future health. If the individual does not have HIV, he should take appropriate measures to avoid getting it. If he has contracted HIV, he should get treatment immediately. As a result there will be increased pressure on health providers to offer appropriate treatment with ART advice and therapy. At the same time, the health systems in countries have to continue to address the potential for a HIV epidemic among high-risk groups through better outreach, media coverage and programs to reduce discrimination and isolation of high-risk group members.

Where the number of HIV cases is increasing along with the rate of coinfection with TB, greater integration of tracking systems is critical. This will require more computerization of records and the ability to transfer files to address different aspects of both diseases. Greater community involvement is also critical along with feedback from regional centers to central data processing locations. Paper files will become too cumbersome as intake numbers swell further.

Although the cost of delivering antiretroviral drugs to the more than 34 million people now living with HIV has decreased substantially, and the availability of these drugs in resource-poor settings has steadily increased, the costs associated with delivering antiretroviral drugs is overwhelming many organizations and public health systems. Estimates put the cost of the funding response to the HIV/AIDS epidemic by 2015 between US$22 billion and US$24 billion per year and between US$19 billion and US$35 billion per year by 2031, with antiretroviral treatment accounting for up to 70% of the total cost of care in the most affected countries.

It is estimated that for every person starting treatment, two are newly infected, a path that is clearly unsustainable.

Given these limitations, there is growing recognition that the search for an HIV Cure is imperative both in terms of the individual and public health benefits it would provide and also an opportunity to potentially avoid the long-term cumulative costs of ART.

The above figures are quoted from the Press release of Inaugural Global Scientific Strategy Towards an HIV Cure launched ahead of the XIX International AIDS Conference in Washington DC. (UNAIDS, 2012a).

In 2011 the United States began a new initiative as a continuation of the President's Emergency Plan for AIDS Relief (PEPFAR), which started in 2003 under the Bush administration. The program is supporting antiretroviral treatments to reduce the transmission of HIV from mother to child as well as counseling for HIV patients in many countries around the world. President Obama also renewed the US commitment to provide ARV therapy for six million people by the end of 2013. PEPFAR is also joining with the Global Fund to Fight AIDS, Tuberculosis and Malaria to build a sustainable response to HIV in countries around the world. One component of these efforts will be to help coordinate required actions with governments in affected countries.

To achieve an AIDS-free generation in the future, new HIV infections have to be reduced dramatically as the number of patients on therapy increases. Looking at the number of deaths from AIDS there has been a significant bump upward in mortality rates in developing countries, which seems to have peaked around 2006 and is now trending downward. This is a good sign. It has to be joined by continued efforts to find and treat those who are HIV positive. We do not know how many people would test positive for HIV and are continuing to be potential sources of the spread of the virus in their communities. What we do know is the historical pattern of diagnosing new HIV infections and the increase in new patients on treatment. What is important in the short run is to bring the ratio of new HIV infections to the increase in new patients being treated to one or less than one. If this can be accomplished in those high-risk countries, the long-run outlook will be substantially brighter, even if there are people with HIV who still need treatment.

PEPFAR has provided a snapshop of this ratio and the underlying country date in its latest report (PEPFAR blueprint: creating an AIDS-free generation). Looking at this ratio for some (but not all) of the countries that are part of the scaling up of the ART program shows there is still much work to be done. See the last column of Table 2.6. It shows that only a few countries have brought this ratio below one and many of the crisis countries are still much above 1. Clearly, there is still much more to do to bring down this ratio in some countries.

The PEPFAR report also provides an up to date summary of programs in four countries as well as a suggested program of actions for the medium term. A baseline which assumes that programs are held at the 2010 level is compared with three alternative scenarios which up the level of coverage of different treatment regimes. These scenarios are described for each country in the next section. A feature of the discussions of these country programs is the careful consideration of who should have ART treatment. As CD4 cell counts fall, the risk of infections and diseases such as TB increase. For those in line for receiving ART, the wait can be a matter of life and death. That is why it is so important to increase the supply of drugs available for ART therapy as quickly as possible so as to prevent unnecessary deaths as a result of drug shortage. While there are rough estimates of those who have HIV, who are at present not receiving ART therapy, we do not know for sure the CD4 cell count status of all of these potential patients and how quickly they might succumb to AIDS and die. We know the morbidity statistics only when it is too late. This is why tracking mortality is critically important for policies that can be implemented to increase the supply of ART to those who are most at risk, that is, with CD4 count below 250.

Zambia As noted in Table 2.6, Zambia has managed to bring the rate of new HIV infections below the rate of increase in new patient intake. It is now past the "tipping point" and can move to a new phase in its fight against HIV. According to the report Zambia can realize a goal of reaching an estimated 80% coverage of those patients with CD4 cell counts below 350 cells/cubic mm in the next four years. This would allow it to avert over 100,000 new infections over this period. Furthermore, Zambia is now reaching most of those HIV patients with CD4 cell counts below 350 and so it can work to expand treatment for those with higher CD4 cell counts and also to provide lifelong treatment for those HIV patients living with a partner who does not have HIV. It is also contemplating an improvement in its program to women with HIV regardless of their CD4 cell counts. There is also discussion of raising the CD4 cell counts level to 550, which would bring many more patients into the treatment program. How this would be funded remains a challenge. Were it to be implemented, it would result in a decrease in the number of AIDS-related deaths by an estimated 118,000 over the next four years relative to the baseline scenario.

Kenya In Kenya also the situation is challenging. A combination of higher levels of ART and increased circumcisions as well as other programs, including condom distribution and community awareness, has helped to bring Kenya to the tipping point. New infections of around 90,000 were just about equal to the increase in new patients in 2011. If Kenya can move to the level of 550 CD4 cell counts, it would be able to admit an additional 500,000 patients per treatment each year. This would avert an estimated 300,000 plus HIV infections and over 250,000 AIDS-related deaths between 2012 and 2016. Whether the healthcare system can effectively deal with the increased patient load is the critical question at this point.

Uganda As noted in an earlier section of this chapter, Uganda had a forward looking response to the HIV/AIDS epidemic in the early days before the epidemic spread throughout Sub-Sahara Africa and to the rest of the world. However, its HIV abatement program has stuttered in recent years as its ART, circumcision and the program to reduce transmission from mother to child have lost momentum. As a result the rate of new infections is about double the rate of new patients being treated (120,000 versus 60,000). To turn this around more resources have to be devoted to ART and also to avert HIV by better outreach to communities, a more intensified circumcision program and more effort to avert contracting HIV through condom use, better community awareness, attention to those men who have two families and school programs to spread the importance of appropriate health and sexual practices. Currently, Uganda has an active circumcision program which is estimated to be the major contributor to avert HIV infections. It could be expanded even further along with ART and mother-to-child transmission reduction programs. PEPFAR estimates that a combination of an increased ART program along with other initiatives could avert over 200,000 new infections and 100,000 fewer deaths between 2012 and 2016 compared to the baseline. Greater funding and buildup in the capacity of the healthcare system would be required to implement these changes.

Cambodia This country presents a case where HIV is being spread by three groups where the epidemic has reached epic proportions. As the blueprint suggests, it is "mainly sexually driven," with sex workers, men who have sex with men and intravenous drug users being the major groups with high HIV incidence. Estimates of the extent of the epidemic are not available from official sources. However, the blueprint suggests that there were 46,000 new infections in 2011, while there were only 9000 plus new patients under treatment. This is one of the highest ratios in the world, at close to five, rivaled only by Nigeria. Because the major

HIV patients are often stigmatized and considered outcasts, there are challenges in Cambodia in determining who has contracted HIV and how to provide information to them so they can seek treatment. With the limited resources at its disposal Cambodia has been able to implement a successful condom use policy and has reduced the HIV rate by 65% between 1998 and 2010. Nevertheless, much more needs to be done on the treatment side, so as to bring the treatment rate in line with the infection rate.

Moving to a more general agenda for all HIV-affected countries, PEPFAR suggests a coordinated set of actions to save lives, make smart investments, share responsibilities of the global community and integrate scientific developments into country programs. The blueprint is well organized and comprehensive in its ideas, but short on details of how the programs are to be financed. Although implementation steps are spelled out in great detail, many of the aspects of the various initiatives themselves have been touched on already in earlier discussions in this chapter.

The road map for saving lives involves the following steps:

- Eliminate new HIV infections among children
- Increase coverage of HIV to reduce AIDS-related mortality and enhance HIV prevention
- Increase circumcision of men to prevent spread of HIV through sexual activity
- Increase access to prevention interventions such as condoms, testing and counseling

The road map for smart investment involves the following steps:

- Target HIV-associated tuberculosis and reduce co-mortality and morbidity
- Increase access and uptake of key HIV services
- Partner with those with HIV to design programs that respond to their needs
- Focus on women, girls and gender equality
- Reach orphans and vulnerable children
- Support young people

The road map for shared responsibility involves the following steps:

- Partner with countries to bring about country-led responses

- Increase support for civil societies as partners in global AIDS response
- Expand collaboration with bilateral and multilateral partners
- Increase private sector mobilization toward an AIDS-free generation

Road map for driving results with science involves the following steps:

- Support implementation research
- Evaluate the impact of combination prevention
- New technologies for prevention and care
- Develop evidence-based approaches to reach people early enough in disease progression to help maintain a strong immune system
- Measure viral load through point of care tests
- Assist countries in adopting new technologies such as point of care HIV tests and TB tests with reduced time for diagnosis and treatment for people living with HIV and TB.

These are all laudable objectives, but the blueprint doesn't spell out from where the money is to be raised. Further, how are the many other countries that are not close to the tipping point to reach the goal of treating more with additional funding while at the same time reducing the number of new patients treated. UNAIDS has posted some broad global numbers for the recent past and the goal by 2015.

HIV/AIDS funding was $300 million in 1996, rising by leaps and bounds to $15.6 billion by 2008 and hopes for $22 billion by 2015. Meanwhile the gap between what funds are needed and funds available grew from $6.5 billion in 2008 to $6.9 billion in 2010. The gap is projected to be $7 billion by 2015, which can be closed if 4.2 million new infections and 1.9 million deaths are to be averted. Fifteen million more people will have access to HIV therapy by 2015 as well if funding is forthcoming. This will bring the numbers of those with HIV who can benefit from ART therapy into virtual balance with those getting ART therapy.

How is the money being spent now and how is the money to be spent in the future? We only have at hand the estimates provided by PEPFAR for interventions and HIV infections averted by four classes of intervention in the three countries reported in the blueprint. Estimates are that ART averted 35% of all HIV infections on average in Zambia, 50% in Kenya and 20% in Uganda. Preventing mother-to-child transmission held the infection to 12%, 10% and 8%, respectively in Zambia, Kenya and Uganda and circumcision 36%, 10% and 40%, respectively in the three countries. Other interventions including counseling and condoms are estimated at 16% and 29%, respectively. There is a lot of variation in the effectiveness of the different classes of interventions in these three countries. It is likely that similar kinds of disparities arise in other countries where the epidemic is claiming lives. Without further evidence, it is not possible for us to say which intervention is most appropriate in any individual country. It is only important to note that all four classes of intervention are effective in cutting the rate of HIV infections. Circumcision acts as a kind of vaccine against transmission, and condoms and other community-based programs cut the rate of transmission, while ART prolongs life of those with HIV and also provides nearly 100% protection against transmission once ART has begun.

At the global level, the *Global Burden of Disease Study 2010* also has suggestions on how to address the HIV/AIDS epidemic. Sidibé, Piot and Dybul (2012) make a series of observations that fill in some of the blanks in the global agenda, but also raise concern with the gaps in funding. They echo the concerns regarding funding and highlight the gap between the estimate funding needs of 20–25 billion per year by 2015 compared with the current yearly funding of about $8 billion, much below the $15 billion mentioned in the blueprint. They stress the importance of making investments to provide care for treating the HIV patients for life. Aside from the funding gap, Sidibé et al. (2012) argue that investments have to be made in a strategic manner for six priority areas, many of which are also mentioned in the blueprint. They are as follows:

Reaching key populations at increased risk (MSM, IV drug users, sex workers)
Eliminating HIV in children
Promoting behavioral changes that reduce risky behavior
Condom promotion and distribution
Care and support of those living with HIV
Voluntary circumcision

Sidibé et al. (2012) also argue for increasing synergies within the health sector such as mother-to-child transmission and HIV–TB programs. And as more patients are brought onto ART, there will be a need to address noncommunicable diseases and opportunistic infections. They mention Pink Ribbon Red Ribbon a community-based help group, that provides additional health services for women living with HIV in Cambodia, Ethiopia, Kenya and Zambia. Following on this idea, they stress the importance of community mobilization and political leadership. More details are available at UNAIDS (2012b).

Reading through the suggestions from the blueprint and Sidibé et al. (2012), there is a communality of interest and a closely aligned agenda for further steps to address the challenges that are going to arise as more HIV sufferers are treated with ARV therapy, and fewer new cases arise as publicity, behavior modification, condoms, circumcision and so on continue to have an impact. As we see it, the issue comes down to money and how to effectively distribute the existing budgets among various options. It also seems that more countries are adopting rational and scientific-based methods for making these allocations and the level of waste and corruption seem to be falling. Whether the funding gap is $8 or 10 billion or some other figure can be worked out with the various funding agencies. Whatever, it is always important to keep in mind that we are talking of millions of human lives that hang in the balance.

2.12 Statistical analysis

We conducted an analysis of the causes of AIDS mortality rate for a broad panel of countries. In order to examine the importance of variables that affect AIDS mortality rate, we utilized pooled regression results in our study. The usual ordinary least squares method tends to assign equal weight or importance to each observation and does not make use of the "information" contained in the unequal variability of the dependent variable. The problem of heteroscedasticity is likely to be more commonly found in cross-sectional than in time series data. Members of the pool may be of different sizes and different economic developments. There is considerable variability in the variables of different countries. In addition, the problem of heteroscedasticity can arise as a result of the presence of outliers. The inclusion or exclusion of an observation that is very much different in relation to the other observations in the sample, especially when the sample size is small, can substantially alter the regression analysis results.

Top 22 high-burden AIDS countries by WHO (2013a) include: Angola, Botswana, Burundi, Cameroon, Chad, Côte d'Ivoire, Democratic Republic of Congo, Ethiopia, Ghana, India, Kenya, Lesotho, Malawi, Mozambique, Namibia, Nigeria, South Africa, Swaziland, Uganda, United Republic of Tanzania, Zambia and Zimbabwe.

Hence, we make use of the generalized least square method (GLS) pooled regressions so that observations that come from populations with greater variability are given less weighting than those coming from population with smaller variability. Thus, it is capable of producing estimators that are best linear unbiased estimators. We report results for the GLS model as well as GLS with fixed country intercept model.

Table 2.7 Statistical analysis of AIDS mortality using GLS

	Pooled GLS	Pooled GLS with fixed effects
C	−60,954.74*	292,007.50*
	(12,331.71)	(27,613.46)
ART	−1733.35*	−229.28*
	(316.65)	(59.61)
HEALTHEXP	6550.38*	−2128.43*
	(1492.63)	(586.65)
HDI	336,139.50*	−444,173.10*
	(58,942.52)	(59,367.55)
R^2	0.724	0.998
No of observations	57	57

Note: The method used generalized least squares regression with fixed country intercepts, with standard errors in parentheses on top burden 22 AIDS countries identified in 2013.
*denotes statistical significance at the 5% level.
AIDS: AIDS estimated deaths (UNAIDS estimates).
ART: Antiretroviral therapy coverage (% of people with advanced HIV infection).
HEALTHEXP: Health expenditure, total (% of GDP).
HDI: Human Development Index.

We explore the impact of the respective health interventions and the general level of economic income and HDI on the AIDS death rate. We make use of AIDS estimated deaths from the UNAIDS database. In general, the variables in the GLS model such as ART, health expenditure per capita and HDI are significant. However, it tends to give the wrong sign for health expenditure per capita and HDI.

To take into account the differing stages of development among the 22 high-burden AIDS countries, we utilized GLS with fixed country intercepts (see Table 2.7) and use the average value of the intercept for all the countries in the sample as well as individual countries' deviation from that overall average. Looking at the importance of antiretroviral therapy coverage on the AIDS mortality rate, we look at the percentage of ART coverage of people with advanced HIV infection. The ART coverage is significant and is negatively related to AIDS' death rate. Health expenditure per capita and HDI play a significant part in reducing AIDS mortality rate, and with the correct *a priori* sign under this new model.[5] The model lends significant support for greater government intervention to reduce HIV infections and mortality rate.

3
Tuberculosis

3.1 Introduction

Tuberculosis (TB) has been around for thousands of years. There is evidence that Egyptians had TB and the disease has ebbed and flowed since then. The word "phtisis" or "consumption" appeared in the Greek literature and was described as being the most widespread disease by Hippocrates. Records from that period suggest that TB was almost always fatal. Those who contracted TB were left alone to die. This is very similar to what happens now in some developing countries where rabies is common and those bitten don't get shots right away. Medical understanding of the nature of TB increased slowly with one of the first breakthroughs coming in the 17th century when it was recognized that changes occurred in the lungs of patients with consumption. The bacteria typically affects the lungs (pulmonary TB) but can affect other parts of the body as well (extrapulmonary TB). At that time it was also recognized that the disease was contagious and that patients should be isolated. Later it was realized that TB germs are spread through the air and those infected can infect others as they cough or spit. Since the lungs are most often infected, TB spreads quickly to others in congested areas and the spread of the disease is reinforced by poor sanitation, crowded living conditions, poor diets and the fact that the TB bacillus can remain in the air for several hours. Someone with an untreated active case of TB can infect as many as 15 other people each year. Those who are contagious probably are sick with a cold and fever and are coughing and sneezing. Those who come in close contact with someone with an active case of TB run the risk of becoming infected. The best way to keep the spread of TB from reaching epidemic proportions is to identify those who might have TB and to refer them to a health clinic as soon as possible. It is easy to test for TB. If the test is positive, those that the person has come in contact with should also be tested. There are drugs available to treat TB.

However, identifying all who might have been infected is not always that simple. Having a cold is not always an indication of TB, even if the cold lasts some time. And if active cases are not identified and treated quickly, the risk of the infection spreading is increased. Those who are run down, anemic, poorly nourished or sick from some other disease (HIV being the most prominent) are more likely to become infected with the TB virus themselves. To complicate matters further, those infected with the TB bacilli don't necessarily become ill with the disease. If they have a strong immune system the bacilli can be walled off by a thick coat and the disease can remain dormant for years. These people will not and cannot spread the disease. However, if their immune system is sufficiently weakened, perhaps as the result of a bad cold sometime later, the coating can be compromised and the person can become ill and thus transmit the disease. This means that, without treatment, there are untold numbers of potentially ticking TB time bombs.

Before the development of antibiotics, TB was treated by a regime of bed rest and isolation from others combined with a healthy diet. For rich people living in the 18th and 19th centuries that meant going to a sanatorium. Dr. Hermann Brehmer, an early innovator in TB care who suffered from TB himself, built one of the first sanatoriums in Germany in 1859.

Many sanatoriums were started in Europe to cater to those diagnosed with TB and some other more adventurous souls went to mountains of India and Nepal for treatment. In 1720, Dr. Benjamin Marten was one of the first to understand how the disease might spread and later built a sanatorium. There are now literally thousands of sanatoria in Europe (Switzerland and Austria mostly) and the United States (Arizona) in the late 19th and early 20th centuries. After 1943, when Albert Schatz, then a graduate student at Rutgers University, discovered streptomycin, an antibiotic and the first cure for tuberculosis, sanatoria began to close. In industrial countries, the spread of TB slowed and the number of new cases fell dramatically as the use of antibiotics expanded in these countries. Furthermore, an effective vaccine was developed in the early part of the 20th century by French bacteriologists Calmette and Guerin and a skin test was developed by Charles Mantoux at around the same time. The vaccine developed by Calmette and Guerin, called Bacillus Calmette–Guérin (BCG), was accepted by the League of Nations and subsequently was adopted and given to babies, either at birth or soon afterward. It is now administered as a vaccine for immunization of newborns against TB in most countries around the world. However, BCG tends to wear off after some years and so TB has continued to spread around the globe and has become particularly virulent in overcrowded slums where diets are poor and medical care is minimal.

3.2 Toll in lives

After HIV/AIDS, tuberculosis claims more lives than any other infectious disease. TB is spread by personal contact through the air. When a person with TB coughs, he or she spreads germs through the air and others need only to ingest a few germs in order to contract TB. The World Health Organization (WHO) estimates that one-third of the world's population is infected with the TB bacilli (WHO, 2013b). If not treated, somewhere between 5% and 10% of those infected will become sick at some time during their lives. They can then infect others. If untreated, TB could be fatal. Worldwide an estimated 1.3 million people died of TB in 2012 and nearly nine million fell ill. TB claimed the lives of adults, leaving ten million orphans. TB is the leading killer of those living with HIV, causing 25% of all HIV/AIDS deaths. Over 95% of TB deaths occur in low- and middle-income countries and is one of the top three causes of death for women in the child-bearing ages between 15 and 44. The TB mortality rate is overly high for a curable disease when short-term courses of first-line drugs that can cure about 90% of the cases have been available for decades.

3.3 Identifying those at risk

3.3.1 Geographic distribution of TB

Globally around 80% of cases occur in 22 countries – see Table 3.1. Between 2000 and 2007, TB incidence has fallen in the three most populous countries in the world – China, India and Indonesia – but has increased in many countries where the HIV incidence is high. Tuberculosis is treatable and curable with the proper medication and care. There are now relatively few cases in industrial countries.

TB occurs in almost every part of the world. WHO reports that in 2012 Asia (58%) had the greatest number of estimated TB cases, followed by the African region (27%), Eastern Mediterranean region (8%) and the region of the Americas (3%). Countries in the African region had the highest proportion of TB cases coinfected with HIV.

Table 3.1 TB cases, 2000 and 2007

Country	Heritage index	TB controls costs/capita	2000 New notifications	2007 New notifications	TB prevalence per 100,000 1990	TB prevalence per 100,000 2004	HIV over 15% in TB cases 2007	Number of cases 2007 ('000s)
India	123	0.1	107	111	586	311		1962
China	138	0.2	36	74	327	220		1306
Indonesia	115	0.4	40	119	443	274		528
Nigeria	116	0.4	21	56	282	573	x	460
South Africa	70	12.3	333	649	769	676	x	461
Bangladesh	130	0.1	54	93	639	444		353
Ethiopia	134	0.4	131	155	323	613	x	314
Pakistan	122	0.3	77	141	430	333		297
Philippines	107	0.4	157	160	799	534		255
Congo	172	1	120	159	209	477		245
Russia	144	9	95	89	69	136	x	157
Vietnam	136	0.3	114	111	365	226		150
Kenya	103	1.1	205	284	125	410	x	132
Brazil	99	0.5	45	39	124	63		92
Tanzania	119	0.7	161	147			x	120
Uganda	78	0.6	123	132	206	472	x	102
Zimbabwe	178	1.6	402	302	409	652	x	104
Thailand	60	0.8	56	86	336	188		91
Mozambique	108	1.4	116	176	287	567	x	92
Myanmar	173	0.3	67	265	411	168		83
Cambodia	157	0.9	148	246	928	696		72
Afghanistan	NA	0.4	34	106				

Sources: WHO (2009, Tables 1.2 and 3.4) and the Heritage Foundation (2013).

3.3.2 Identified parties at risk

TB affects mostly young adults, although there are new cases in all age groups every year. TB is also more common among men than women but it remains among the top three causes of death among women worldwide. Those who have HIV are anywhere from 20 to 35 times more likely to contract TB and this is one reason for the rapid spread in countries where there is an HIV epidemic. Often the diagnosis of HIV follows the discovery that the patient has TB. TB is also more prevalent if patients have other conditions that impact the immune system. Tobacco use increases the likelihood of contracting TB as do crowded living conditions in slums and shanty towns. WHO estimates that more than 20% of TB cases worldwide are the result of smoking. Symptoms include persistent cough, sometimes accompanied by blood or sputum, chest pains, fever, night sweats and weakness. It can also be accompanied by weight loss. It is hard to diagnose in children.

3.4 Identification and treatment of the TB epidemic

3.4.1 Active versus latent TB

While many people have been exposed to TB and have inhaled the virus, some have strong immune system and are able to contain the bacilli. These individuals are said to have latent TB. If the individual is diagnosed with latent TB, he is not sick or contagious. However, he may need to take medicine for latent TB, depending on a variety of factors including intensity and duration of contact with someone who has active TB, whether he has diabetes, kidney problems or other medical conditions, including some cancers or those using medications to suppress the immune system or where there is some evidence of old TB from a chest X-ray. Those with HIV are particularly susceptible. The medicine recommended for treating latent TB is the drug isoniazid (INH). Taken daily for four to nine months INH will kill the TB bacilli. Studies also show that 10% of those individuals with latent infection could eventually progress to active TB, which, if left untreated, could lead to death.

If the individual has active TB, he will be contagious for a few weeks after beginning medication. If he does not take medication, TB will remain active and it will eventually be fatal in many cases. However, once medication is started, the active phase is over after a few weeks and patients are no longer contagious. The drug regime for active TB is more complicated than the regime for latent TB. It usually contains a cocktail of several drugs taken together.

3.5 Measures for the TB epidemic

3.5.1 Vaccination to prevent TB

BCG is a vaccine that has been widely used to protect against TB since the 1920s. It continues to be the only vaccine used to prevent TB. The vaccine has been in use for almost a century; however, its effectiveness is limited, even though it is currently used to vaccinate babies throughout the world. In one of its circulars (Initiative for Vaccine Research – IVR), the World Health Organization says that the strain was carefully subcultured every three weeks for many years. Eventually the vaccine was distributed to several laboratories throughout the world and WHO estimates that one billion people have received BCG. Over time the vaccine lost its effectiveness against lung disease, but is still effective in protecting against TB in other parts of the body and this is the reason for its continued widespread use. Recent work at the Vanderbilt Medical Center, led by Dr. Douglas Kernodle, reported a breakthrough that has the potential for revitalizing the ability of BCG to arrest the development of pulmonary TB (see Vanderbilt University Medical Center, 2009) and the Aeras Global TB foundation has already licensed modification technology developed by Kernodle and his colleagues. WHO (2013c) also reports that plans are in the pipeline for ten vaccines for TB prevention and two immunotherapeutic vaccines to improve responsiveness to chemotherapy or prevent relapse or re-infection. Hopefully these measures will provide a new step forward in vaccinating against TB in early childhood. However, there is still no vaccine that is effective in preventing TB in adults.

3.5.2 Identification of TB

In the meantime reliance will continue to be placed on identification of TB using smear tests and the subsequent application of direct observed therapy (DOTS) protocols if the individual is found to be infected with TB. The smear test is performed using a small needle to put a few drops of a test solution under the skin. The test area may swell and itch. Patients are told not to scratch as that could comprise the results of the test. The patient returns after two to three days and is given the results. If the test is positive, there are TB germs in the body and the patient is instructed to begin to take medicine, usually for up to six months and according to the DOTS protocol. Globally, the smear test is the most widely used test for TB. Sometimes a blood test is an alternative to a smear test. A small blood sample is analyzed by a laboratory to test how strongly a person's immune system reacts to TB bacteria and the results are available in a few days. Alternatively, a sputum smear can be analyzed, which also requires laboratory analysis and a second visit to a clinic. A third alternative is a chest X-ray, which can test for lesions in the lungs. In any event, whichever of the three protocols is adopted, the diagnosis of TB requires a network of laboratories, health professionals and/or X-ray equipment to make the diagnosis. It also risks loss of patients who do not return for a second visit or to find out the results of the test. For developing countries this can be a big barrier to effective diagnosis. Furthermore, as noted earlier, the treatment of TB requires the patient to take medicine every day for several months under the supervision of a health professional. This also requires manpower.

Recently an alternative called Xpert MTB/RIF has been developed which provides a TB diagnosis in a few hours. Xpert MTB/RIF has been developed by a Swiss drug firm based on a sputum sample. No blood test is required and the results are available in a couple of hours, not days or weeks. The patients can get the results right away and this reduces the risk that they may never return to get the results. If the patient doesn't return for treatment and has active TB, the virus could easily be spread to many others. To successfully implement Xpert MTB/RIF a stable electrical supply, security against theft, trained personnel, adequate storage space, annual calibration of the instruments by a commercial supplier and biosafety precautions similar to those for direct sputum microscopy are required. Aside from electricity and safety from theft, this requires some modification of the sputum smear protocol but probably not any additional personnel. Furthermore, the infrastructure for following up the treatment of patients diagnosed with TB will remain unchanged. The only difference is that patients will get results in an hour or two and can begin treatment immediately if they are diagnosed with TB. This alternative has reduced the diagnostic time and the need for a return trip to the clinic to get results. It also allows treatment to begin immediately, reducing the chance of infected patients from spreading TB to others that much sooner. "The tests can be performed by routine staff with minimal training and these results retained the accuracy seen in previous controlled studies that were undertaken in reference centres" (see Boehme et al., 2011).

Progress in implementing the installation of the MTB/RIF technology, training staff and integration into the DOTS protocol is now underway around the world. The MTB/RIF technology has been endorsed by WHO and leading medical journals including the *Lancet*. Rollout orders by country as of Q4 2011 are displayed in Table 3.2.

Table 3.2 MTB/RIF machines ordered through Q4 2011

Country	Through Q3 2010	2010 Q4	2011 Q1	2011 Q2	2011 Q3	2011 Q4	Total
Algeria						4	4
Azerbaijan	4				4		8
Bangladesh					12		12
Botswana			4			48	52
Brazil				4	4	52	60
Cambodia		4	12		8	16	40
Central African Republic					4		4
China		16					16
Colombia					8		8
Democratic Republic of Congo					8		8
El Salvador						4	4
Ethiopia		8			4		12
Gambia						4	4
Georgia		4	4				8
Guatemala				4			4
Guinea					4		4
Haiti			4			8	12
India	6		4	4	4		18
Indonesia					68		68
Kenya	12		16	4	24	16	72
Kyrgyzstan			4			24	28
Lesotho			4		4	8	16
Madagascar						12	12
Malawi		4	4	4		44	56
Mozambique		4	8		8	16	36
Myanmar					8		8
Nepal	4					28	32
Nigeria					36	24	60
Pakistan		4			96		100
Peru	4			4			8
Philippines	4				88		92
Moldova						68	68
Russia					12	4	16
Senegal					4		4
Somalia						8	8
South Africa	8	8	244	101	282	456	1099
Swaziland			8	12		20	40
Tajikistan				8			8
Tanzania	28	4		4	6	12	54
Thailand					16	12	28
Timor Leste					4		4
Trinidad and Tobago						4	4

Uganda	4	16	6		28	6	60
Uzbekistan					12		12
Vietnam						22	22
Zambia		8	2	4	4	24	42
Zimbabwe	4		16	4		12	36

Source: WHO (2014).

South Africa, where the AIDS and TB epidemics have spread rapidly in the past few years, has placed the most orders. Other countries in Africa and Asia are also placing orders. However, more resources need to be devoted to replacing old technology requiring laboratory analysis with the new machines as soon as possible. This will free up resources to increase the identification of new cases and reduce the spread of TB. It will also close the gaps that sometimes arise between the initial test for TB, which under the old testing techniques could take a week or more, and the final decision as to whether the patient has TB and needs to be treated immediately. Some patients never come back after the first visit when the diagnosis begins and others may come back after some time, having had the opportunity to infect more individuals. These lags can be detrimental to TB treatment efforts, further undermining the DOTS program which depends on timely diagnosis, treatment and eventual cure.

Work at the Harvard School of Public Health, conducted by Joshua Salomon, professor of public health, designed to investigate the potential health and economic consequences of implementing the Xpert test in several African countries (Botswana, Lesotho, Namibia, South Africa and Swaziland) found that replacing the current diagnostic test of sputum smear microscopy with Xpert would prevent 132,000 TB cases and 182,000 deaths in Southern Africa over ten years. This would reduce the proportion of the population with active TB by 28% (see Menzies et al., 2012).

The cost of widespread implementation of Xpert in Southern Africa was estimated at $460 million over ten years. Much of the additional cost would arise from the tests for TB and HIV, which would result from this new and user-friendly technology. In addition, the new test also provides information on TB drug resistance not previously available with sputum smear microscopy. Finding out those with drug resistance would require additional tests and therapy for those with multidrug-resistant TB. There would also be side benefits for those suffering with

HIV. Xpert would find more TB cases and also more individuals coinfected with TB and HIV. Survival rates for HIV patients would increase as would those receiving HIV treatment. Would all of these additional costs be outweighed by benefits? According to WHO standards, the cost per year of healthy life gained would be within the WHO guidelines of a cost-effective treatment in these African countries. However, the cost-effectiveness of the treatment depends to some extent on the mutual benefit gained by treating HIV and TB in a high HIV prevalence environment.

Despite the efficacy and effectiveness of this new diagnostic tool, it is encouraging to note that recent research has explained how smear microscopy technology is being improved and updated to require only one visit to a clinic with a result that is more reliable.

Even under the best conditions, smear microscopy has substantial limitations: sensitivity is low and drug resistance is not detected. Rollout of same-day molecular tests such as Genotype MTBDRplus (Hain Lifescience, Nehren, Germany) or Xpert MTB/RIF (Cepheid, Sunnyvale, CA, USA) will address these restrictions. These tests generate results within hours, and with the provision of same-day microscopy, assessment of two sputum smears plus molecular testing within one visit will be possible.

However, at present most patients with tuberculosis have access to only smear microscopy. In 2010, of 36 countries with the greatest burden of tuberculosis and multidrug-resistant tuberculosis, 20 had less than one laboratory capable of doing culture for every five million people. More than 80% of the estimated 8.8 million people with tuberculosis live in high-burden countries. We estimate that less than 10% of patients with tuberculosis in low-resource settings had their disease proven with culture or molecular biological approaches. Therefore, assuming a conservative estimate of 20% default, more than 1.5 million people will have a missed or delayed diagnosis every year. In view of the vast numbers of patients involved, incremental improvements in smear microscopy will lead to substantial increases in the numbers of patients detected at little or no cost.

What this account from WHO fails to note is that eventually the new diagnostic regime will eventually supplant smear microscopy in most countries. In the meantime an alternative protocol has been suggested that uses smear microscopic examination but relies on two sputum smears taken in the morning and the evening of the same day. This protocol would have the same limitations as existing smear tests but it would hopefully reduce the number of patients who drop out and never complete a course of treatment. These patients will go on to infect others and perhaps spread a more virulent form of the virus.

3.5.3 Taking medication for active TB – the DOTS program

The DOTS was introduced globally in the 1990s and has been an effective implementation tool for treating active TB. For both latent and active TB therapies to be effective, medication has to be taken **every day**. In a DOTS program a healthcare worker makes sure the individual takes his medication every day. So far it is the only proven way to stay on schedule although mobile devices are now being used experimentally to track patients with videos or photos. Patients taking their medications are shot taking their medication and these photos or videos are then sent back to a central location. Without joining a DOTS program, there is a risk that patients will stop taking their medication once they feel better. Doing this creates an opportunity for the TB bacilli to become stronger and more difficult to cure later on. The Stop TB Strategy of which DOTS is the primary component has six items in its strategic tool kit and is part of the Global Plan to Stop TB launched by WHO in 2006. These initiatives were a component of a program to implement the Millennium Development Goal (MDG) of halving the prevalence and death rates from TB by 2015 compared with 1990 and that at least 70% of active TB cases should be successfully treated by 2015. The DOTS strategy has several components. First, active TB is typically detected and diagnosed by blood analysis from smear-positive microscopy. Second, standardized chemotherapy is adopted for a period of six to eight months for all smear-positive cases including DOT during the intensive phase (a few months). In cases where there has been a relapse or treatment might have been suspended a different regime may be called for. A typical protocol would involve a six month treatment with a cocktail of five drugs (Isoniazid, Rifampicin, Pyrazinamide, Ethambutol and Streptomycin). As noted, the recommended dosage is daily, although WHO has recently issued a directive that three doses a week is acceptable as long as patients are supervised by a health professional. At the end of treatment, patients take a blood test or a chest X-ray to determine if they are free of TB.

3.6 Mathematic models of the spread of TB

Mathematicians and statisticians have developed models of the spread of TB. The fundamental approach is to set up a system of differential equations that outline the pattern of infection, spread and cure. These equations are solved using Mathlab, a mathematic computer program that produces a set of results that plot the evolution of the disease over time. In China, a group of mathematicians have constructed such a system to model the various aspects of the spread of TB. They split the model into two components for two different populations – those for which individuals receive diagnosis and treatment and those for which there is no treatment. For those who are treated, they suggest common sense solutions based on their model. These include lowering the incidence of transmission and incidence by quick and effective action to control the spread of the disease. However, for the second population, for which they had no reliable data, they suggest testing migrants from rural areas where there are fewer centers for treatment and also improving the living conditions in those areas, reducing congestion and improving diets all of which will help to slow the spread of the disease.

As far as we know there have been no attempts to develop models which encompass the full range of possibilities for the identification, spread and treatment of TB in large populations, recognizing that some members of the population will be untreated and they will spread the disease. The Currie et al. (2005) paper is a very good start. WHO is depending on the adoption of DOTS to slow the spread of TB and is imposing a protocol for the proportions of patients identified and treated to control the spread of TB over time. However, DOTS, as it is currently implemented, may not be enough. Not enough cases are being detected and of those that are detected, not all are treated until they are cured.

3.7 Spread of TB and diagnosis

As noted earlier, the most important step in the identification and treatment of TB is diagnosis. Since the infection is spread through the air, it is hard to know who might be infected, although close contact is needed to spread the disease. In an environment where TB is endemic and may have already spread in many people, it is paramount that everyone in the society be aware of the symptoms and seek speedy diagnosis and treatment. Timely diagnosis can lead to immediate treatment and minimum risk of further spread from infected patients to others. The best treatment protocol in the world will fail to contain the spread of the disease if too many infected individuals are diagnosed after long delays and they have time to spread the disease further. This is why an effective public health service and a strong information network is the foundation of effective TB containment. At the same time, it is equally important to monitor those who are being treated remain in the treatment program until they are completely cured. In many countries the dropout rate is much higher than the recommended rate of 10–15% and can be as high as 50%. These patients who have been taking medication for some time and have now quit run not only the risk of infecting others but may have also gotten a more virulent and difficult kind of TB which is more expensive to cure. Therefore, it is critical that dropout rates be reduced by more effective monitoring of patients either by health personnel or by members of the community. Modern technology can be of help, either by taking photographs of patients when they take their medications or having family members report on compliance.

In poorer countries with effective healthcare systems, TB rates are much lower than in countries with similar living standards but less effective healthcare systems. For example, in Sri Lanka it is estimated that prevalence of TB is 79 per 100,000 population and the incidence of new cases is much lower, at 27 per 100,000. On average, based on global surveillance, authorities estimate that 85% of new cases are detected by the present monitoring system and the treatment success rate is 87%. This means that the Sri Lankan program is quite effective in finding and treating new cases. In Sri Lanka the public health system is not catching and treating all cases, but the spread of TB has been cut by 75% to the current rate of 79 cases per 100,000 population from 234 per 100,000 in 1970. The incidence rate of new smear-positive cases is estimated to be 27 per 100,000 population. The country has achieved the global Millennium targets for case detection and treatment success rates. The case detection rate for 2007 was 85.6% and treatment success for the 2006 cohort of new smear-positive cases was 87%.

Compare the Sri Lankan experience with that of India and Pakistan, Sri Lanka's neighbors. TB treatment programs have been much less successful in these two countries. It is estimated that prevalence of TB is over 300 per 100,000 population in both countries, about three times the rate in Sri Lanka, a country with a similar living standard to both Pakistan and India. However, some parts of India have also managed to reduce the TB epidemic as a result of more effective public health programs. Kerala, one of the Indian states in the southeastern part of the country, has achieved much greater success than India as a whole. The key to success has been finding those who have TB and treating them effectively. That can only be done with a lot of effort on the part of the public to be aware of potential TB sufferers combined with well-publicized symptoms of the disease. This has to be accomplished within a healthcare system that has enough resources to effectively treat those patients that are identified as carrying the active form of the disease. In high-risk environments such as when HIV rates are high, even latent TB should be identified and treated immediately (see following section 3.9).

3.8 Multidrug-resistant TB

Multidrug-resistant TB (MDR-TB) is a form of TB where the bacteria do not respond to the standard, so-called, first-line drugs of isoniazid and rifampicin. This resistance can be the result of several factors including inappropriate treatment where the patient didn't take the appropriate dosage for a long enough time, did not complete DOTS treatment or was taking poor quality medicines. MDR-TB is more difficult and costly to treat using "so-called" second line drugs, which might not be available. Treatment is much longer, taking up to two years. For these reasons it is critically important that diagnosis be accurate and the DOTS regime be systematically followed. In some cases patients become immune to MDR-TB drugs and fall into another category, extensively drug-resistant tuberculosis (XDR-TB), which is also hard to cure. Globally in 2012, there were an estimated 450,000 cases of MDR-TB, over half in China and Russia. About 10% of MDR-TB cases had XTR-TB. Fatality rates for MDR-TB and XTR-TB are probably higher than for ordinary TB but hard data are not available. WHO (2013c) acknowledges the immense challenge of achieving the targets for diagnosis and treatment of MDR-TB and how it has resulted in a public health crisis in many countries. Worldwide and in most countries with a high burden of MDR-TB, less than one-quarter of the people estimated were detected in 2012.

The high levels of mortality and large numbers of patients being lost to follow-up have resulted in global treatment success rate to be under 50%.

3.9 Coinfection with HIV

It is estimated that about one-third of those infected with HIV (34 million worldwide) are also infected with the TB bacteria. Rates of infection have skyrocketed in much of Sub-Sahara Africa (see Box 3.1). Coinfection with HIV is one reason but high rates of poverty, excessive overcrowded living conditions and treatment programs, which are both understaffed and underfunded, are also to blame. The strong presence of HIV in many countries has served to complicate the treatment of

TB. HIV patients are highly susceptible to contracting TB, perhaps as much as 20–30 times more likely than others in the community. As a result of this susceptibility factor, many HIV patients become infected with the TB virus. This is evident from comparing the column with over 15% of HIV cases with the change in prevalence rates of TB from 2000 to 2007 in Table 3.1. Note that in many countries where the TB/HIV coinfection rate is more than 15%, the TB prevalence rate has increased rather dramatically between 1990 and 2004, whereas in the other top 20 it has fallen. Treatment protocols where TB is coinfected with HIV are more complicated and the TB infection rate is much higher than when patients are free of HIV. Furthermore, there are many countries where the prevalence rate of TB is over 200 per 100,000 residents. All of this suggests that there can be a TB outbreak of epic proportions wherever there is coinfection with HIV. Recent data suggest that an estimated 25% of those who die of HIV also had TB. Globally there are over a million new cases of HIV-positive new TB cases with the bulk of them (around an estimated 80%) occurring in Africa. For this reason the compliance with treatment protocols for TB is even more compelling in high-incidence environments where HIV is widespread.

It should also be noted that the list of high-TB countries can be recast in terms of rank by incidence, mortality and HIV. The top 12 countries in these categories are displayed in Table 3.3. Note that the

Table 3.3 TB incidence, mortality and incidence of HIV in TB cases

Country	TB incidence 2004 per 100,000 pop	Country	Mortality 2004 per 100,000 pop	Country	2004 HIV percent of TB patients
South Africa	718	Zimbabwe	151	Zimbabwe	68
Zimbabwe	674	South Africa	135	South Africa	60
Kenya	619	Kenya	133	Mozambique	48
Cambodia	510	Mozambique	129	Tanzania	36
Mozambique	460	Cambodia	94	Kenya	29
Uganda	402	Uganda	92	Nigeria	27
Congo	366	Afghanistan	92	Congo	21
Ethiopia	352	Nigeria	82	Ethiopia	21
Tanzania	344	Ethiopia	79	Uganda	19
Afghanistan	333	Congo	79	Brazil	17
Philippines	293	Tanzania	78	Cambodia	13
Nigeria	290				

Sources: WHO (2013) and World Bank (2013).

countries are generally the same in all the three lists. Countries with high TB incidence, mortality and coinfection with HIV are generally the same in all three cases, that is, by TB incidence and mortality and by the degree of coinfection with HIV. These observations strengthen the importance of dealing with TB and HIV at the same time and with the same focus.

Box 3.1 TB in South Africa

The tuberculosis and HIV/AIDS epidemics in South Africa are creating an enormous public health challenge. The country accounts for upward of 20% of the global burden of HIV infection though it has less than 1% of the world's population. Because of the rapid increase of coinfection with tuberculosis, South Africa also has one of the most serious tuberculosis epidemics in the world (refer to Table 3.1). The roots of these epidemics can be traced to apartheid, when there were overcrowded urban squatter settlements, a large flow of migrant labor moving back and forth between the cities and rural towns and extremely poor provision of public health services for blacks. Hundreds of thousands of blacks (usually men) working in cities were forced to live in filthy, congested and poorly ventilated single-sex hostels. Prostitution was rampant (called town wives in the vernacular) and the men usually had wives and families in their rural home towns. Moving back and forth between their jobs in the cities and the mining sector and their villages in the countryside, these temporary migrants carried tuberculosis and sexually transmitted diseases with them.

The diseases spread throughout the 20th century and now present the most important public health challenge facing the country. The public health response to these diseases has been inconsistent. The apartheid government did almost nothing to contain the HIV/AIDS epidemic until 1990, when the HIV epidemic was acknowledged by the Maputoa statement on HIV/AIDS in Southern Africa, issued jointly by the outlawed African National Congress (ANC) and a range of other antiapartheid groups. In 1993 the National AIDS Convention of South Africa was created and it contained representatives of the apartheid government and HIV/AIDS activists. After the end of apartheid, the Mandela government did not give a high-profile response to the epidemics. There was controversy surrounding the cabinet support for a toxic industrial solvent as a cure for AIDS and refusal to fund a program to provide funds for a drug that was proven to prevent mother-to-child transmission of HIV.

There was, however, support for the implementation of DOTS beginning in 1995 and included a record keeping system and central coordination of disease monitoring and control. Despite these new initiatives, the number of TB cases continued to rise along with the spread of HIV/AIDS. This was not helped by disagreements within the government, including one minister of health, who denied that AIDS was transmitted through the blood or sex and that HIV did not cause AIDS. This came to a headstand in 2000 when the XIII International AIDS conference was held in Durban and served to rally wide support from community organizations, trade unions, activists, scientists and healthcare workers for the end to inequities of access to treatment. In 2001 the Constitutional Court ruled that the government had to provide nevirapine to pregnant women and the program for treating HIV/AIDS moved forward and in 2003 ART began to be provided free to the public.

By 2007 a Tuberculosis Strategic Plan for South Africa was adopted. However, by then there was a growing epidemic of multidrug-resistant and extensively drug-resistant tuberculosis cases on the books as well as coinfection with HIV.

During apartheid TB treatment for the poor was minimal and it spread through crowded slums and poor villages. Whatever treatment there was consisted of bed rest with isoniazid, streptomycin and para-aminosalicyclic acid treatment for 12–18 months and it was usually unavailable to the poor who did not have the resources to stay in a hospital bed for a year or more.

As the DOTS protocol became widely adopted, rifampicin-based treatment was shorter and patients were not required to stay in bed. However, the indigent were still poorly served. Nevertheless, whatever gains in TB control, which might have manifested from the new DOTS regime, were overwhelmed by the coinfection with HIV and the growth in more intractable forms of the TB virus. Between 1986 and 2006 the case notification rate for TB increased from 163 per 100,000 population to 628 per 100,000 in 2006. There were over 340,000 TB cases, the fourth largest number in

Box 3.1 (Continued)

the world after China, India and Indonesia, countries with much larger populations (50 million versus over a billion for India and China and 250 million in Indonesia). Those patients with HIV had as much as a 10–20 times higher chance of contracting TB as the general population and the chance of someone with latent TB. Put another way, the rate of latent TB becoming clinically active increases from a lifetime risk of 10% in the general population to an **annual** risk of 10% for those who are coinfected with HIV. So the five year probability of contracting TB goes up five times in five years.

3.9.1 Modeling TB and HIV interactions

Mathematical techniques can be used to focus on situations where HIV and TB are both prevalent. When infection rates for both HIV and TB are high, deaths from TB could be 100% higher than in communities where none of the population is HIV infected. For example, one model suggests that if 30% of individuals with latent TB are treated, then the active TB rate could be cut by over 90% in a decade. There are a number of other models using a similar technique to model the spread of TB in a closed village environment and the spread of diseases among animals. Furthermore, Currie et al. (2003) suggest that the best way to manage TB epidemics that are the result of coinfection with AIDS is to find and treat TB cases, rather than to solely prevent or mitigate the effect of the HIV infection. These results are robust under a variety of assumptions and are similar for epidemics in Uganda, Kenya and South Africa, three countries where the HIV epidemic is in early (Uganda), intermediate (Kenya) or late stages (South Africa).

This seemingly counter intuitive conclusion is explained by the fact that curative measures directed at TB reduce transmission and deaths irrespective of whether the patients are coinfected with HIV or not. If measures are directed at only those who are coinfected, many cases of TB would be overlooked. Even though the epidemic of TB has spread to many HIV-positive patients, there are still substantial numbers of potential TB patients who would be overlooked by a strategy that focuses on coinfection alone. Currie et al. (2003) conclude that as little as a 1% increase in case detection of TB could result in averting TB in 3200 cases in Uganda, 6700 cases in Kenya and 2900 cases in South Africa over the next ten years. Similar reductions in deaths of 2000, 4900 and 22,000 would result. As noted in the previous section, the bottom line is that the DOTS strategy has to be strengthened and the TB identification rate has to be increased if substantial progress in dealing with the TB epidemic is to be achieved.

Recently, additional evidence has been presented for treatment in South Africa by Dr. Salim A. Khan, which has been summarized in Chapter 2 and is repeated here as follows.

For a patient with HIV and TB, neither anti-TB drugs nor antiretroviral (ARV) alone is likely to increase life expectancy. However, the two therapies used in tandem should be the protocol for treating both diseases. Furthermore, it is not recommended to delay the treatment of HIV until TB treatment has ended. Trials by Dr. S. A. Kalim have yielded strong results that the two should be treated together. Work with his colleagues found that patients waiting to complete TB treatment before beginning HIV therapy were 50% more likely to die than patients being treated for both diseases simultaneously. See http://www.voanews.com/articleprintview/401302.html. He cautions to not wait for them to finish their TB treatment but rather to start HIV therapy at the same time as the DOTS protocol for treating TB begins.

Both Currie et al. (2003) and Khan's research findings suggest that both TB and HIV should be treated at the same time. If TB is found, treat it and if it is found to be coinfected with HIV treat both at the same time. Don't wait for the cell count to go down to "acceptable" levels to treat HIV. Start as soon as the results are positive for HIV.

It may also be useful to survey other field studies that employed this protocol and compare the results with more conventional programs where TB treatments have been completed before HIV therapy was begun.

3.9.2 WHO strategy and coinfection with HIV

Given this background, it is useful to examine the stance of WHO with regard to detection and treatment of TB. The standard recommendation for TB treatment suggested by WHO is to adopt what has been called a "passive" approach to this TB epidemic. The process of identification and treatment begins when patients ask for treatment, either in hospitals or in treatment centers. After TB has been identified, patients enter into the next phase of the DOTS protocol and emerge free of TB at the end of the course of drug therapy.

The data in Tables 3.1 and 3.3 suggest that this passive approach needs to be revamped and modified, particularly in countries where there is a high probability of coinfection with HIV. Recent research findings back up this view. TB is spreading rapidly in the high-incidence countries and a different approach needs to be adopted by WHO and governments in these 22 high-risk countries. In addition, the donor community has to realize that there is a growing threat of TB and that resource to mount a much more vigorous global TB campaign needs to be mobilized. As noted earlier, the major reason for the dramatic uptick in TB is the rising incidence of HIV and coinfection with tuberculosis. In South Africa, a recent symposium echoes the suggestion that more aggressive methods need to be employed to identify tuberculosis and that latent case of tuberculosis should be treated with isoniazid prevention therapy (IPT). Churchyard and Eldred (2008) note that the aggressive use of IPT would reduce active TB by about a third in people with HIV.

However, this has not been happening. WHO reported in its 2009 TB report that only 29,000 people with HIV were started on IPT. Globally there are an estimated 33 million people infected with HIV and it is estimated that close to 40% of those are eligible for IPT therapy. This translates into around 12 million people globally. Compare this with the 29,000 people actually being treated. According to Churchyard and Eldred about half that number, six million people, should be receiving IPT treatment globally, not 29,000. Most of these new patients would be in the top 22 countries where both TB and HIV incidence rates are extremely high. Furthermore, the majority of AIDS deaths are a result of TB infections and so by curing TB the death rates from AIDS would also be cut.

An effort to start those with HIV on antiretroviral therapy (ART) has been much more successful, although still woefully short of full compliance and it still leaves many millions without treatment. Some estimate that at least half of those patients with HIV and who would benefit from ART are not being treated. There are also untold numbers with HIV that have not been identified and who are spreading the disease. Furthermore, Murray and Salomon (1998) argue that a massive preventive therapy campaign could reduce the spread of tuberculosis and have a significant impact in reducing the size of the epidemic over the next few decades. They also argue for more vigorous research to find a single contact treatment. They contend that

> tuberculosis program managers and control specialists must develop more ambitious objectives for tuberculosis control over the next half

> century. Tuberculosis is likely to remain one of the leading causes of death in the 21st century but it is also one of the few for which there are a number of existing potential new interventions that can make a dramatic difference. A major rethinking of global tuberculosis strategy can occur only if the size of the problem and the potential for action are recognized more widely.
>
> (p. 13885)

Murray and Salomon argue that rather than a passive strategy, active case finding as the primary strategy could easily reduce tuberculosis mortality by one-quarter to one-third. They note that IPT has been recognized for decades but that it has a small risk of toxicity. For this reason it has not been recommended in countries where rates of tuberculosis are low. However, in the current global environment and particularly in Africa and parts of Asia, where major gains in the reduction of mortality and the spread of TB can be achieved by greater use of IPT, a change in direction to a more active policy would have an enormous positive impact. It would also blunt the rising impact of TB/HIV coinfection on mortality. Corbett et al. (2003) calculate the case fatality rate (CFR) for HIV-related TB to be over 50% in many developing countries. Similarly, the contribution of TB to AIDS deaths is substantial. Corbett et al. echo the concern of Murray and Salomon and Churchyard and Eldred.

> There is a urgent need to implement a strategy of extended scope combining intensified TB case finding and treatment, HIV prevention, and the identification and treatment of latent MTB in coinfected individuals. Controlling HIV-related TB will require a massive global effort.
>
> (pp. 1018–1019)

This change in direction in TB policy would complement ongoing research efforts such as finding a single contact treatment and strengthening the effectiveness of BCG. In any case more resources have to be made available to tread TB, particularly in several top 20 countries where HIV rates are also high. In many cases it is also suggested that more be allocated to the integration of HIV and TB into the provision of healthcare services in countries with high exposure to both HIV and TB, particularly the 12 countries listed in Table 3.3.

Anand et al. (2010) indicates that IPT has been adopted as a national policy for people living with HIV in only half of the 41 countries responding to the survey. However, only six out of 21 countries have implemented this policy on a national scale. Furthermore, despite WHO guidelines that all HIV patients be screened for TB, only around 2% of people living with HIV worldwide were screened for TB. In Sub-Sahara Africa this abysmal record is compounded by lack of drugs and poor supply-chain management.

3.10 Coinfection of TB and diabetes

The incidence of diabetes has increased rapidly in industrial countries and also in developing countries as the use of refined sugar products has increased. Both type I and type II diabetes can threaten an escalation in TB and can complicate TB treatment. According to the Harvard School of Public Health, diabetes increases a person's chance of getting active TB by threefold compared with people without diabetes. There are an estimated 285 million people with diabetes worldwide and there is a definite risk of coinfection of TB and diabetes, even though diabetes is not a communicable disease. A nine-month pilot bidirectional screening program was started in China in 2001 and evaluated in 2012. China has an estimated 1.5 million new TB cases each year and 270,000 deaths according to James Mullins (2012). Individuals with either TB or diabetes should be examined and strategies developed to treat those with both diseases. Like TB, diabetes affects the poor disproportionally. Eighty percent of those with diabetes are found in low- or middle-income countries. To look at coinfection of the two diseases, the pilot project was implemented in 11 clinics/hospitals in Beijing and in the south of China. The six TB clinics/hospitals screened TB patients for diabetes and the five others screened those with diabetes for TB. TB case notification rates in screened diabetes patients were several times higher than those of the general population. For screened TB patients, the rate of diabetes was small and most patients already knew they had diabetes. Putting diabetes screening into routine healthcare setting and also into TB clinics can improve the diagnosis of TB among those with diabetes. Diabetes is diagnosed by a simple fasting plasma glucose test which measures blood glucose in a person who has not eaten anything for at least eight hours. This test is used to detect both diabetes and prediabetes.

The protocols described and adopted in China have also been followed in India. They need to be installed more generally in healthcare settings throughout these two countries with over two billion people and in other developing countries. Before scaling up to the national level, care should be taken to carry out analysis of the cost-effectiveness of these programs even though on the surface they look like a good investment. Blood glucose tests are simple and easy to administer. The benefits are most likely to come from screening diabetes patients for TB.

3.11 Some general limitations

Aside from the complications such as coinfection with HIV and MDR-TB, presently there are other risks to a continuation of the present DOTS protocol as it is now implemented in many developing countries.

1. Because of shortages of health personnel many people with active TB may go undetected. Without treatment they spread the disease and if untreated could die. Remember that TB is highly contagious, particularly where living conditions are crowded and sanitation is substandard.
2. Some patients have found the DOTS regime too difficult to follow for a number of reasons. Dropping out puts them at risk for contracting multiple drug-resistant TB and this raises the cost of treatment dramatically. It also increases the risk of further spread of this strain of TB which is more difficult and costly to cure.
3. Living too far from a treatment center to travel to and from every day as required by DOTS.
4. Not being able to afford the travel cost required for treatment.
5. Not being able to afford a proper diet that would help insure against the side effects of the therapy.
6. Stopping the DOTS protocol before treatment is completed and patients are cured. This can lead to the recurrence of the illness and perhaps to MDR-TB.
7. Going to health providers outside the DOTS framework where they are given different and often inferior drugs. Dropouts from these programs are not monitored and also suffer the risks associated with MDR-TB. As noted earlier, MDR-TB is a more virulent form of the TB virus, which is more difficult and costly to treat.
8. Lack of support of family and friends in their local communities.
9. Lack of health professionals or others that can help administer drugs at home without the need to visit a health center every day.
10. The social stigma of having TB, which can lead to stopping treatment. In Imo State in Nigeria, stigmatization and discrimination dissuaded many people from accessing the state's 41 TB treatment centers. As a result treatment coverage is a paltry 14% and the case detection rate is only 27%.

11. Because of the stigma of having TB, patients go to great lengths to avoid going to DOTS clinics. To deal with these problems, officials are now recommending that TB treatment be bundled with other health service.
12. The stigma attached extends to health workers, many of whom have quit their jobs amid concerns that they are becoming infected with TB. This lack of knowledge about the spread of the disease and the fact that patients are no longer contagious shortly after they have been diagnosed and begun treatment needs to be recognized by everyone in the treatment chain.

3.12 Millennium Development Goals

For tuberculosis, the Millennium Development Goals can be summarized in one line, that is, to have halted by 2015 and begun to reverse, the prevalence and death rates associated with tuberculosis and also to increase the proportion of tuberculosis cases detected and cured by DOTS. The goals for the DOTS programs are not specified. The latest data available suggests that many countries have already achieved this goal, which is quite modest when one recognizes how many people are still being infected every day. On the other hand, the countries with the most cases, mostly in Africa and compounded by the high incidence of AIDS, are making little progress in reducing the incidence of TB. The TB epidemic is complicated by the fact that patients with HIV/AIDS are much more likely to contract TB because of the compromised state of their immune system. Estimates made by WHO suggest that HIV-infected individuals are as much as 15 times more likely to contract TB than the general population. Furthermore, as noted earlier, WHO policies still stress a more passive approach to the growth in tuberculosis epidemic and nearly exclusive reliance of DOTS. Latest figures from WHO (2013d) show that there are some positive developments over time such as an increase in the treatment success rate of TB from 69% in 2000 to 87% in 2011. Global TB mortality rate has fallen by 45% since 1990 and appears to be on target to achieve the MDG of a 50% reduction by 2015. However, the rate of decline in TB remains slow at 2% per year. Prevalence of active TB disease in the community has only fallen by 37% from 1990 to 2012. Out of the 22 high-burden countries identified, 50% of the countries are not on track to achieve the reduction in incidence, prevalence and mortality in line with targets. They include the Democratic Republic of the Congo, Kenya, Mozambique, Nigeria, South Africa and Zimbabwe, Afghanistan, Pakistan, Bangladesh, Indonesia and Russia.

We believe that the goals for a global TB program to identify, treat and eradicate TB should be much more ambitious than spelled out in the Millennium Development Goals. This would include a significant reduction in the rate of TB infection and improved treatment outcomes. With proper funding, human development support and community involvement it should be possible for the countries in Africa to achieve the cure rate of countries such as Sri Lanka over the next decade or so.

3.13 Future

WHO is convinced that concentrating on the spread of the TB epidemic and by putting significantly more resources into testing and treatment, there is the likelihood that the incidence of TB, along with mortality, will continue to dwindle over time. However, as yet there is no evidence that DOTS is slowing the spread of TB. However, there are a number of new developments and future prospects seem promising. Progress can be accelerated by Xpert MTB/ RIF and exploring new versions of the BCG being developed by Kernodle and his associates.

Furthermore, and as noted in the previous section, finding out who has TB and starting treatment immediately is crucial. Much more can be done by developing programs to lift the level of public awareness. Such programs should stress the importance of proper ventilation and avoid being cramped into small spaces where the TB bacteria can easily spread. People should also be sensitized to the threat of spreading TB through coughing, clearing the throat and even talking. Being more aware of the beginning signs of a TB infection is also critical and one should visit a clinic to have a smear test if TB is suspected.

The WHO strategy is designed to be effective in low-income developing countries that lack well-developed or manpower-intensive health services and the short course chemotherapy will replace the prevailing treatment. This new protocol is designed to achieve a higher cure rate by increasing patient compliance, reducing the number of patients under treatment at a given time and preventing the emergence of drug-resistant TB by using isoniazid and rifampicin, rather than isoniazid alone or other drug combinations. It is anticipated that the cure rate will be increased by cutting the time under treatment and better monitoring of intake of patient's medications.

The spread of the Xpert MTB/RIF technology in cooperation with DOTS should help to make the entire process of testing and treatment easier, quicker and user-friendly. Higher rates of treatment and diagnostic success have brought down the fatality and infection rates in many countries and should continue to do so in the future. However, rates of infection have climbed in Africa and parts of Asia along with the spread of HIV/AIDS and coinfections with TB. Globally more resources have to be devoted to all aspects of identification and treatment with particular attention to coinfection with HIV/AIDS and the spread of drug-resistant TB.

It is becoming clear that the DOTS protocol does not always work and that some or even many patients do not take their medications every day as recommended. When this happens, the threat of MDR-TB increases. Indeed, there is mounting evidence that MDR-TB is spreading and that the DOTS system is breaking down in many locations.

3.13.1 Better enforcement of DOTS

For all of the reasons mentioned earlier in Section 3.11, a broader society-based approach is needed, which includes participants from a variety of sectors outside the health professions.

A civil society perspective: TB case identification and treatment

Ideally a TB program would have three interrelated components. The first would be an ability to identify all citizens with either latent or active TB through a screening process. This would involve a smear test, Xpert MTB/RIF test or chest X-ray.

The identification process cannot rely completely on patient intake in clinics or hospitals. It has to search for new cases of TB in the community by seeking out family and friends of those who are currently being treated or in communities where the risk of TB infection is high. This could be because of high incidence of TB in nearby locations, where there are some cases of coinfection with HIV/AIDS, where there are cases of MDR-TB or where environmental factors such as extensive poverty, poor diets, crowded living conditions and/or poor sanitation suggest the TB epidemic could be spreading.

The ability to identify new cases and bring them in for treatment will depend on the ability to mobilize public opinion and raise awareness of the TB treatment as well as the ability to recruit and mobilize health activists and healthcare workers in villages and in local districts in urban areas and cities. There are examples of successful programs in Bangladesh, Tanzania and Thailand that should be studied and adopted by other countries.

The main feature of these programs is a process of identification of patients that combines walk-ins to clinics with referrals from people in the community, community members who work with health professionals to obtain proper drugs for patients and make sure patients take their medication and follow up through the course of treatment to completion.

By including members of the community as part of the identification and treatment of TB, success rates have increased dramatically at a small additional cost. The key is the involvement of the wider civilian community.

The second component is an enhanced ability to draw private sector doctors and health practitioners into the DOTS system. This would include upgrading their treatment protocols and entering their patients into a national database. What happens now is that many patients are either receiving improper treatment from private providers outside the DOTS system or patients are dropping out before completing the course of medication. In either case the risk of infection to others and the spread of MDR-TB is increased. A system that has such a large and unregulated private sector component is at risk for rapidly spreading either TB or MDR-TB.

It would be extremely insightful if small-scale projects could be developed, which refine these features in a setting where results could be compared with other communities where community involvement is not as strong.

Hence, much more needs to be done to make the DOTS system both full proof and extending it to more patients. This is the first and most important part of a three-part process for future control of TB. The **beginning step** in the process is to find all the cases of contagious TB and treat them with DOTS. If DOTS is not observed, then there will be an even bigger problem as MDR-TB is much more difficult and expensive to cure and mortality rates will also increase. To ensure that DOTS does work, more heath care resources have to be allocated to monitoring patients to make sure that they take their medication. Aside from monitoring at health centers, more local personnel can be trained to deliver the drugs and observe patients as they take them. An alternative is to use cell phones or Skype to have a real-time record to monitor compliance. This could be a component of a broader move to an electronically based system of diagnosis and treatment is discussed in more detail later in this chapter. Cash incentives can also be offered to patients that complete their course of treatment and also to health workers or trained village residents that monitor compliance. The importance of this step cannot be overemphasized. If DOTS breaks down, the result could be worse than no treatment at all. Better and more effective use of community health workers is required. In Bangladesh there is an extensive network of female community health workers (*shastho shebikas*) who routinely look for new TB cases and refer them to health clinics. They also administer DOTS and encourage cured patients to also help in the TB program.

The **second** step is to visit households where there are active cases of TB and then check and treat the most likely cases, most likely those who are sleeping in the same room, children, those with HIV and diabetics. It is important that this follow-up is timely. Fifty percent of the lifetime risk for getting TB occurs in the first year of exposure. If the skin test is positive for these individuals, then they are to begin treatment. The skin test is for latent TB only. If active TB is suspected, then a blood test or the new Xpert test is recommended.

Third, find all the high-risk groups in the village, the region and the country (HIV, malaria and diabetes) and undertake targeting testing for both latent and active TB.

In addition to this three-step process, there are seven additional steps that need to be taken to reduce the threat of the TB epidemic getting worse over the next few decades. The time line is unclear for some of these steps, yet the efforts have to be made now.

1. Continue to fund research to find a vaccine that will cure TB. This is difficult since the virus can go to sleep, making it hard to identify when it is not contagious. Yet this is the Holy Grail and the long runway to eradicate TB completely. WHO has recently developed a strategic blueprint for the next decade as part of its Stop TB Partnership Working Group Plan on new TB Vaccines. Representing consensus reached by the TB vaccine community, top scientific experts have set out a global plan of action for developing the vaccines that are seen as critical to eliminating the disease. In March 2012, the journal *Tuberculosis* published a special issue containing a new TB vaccine blueprint, editorials and opinion pieces. The blueprint outlines five keys to progress: creativity in research and discovery; correlates of immunity and biomarkers for TB vaccines; clinical trials harmonization and cooperation; rational selection of TB vaccine candidates; and the critical need for advocacy, community acceptance and funding. Currently sixteen vaccines have been advanced to clinical trials and 12 are now being tested in the field. Details of the complete blueprint, including relevant opinion editorials, is available at http://www.stoptb.org/wg/new_vaccines/.

2. Ensure better living conditions for the poor who are susceptible to TB. This includes less crowding and more ventilation and ensuring that everyone has his or her own bed. It also involves putting suspect

patients in isolation if possible and certainly away from others and with better ventilation. They should spend some time outside as healthcare TB germs are killed by sunlight.

3. Improve access to healthcare and gather information about TB, its symptoms and how it spreads more readily in poor communities.

4. Medical care should be followed as suggested in the three steps reviewed earlier.

5. Educational initiatives have to be strengthened so that the general public is made more aware of symptoms, where to seek treatment and the medication regime that is to be followed. Print media, radio, television and the Internet resource have to all be brought into play.

6. Work place information has to be provided, particularly where conditions are crowded such as textile factories, construction sites (such as where workers sleep in the buildings) and also in prisons.

7. Finally, the political will to deal with this epidemic has to be energized, perhaps with speeches by popular politicians, movie and other media stars, sports figures and others whose faces are familiar to the public.

It is also critical to begin to implement a diagnosis, treatment and tracking system that is based on electronic file management and patient identification with an electronic signature.

3.13.2 Resource allocation and requirements

What is the best strategy for allocation of scarce resources for the direct treatment of TB and also for use of public health resources to increase public awareness of the TB threat and to marshal manpower in the private sector to assist in case monitoring and treatment? The approach favored by some is to put more stress on human development. The motivation for this way to deal with the growing TB epidemic comes from an understanding of the interaction between HIV/AIDS and TB as well as the needs of growing populations. The disease spreads more quickly in poor neighborhoods. This reemphasizes the need to focus on finding out who has TB and then treating the person quickly and expeditiously.

According to this approach, which is favored by the Stop TB Partnership, human resource development is the most effective and perhaps the only way to deal with the epidemic. The methods for diagnosing

TB need to be extended to target more people who have been exposed. Once these people have been identified, they can be channeled into programs that implement the DOTS procedures, which have been established over the last few decades and which have provided effective treatment. This will require more technicians and lay people who have to be trained to recognize symptoms as well as to deliver medication and monitor patient compliance. It also has to be integrated with a more sophisticated electronic system based on patient id and record keeping.

Effective implementation of DOTS is labor intensive and will require additional manpower to work well. Furthermore, recent development in increasing the speed and user friendliness of diagnosis should make it easier to convince patients to begin and then to return for further treatment. The key to success is getting them to visit the health provider. If they are sick and reside a long way from a clinic, they may never seek treatment, spread the disease to others and die without care. Capturing people in the healthcare safety net is the first and most important step in the process. We do not know what proportion of those with TB are diagnosed or treated. Estimates made by WHO and other agencies are aiming for 70% detection and treatment of cases in the next few years. This is guesswork based on back casting of new cases from already existing cases as well as some detailed health surveys in a few countries. An 85% cure rate is also projected and this appears to be attainable since it is based on the treatment success rate in the past and the continued use of the DOTS protocol on a global basis. However, such an optimistic cure rate still leaves 15% of those infected to spread TB to others.

These projections are probably optimistic and may take some time to be reflected in the data. Careful research at the WHO suggests that DOTS protocol have not yet made an impact on either the diagnosis or treatment of TB globally. Furthermore, the methods used for these projections have been based on decade averages and a different estimating technique could lead to a different result.

Another approach, which is based on lagged response of detection and treatment in a time series model, is also explored. Even if such an approach proves to be more optimistic as to the effectiveness of DOTS, the growth in TB connected with the HIV/AIDS presents challenges and complications which alone would argue for a more focused and coordinated approach to building up the human resource base with greater emphasis on community awareness.

Before outlining such a proposal let's see where we are in terms of the World Health Assembly targets for TB and the ways that the Stop TB Partnership plans to go about implementing its strategy. As noted earlier, the strategy begins with the target of a 70% diagnosis rate under the DOTS strategy along with an 85% cure rate for those diagnosed. So there is nothing new here. According to the Stop TB Partnership, this would reduce the global burden of TB by 50% relative to 1990 levels by 2015. This would involve reducing average prevalence to 155 per 100,000 and deaths to 14 per 100,000. By 2015 the number dying should be less than one million per year including those who are co-infected with HIV.

Is the data that we have up to the present time (2014) consistent with these projections? What further acceleration in success would need to be achieved to reach these goals? From the data available until the end of 2007, it does not appear that these projections are realistic for the countries in Africa where HIV coinfection rates are high. For large population countries where the coinfection rates are not high, the death rates and prevalence rates have been reduced and in some cases these reduction are to rates consistent with the forecast. However, this does not mean that the countries with high rates of TB prevalence can't do better. China has adopted a program which has led to some success. However, there is a large residual population that remains untreated and was not included in their study. In all cases an effective program requires more resource and also a better tracking and monitoring system.

There are an inadequate number of laboratories and shortages of health staff. The logistics of health facilities in relation to the location of TB cases needs to be reviewed in all high-incidence countries. New protocols, which are now being adopted for vaccination with improved BCG strains, implementation of the new protocols for diagnosis and treatment with Xpert MTB/RIF, require additional training, upgrading of facilities and renewed efforts to make DOTS protocols even more widespread. Public awareness campaigns also need to be mounted to increase awareness of TB, how it infects, how it is spread and how and where to seek treatment. Without further upgrading the knowledge base of the general population, many more cases will go undetected and the disease will spread further.

In the disease control priority project culminating in the massive report on *Disease Control Priorities in Developing Countries* (now in its second edition), Dye and Floyd (2006, p. 305) argue that based on WHO analysis

> Some of the poorer countries among the 22 are now receiving sufficient external assistance to fill the gaps in their budgets for TB control, principally from the Global Fund to Fight AIDS, Tuberculosis and Malaria. Consequently the total reported budged deficit

> for the high-burden countries in 2005 was remarkably small – just $119 million – and concentrated in the poorer countries.

Compare this rather optimistic statement with the data in Table 3.3. Does it look like the TB program is under control? The answer is a resounding NO. Much more needs to be done. More resources have to be mobilized and case identification rates have to be increased to curb the spread of TB. Once identified, patients have to be treated effectively so there are many fewer dropouts that can move on to re-infect others, perhaps with a more virulent strain on the virus. How much more money and effort is needed? To assess these needs a detailed assessment for each of the 22 countries needs to be made. Before doing this, we need to fill out the agenda for MDR-TB and coinfection of TB with HIV.

3.13.3 To deal with TB/HIV and MDR-TB

As noted earlier, special efforts need to be made to deal with TB/HIV, MDR-TB (multidrug-resistant TB) and XDR-TB (extensively drug-resistant TB). These challenges require more resources, better science on the ground and a different set of protocols to deal with these cases. Such concerted efforts need to be mounted immediately in all countries where these strains are more common and the international community must be involved. These new strains can be spread from person to person, creating a new wave of the TB epidemic that is much harder to cure.

3.13.4 What to do about TB coinfection with HIV/AIDS?

In analyzing the spread of the TB epidemic in the top 20 countries and in more detail in three of these countries (Bangladesh, Brazil, Thailand), it is clear that the spread of TB combined with the coinfection with HIV/AIDS and the spread of drug-resistant TB is overwhelming the healthcare systems of many countries. While TB rates (prevalence) have fallen in 11 countries since 1990, rates have increased in eight others. In countries where HIV/AIDS coinfection rates are high, the incidence of TB has increased significantly over the past two decades in all but one country. This is true even where the overall incidence of HIV/AIDS is low. This is because the spread of TB among HIV-positive patients is so much higher than the spread rate in the general population. Furthermore, even where TB rates have fallen somewhat they are still unacceptably high and continue to put a burden on healthcare systems (see Table 3.4).

Table 3.4 TB, coinfection with HIV and an index of economic freedom

Country	Per 100,000 1990 TB prevalence	Per 100,000 2007 TB prevalence	HIV prevalence over 15% in TB cases 2007	2007 number of cases ('000s)	Heritage freedom ranking 2010/of 180
India	586	283		1962	123
China	327	194		1306	138
Indonesia	443	244		528	115
Nigeria	282	521	X	460	116
South Africa	769	692	X	461	70
Bangladesh	639	387		353	130
Ethiopia	323	579	X	314	134
Pakistan	430	223		297	122
Philippines	799	500		255	107
Congo	209	666		245	172
Russia	69	115	X	157	149
Vietnam	365	220		150	136
Kenya	125	319	X	132	103
Brazil	124	60		92	99
Tanzania		337	X	120	110
Uganda	206	426	X	102	78
Zimbabwe	409	714	X	104	178
Thailand	336	192		91	60
Mozambique	287	504	X	92	108
Myanmar	411	162		83	173
Cambodia	928	664		72	157

Sources: WHO (2009) and Heritage Foundation (2013).

Because their immune systems have already been weakened, TB is much more likely to spread to those who have already been infected with the HIV virus. Because patients who have been diagnosed with HIV are much more prone to TB infection, the protocol for testing for TB among HIV patients is critical. Furthermore, in a patient where HIV might be suspected, TB could be an early warning sign. Therefore, WHO recommends that patients who have TB symptoms, or have a confirmed case of TB and those who live in an environment where TB is widespread should be tested for HIV. See WHO (2008) and Raviglione, Reichman and Hershfield (2006).

A TB diagnosis can be the first sign that a person has HIV. Furthermore, if a patient has HIV, it has an impact on his or her TB treatment. Co-trimoxazole preventive therapy should be initiated as soon as possible and given throughout the TB treatment phase. It is also important to test family members for HIV when the patient has TB. HIV-positive

TB patients could have household members who are also living with HIV. Using a family framework for HIV testing, other family members should be encouraged to take an HIV test. Where one member of a couple has been diagnosed with HIV and the other has not, counseling can help to prevent the spread of HIV. Within a family-centered approach to HIV testing, once a family member is identified as having HIV, health workers should encourage and actively facilitate HIV testing for other family members. This could be done, where possible and appropriate, through couples or family testing and counseling services. Isoniazid therapy may also be appropriate.

Isoniazid can be used to prevent people who have had contact with tuberculosis bacteria from getting TB and may be appropriate therapy for up to six months or a year. However, there are possible side effects including liver damage, particularly for those patients with weak livers from alcohol use or use of injection drugs. Careful monitoring is critical and lab tests may be necessary to test response to isoniazid. Because of general resistance to testing for HIV, it is suggested that HIV and TB testing be done at the same time if possible.

Coinfection of HIV and TB has been responsible for the rapid rise in TB in nearly half of the top 22 TB countries shown in Table 3.1. The rates of TB have increased several fold in some countries, increasing the healthcare burden of TB dramatically. When combined with the burden of treating HIV-positive patients, this has resulted in a rapid deterioration in the ability of health systems in these countries to deal with both epidemics. The WHO (2009) report provides some estimates of this shortfall. The number of TB, HIV and Antiretroviral Facilities (ART) for six of the high-TB/HIV countries are displayed in Table 3.5.

Data from these countries account for about 15% of the total number of HIV-positive TB cases worldwide. WHO has indicated that the estimated coinfection rate (i.e., HIV-positive TB cases) has increased dramatically. The estimated incidence of HIV in TB cases rose from 9% to 22% of total TB cases between 2005 and 2007 in the countries in Table 3.3.[1] However, the number of patients placed on ART did not keep pace suggesting that an increasing number of HIV-positive TB patients were not receiving ART. The use of co-trimoxazole prophylaxis (CPT), a drug given to HIV-exposed children as well as those living with HIV, has increased rapidly. CPT is being used for scaling up HIV care in resource-limited settings where ART may not be readily available. In most countries the number of facilities offering ART is much smaller than the number of TB facilities. For the future, combining TB and HIV facilities is a logical step to ramp up the treatment of patients with TB and HIV and also increasing the access to ART for those patients with HIV.

Both ART and CPT increase the survival rate for patients suffering from HIV and TB. Antiretroviral therapy improves survival in HIV-positive patients. In addition, according to WHO, ART reduces TB rates by up to 90% at an individual level and also reduces the chance of recurrence by around 50%. Depending on availability, ART should be initiated for *all* people living with HIV along with active TB disease (see Bpharm et al. (2006), Lawn and Churchyard (2009) and Golub et al. (2008)). At the present time ART is not as widely available as it should be to keep the death rate from HIV from escalating. Estimates suggest that as many as two-third of all those suffering from HIV are not being treated with ART. For details see the Chapter 2 on HIV/AIDS.

Similarly, where there is a high incidence of HIV/TB coinfection stronger efforts need to be made to provide chemotherapy to individuals with latent/inactive TB. Mathematical modeling by Heymann (1993) suggests that in communities where 20% of the population is infected with HIV and 25% received treatment for TB, deaths would be 100% higher than in communities where none of the population is HIV infected. It also suggests that active TB could be cut by over 90% in a decade by providing chemotherapy to 30% of individuals with inactive TB. These results suggest that much greater efforts must be made to treat both active and latent TB cases where there is a significant level of HIV coinfection. This will require a reorientation of the TB programs in these countries to not only identify those individuals who present symptoms

Table 3.5 Provision of TB treatment, HIV testing and ART 2007

Country	Number of facilities providing TB treatment	Number of facilities providing HIV testing/ counseling	Number of facilities providing ART
Democratic Republic of Congo	1205	286	209
Ethiopia	833	1005	272
Myanmar	324	291	32
Rwanda	450	312	165
Uganda	1261	554	286
Tanzania	2500	1035	204

Source: WHO (2009, Box 2.5 Table, p. 47).

Table 3.6 Tuberculosis screening questionnaire

	Yes	No
1. Has the individual had a cough for more than 2 weeks?	[ ]	[ ]
2. Has the individual had fevers for more than 2 weeks?	[ ]	[ ]
3. Has the individual had an observed weight loss for more than 3 kg in the last 4 weeks?	[ ]	[ ]
4. Has the individual had night sweats for more than 2 weeks?	[ ]	[ ]
5. Has the individual been in close contact with someone with TB in the past year? (optional)	[ ]	[ ]
6. If done, does the patient have a Tuberculin Skin Test (TST) induration of more than 5 mm? (optional)	[ ]	[ ]
If 'Yes' to Question 1, patient is a pulmonary TB suspect, regardless of answers to other questions, begin evaluation for TB.		
If 'No' to Question 1 but 'Yes' to any other question, patient is a TB suspect. Begin evaluation for TB.		
If 'No' to all questions, patient is not a TB suspect. Repeat TB screening in 3–6 months time.		

Source: Howard and El-Sadr (2010, Figure 1, p. S239).

of active TB but also to screen the general population for latent TB. Such a reorientation has not been suggested by WHO or other agencies dealing with tuberculosis and HIV. The spread of TB to the general population can be prevented by this therapy.

To identify potential TB patients, a simple screening questionnaire has been used effectively in several countries in Southern Africa (Table 3.6).

To reduce the risk of TB transmission in HIV cases, WHO recommends prompt identification of persons with TB symptoms, separating infectious patients from others, controlling spread through cough hygiene including masks and minimizing time spent in healthcare facilities if TB is suspected and/or diagnosed. These measures are particularly important where TB and HIV facilities are shared. Those suspected of having TB should be treated immediately. When there is also a risk for MDR and XTR TB, the risk of infection is multiplied and screening takes on an added dimension (see next section).

One advantage of having HIV and TB facilities is that they can both benefit from cross-fertilization of therapies and increase the efficiency of treatment. In Rwanda both HIV and TB patients are treated in a sequential fashion with TB care at the TB clinic for the duration of their treatment and then transferred to the HIV facility. During TB treatment, patients' HIV status is determined and CD4 cell counts are taken for those with HIV and trimethoprim-sulfamethoxazone (an antibacterial agent that helps to prevent infection in those patients where the immune system has been weakened) and antiretroval therapy are dispensed to those infected patients.

Nutrition of those with coinfection of TB and HIV is also important and is often neglected. This is especially important in low-income and food insecure environments where lowered immunity and the burden of strong drugs on the system have to be matched with a good diet. The exact nature of dietary interventions needs to be explored more intensively in individual country environments.

The three "I's"

In general, WHO recommends implementing the three "I's" for those patients with TB and HIV coinfection. These are Isoniazid preventive treatment (IPT), intensified case finding (ICF) for active TB and TB Infection Control (IC). These are key public health strategies to decrease the impact of TB on people living with HIV.

- Isoniazid preventive treatment (IPT), TB preventive therapy with INH is safe and effective in people living with HIV, reducing the risk of TB by 33–62%.
- Intensified case finding (ICF) for active TB cases involves screening and diagnosing TB in people living with HIV. This can be challenging but TB is curable in people living with HIV.
- TB Infection Control (IC) is essential to keep vulnerable patients, healthcare workers and their community safe from getting TB.

3.13.5 What to do about MDR-TB?

Treatment of drug-resistant tuberculosis

About 12 million people worldwide have tuberculosis and about 650,000 have multidrug-resistant tuberculosis. Children comprise about 10–15% of the tuberculosis burden and it is estimated that about the same proportion applies for MDR-TB, although accurate figures are not available. MDR-TB is undetectable in children. Because of this, and the general problem of identifying MDR-TB in adults, the number of drug-resistant TB in children is still unknown.

Green light committee initiative for MDR-TB

The TB virus has been able to mutate and develop resistance to conventional drug therapy. These new strains of TB require special therapy and different drug cocktails to attack the virus. There are many technical aspects involved in designing a country's multiple disease resistance tuberculosis (MDR-TB) strategy and integrating it into national programs. The so-called Green Light Committee (GLC; www.who.int/tb/challenges/mdr/greenlightcommittee) has been designed to facilitate the formulation of national strategies to incorporate MDR-TB approaches. The GLC is a subgroup of the MDR-TB Working Group of the Stop TB Partnership. It is also an advisory body of WHO that promotes and monitors MDR-TB treatments. WHO has developed five categories of drugs that are used to treat MDR-TB. Without going into greater detail suffice it to say that there are several so-called first-line agents. These are pills taken orally that have proved effective in combating MDR-TB in many circumstances. If these drugs are not effective, there is an array of injectables that are available as well as three other classes of drugs that can be used in particular circumstances, depending

Table 3.7 Groups of drugs to treat MDR-TBa

Group	Drugs (abbreviations)
Group 1: First-line oral agents	• pyrazinamide (Z) • ethambutol (E) • rifabutin (Rfb)
Group 2: Injectable agents	• kanamycin (Km) • amikacin (Am) • capreomycin (Cm) • streptomycin (S)
Group 3: Fluoroquinolones	• levofloxacin (Lfx) • moxifloxacin (Mfx) • ofloxacin (Ofx)
Group 4: Oral bacteriostatic second-line agents	• para-aminosalicylic acid (PAS) • cycloserine (Cs) • terizidone (Trd) • ethionamide (Eto) • protionamide (Pto)
Group 5: Agents with unclear role in treatment of drug-resistant TB	• clofazimine (Cfz) • linezolid (Lzd) • amoxicillin/clavulanate (Amx/Clv) • thioacetazone (Thz) • imipenem/cilastatin (Ipm/Cln) • high-dose isoniazid (high-dose H)b • clarithromycin (Clr)

Source: WHO (2008a, p.ix).

Table 3.8 General principles for designing MDR-TB treatment regimens

Principles	Comments
1. Use at least four drugs certain to be effective	The more of the following factors are present, the more likely it is that the drug will be effective: • Resistance to these drugs is known from surveys to be rare in similar patients. • Drug susceptibility testing (DST) results show susceptibility to drugs for which there is good laboratory reliability: injectable agents and fluoroquinolones. • The drug is not commonly used in the area. • For decisions about an individual patient – no prior history of treatment failure with the drug; no known close contacts with resistance to the drug.
2. Do not use drugs for which there is possibility of cross-resistance	• Many antituberculosis agents exhibit cross-resistance both within and across drug classes.
3. Eliminate drugs that are not safe	• Quality of the drug is unknown. • (For decisions about an individual patient – known severe allergy or unmanageable intolerance; high risk of severe adverse drug effects such as renal failure, deafness, hepatitis, depression and/or psychosis.)
4. Include drugs from Groups 1–5 in a hierarchical order based on potency	• Use any of the first-line oral agents (Group 1) that are likely to be effective. • Use an effective aminoglycoside or polypeptide by injection (Group 2). • Use a fluoroquinolone (Group 3). • Use the remaining Group 4 drugs to complete a regimen of at least four effective drugs. • For regimens with fewer than four effective drugs, consider adding two Group 5 drugs. The total number of drugs will depend on the degree of uncertainty, and regimens often contain five to seven.

Note: Avoid streptomycin even if DST suggests susceptibility because of high rates of resistance with resistant TB strains and higher incidence of ototoxicity.
Source: Adapted from WHO (2008a, Table 7.3).

upon the level of resistance and the experience with the two first-line agents. These five categories of drugs are listed in Table 3.7 and the general principles for treatment regimes in Table 3.8. Obviously, there is much left to the discretion of the health professional supervising the course of treatment as well as availability of drugs, the reaction and health of the patient and other local factors and conditions. The cost of treatment and the requirements for experienced health practitioners escalates as the scope of treatment and the spread of MDR/TB increases.

The general approach to selecting the appropriate dosages and mixes of drugs for individuals should be guided by the general principles outlined in Table 3.8.

Treating children with MDR-TB

Globally, children comprise about 15% of all MDR-TB cases. A meta-analysis of a number of studies carried out by Ettehad et al. (2012) investigated the results of eight studies carried out on children with MDR-TB. Despite some limitations and lack of standardization of the reporting and collection process in cases of childhood tuberculosis, the authors concluded that when children are treated for MDR-TB the results are as good as or better than those reported for adults. To develop better treatment protocols for children, the authors suggest that outcomes be reported for cases where children are involved.

Need to reduce the spread of the MDR-TB virus

In 2008 an estimated 440,000 cases of MDR-TB were diagnosed. Over 50% were in China and India. The highest concentrations as a percentage of all new TB cases were in the former Soviet Union, ostensibly because of poor implementation of DOTS or failure to adhere to DOTS protocol. Currently, the progress toward targets for universal access to diagnosis and treatment of MDR-TB is still way off target (WHO, 2013d). Twelve countries accounted for 80% (237,000) of estimated MDR-TB cases among notified TB patients in 2012 (see Table 3.9).

There are several ways that MDR-TB can be contracted and spread. If those enrolled in a DOTS program fail to take their medication for the prescribed length of time, they are highly susceptible to a relapse, which can take the form of MDR-TB. Those with MDR-TB, which is undiagnosed and untreated, can also spread MDR-TB in the same way that the usual form of TB is spread through close personal contact. Evidence presented by Eva Nathanson et al. (2010) suggests that 75% of MDR-TB cases occur in new patients that have not been diagnosed and who have not previously received treatment for TB. The remaining cases are

Table 3.9 Estimated MDR-TB cases among notified TB patients, 2012

	Best estimate	Uncertainty interval	Number of notified MDR-TB cases in 2012
India	64,000	49,000–79,000	16,588
China	59,000	52,000–66,000	3007
Russia	46,000	43,000–49,000	13,612
Philippines	13,000	10,000–16,000	679
Pakistan	11,000	0–29,000	1602
Kazakhstan	8800	8700–9000	7608
South Africa	8100	6900–9400	15,419
Indonesia	6900	5200–8500	428
Ukraine	6800	6500–7000	6934
Myanmar	6000	4600–7500	778
Uzbekistan	4000	3700–4300	1728
Bangladesh	4200	3100–5200	513

Source: WHO (2013d, Table S4, p. 9).

most likely a result of the failure of a DOTS program to affect a cure or else treatment of the patient outside the DOTS framework. The spread could have also occurred as a result of past treatment of patients who then spread the disease. These patients could have been treated either in a DOTS program where patients were not monitored effectively or in private clinics outside the DOTS framework. Whatever the reason, the number of MDR-TB cases is increasing and needs to be addressed. Weak laboratory capacity remains a global problem, particularly in poor countries, and the time needed to diagnose MDR-TB is quite long – up to two or three months – and in the meantime the patient might be spreading the TB germs. Nathanson et al. argue that

> The failure to adequately fund a response to MDR tuberculosis would have a catastrophic consequence in terms of both human lives and tuberculosis control in general.
>
> (p. 1052)

In general, greater surveillance, more funds and more health professionals are needed if the Stop TB initiative is to achieve its objectives of treating 50 million people for TB and enrolling three million patients who have both HIV and TB. The goal of the WHO, however, is not to roll back the prevalence and death rates to much lower levels by 2015, but rather to return to the situation that existed in 1990.

We can do better. China and a few other countries have shown that we can do better. What will it take? Nathanson et al. suggested that for MDR-TB alone it would take several billion dollars to treat the estimated 1.3 million cases between 2010 and 2015. Additional details of a proposed control strategy are displayed in Table 3.10.

Table 3.10 Critical challenges in the control of MDR tuberculosis and XDR tuberculosis and potential solutions supported by the WHO[1]

Goal	Problem	Proposed solution
Finance control and treatment for MDR-TB and XDR-TB	Estimated cost for 2010–2015 is $16.2 billion (in US$), increasing annually from <$1.3 billion in 2010 to $4.4 billion in 2015; funding needed is already in excess of the planned national MDR-TB budgets for 2010	Maximize use of domestic resources while targeting resources from the Global Fund to Fight AIDS, Tuberculosis and Malaria, UNITAID and other external funding mechanisms
Abolish financial barriers	In countries with a high burden of MDR-TB, treatment costs for a single patient constitutes more than 100% of the gross national per capita income	Improve healthcare financing schemes to strive for universal access to prevention and control; decentralize services to reduce indirect costs; promote patient adherence to treatment; and subsidized care provided in the private sector
Engage all care providers in appropriate MDR-TB prevention and control	A substantial proportion of patients seek care from providers who do not follow internationally recommended standards of treatment	Engage diverse providers (public, voluntary, private and corporate) to align TB-management practices with WHO International Standards for TB Care

Optimize MDR-TB and XDR-TB management and care	Persons with infectious MDR-TB and XDR-TB remain in the community for long periods of time because of delayed diagnosis and initiation of treatment with second-line anti-TB drugs; hospitalization of patients with MDR-TB or XDR-TB poses problem of nosocomial transmission and is costly and inconvenient for patients	Ensure timely diagnosis and treatment initiation for patients with MDR-TB or XDR-TB; implement appropriate models of care, preferably outpatient, to ensure patient-centered care, avoid disease transmission in healthcare facilities and make rational use of financial resources
Address laboratory crisis	In 2008, in 27 countries with the highest burden of MDR-TB, only 1% of patients with newly diagnosed TB and 3% of patients with previously treated TB underwent drug-susceptibility testing	Strengthen laboratory services by using new molecular technologies
Ensure access to quality-assured anti-TB drugs	Use of counterfeit and poor-quality anti-TB drugs, which can lead to development and amplification of drug resistance, is well documented, but there is no accurate estimate of the scale of the problem	Secure affordable, quality-assured anti-TB drugs using national procurement mechanisms while building up a reliable second-line anti-TB drug market, with manufacturers investing in increased volumes and improved quality
Restrict availability of anti-TB drugs	Wide availability of anti-TB drugs over the counter in retail pharmacies encourages self-treatment and the purchase of inadequate quantities and combinations of medicines	Restrict drug availability to accredited providers by combining government policy, agreement with providers and industry on improved marketing practices, and optimization of the protocol for drug management and supply specified by the national TB program

Table 3.10 (Continued)

Goal	Problem	Proposed solution
Prioritize TB infection control	Ongoing transmission of MDR-TB and XDR-TB occurs in healthcare facilities and congregate settings because of inadequate infection control	Engage wide range of stakeholders across the health system (e.g., hospital administrators, architects, engineers and healthcare workers), including those concerned with control of other infections with airborne potential, such as influenza, to implement infection-control policies
Address global health workforce crisis	Shortage of trained staff to effectively manage the 1.6 million MDR-TB cases expected by 2015 is exacerbated in many low-income countries by active recruitment of staff by industrialized countries	Revise or update strategic plans for increasing the TB healthcare workforce (including private healthcare providers) to improve basic TB control and to scale up MDR-TB control
Improve surveillance systems	Estimates of the burden of drug-resistant TB globally and by country remain incomplete and less than accurate	Establish or strengthen continuous surveillance systems for drug-resistant TB
Invest in research and development of new diagnostic tests, drugs and vaccines	Tools for prevention, diagnosis and treatment of TB and drug-resistant TB are obsolete	Ensure collaboration between development and technical agencies to facilitate development and field testing of new tools for prevention, diagnosis and treatment of TB

Note:[1]The international group known as UNITAID purchases and distributes diagnostic tests and drugs used in the treatment of HIV–AIDS, malaria and tuberculosis. AIDS denotes acquired immunodeficiency syndrome, MDR-TB multidrug-resistant tuberculosis, TB tuberculosis, WHO World Health Organization and XDR-TB extensively drug-resistant tuberculosis.

Source: Nathanson et al. (2010, p. 1053).

In addition to surveillance, funding and more health professionals, healthcare systems need to be integrated to take care of all the different kinds of TB that can arise within any healthcare system. The healthcare network needs to be able to integrate private care physicians and clinics into the national network so that patients receive the same level and consistency of care no matter where they are treated. Medicines of questionable quality have to be banned and penalties imposed for those who prescribe them. A better tracking system also has to be put in place based on electronic records rather than paper files.

3.13.6 Improving the delivery of TB diagnosis and treatment and keeping the public informed

TB diagnosis and control requires systematic efforts from finding out who has TB through to complete cure. If any steps are skipped or implementation is weak, the system fails and the number of TB cases continues to grow. The coinfection of TB and HIV requires different tactics, along with close coordination with health officials involved with HIV/AIDS. In this section we are concerned with smear-positive TB cases without complications of coinfection as well as coinfection with HIV/AIDS as well as MDR-TB (drug-resistant strains).

In 2006, Public Health Watch presented a detailed series of five TB policy reports on TB from a civil society perspective. These five countries (Nigeria, Bangladesh, Tanzania, Brazil and Thailand) are among the 22 high-burden countries identified by WHO. In this section we summarize these findings and make some suggestions for future TB policies. The recent revision to the WHO guidelines for the once-a-day DOTS is also explored. This review is offered by Public Health Watch from the perspective of implementing processes and programs that can actively address TB diagnosis and treatment. Many agencies both public and private including nongovernmental organizations (NGOs) as well as the medical community and the general public are involved.

Is there political commitment?

In 2000, 20 high-burden countries signed the Amsterdam Declaration to Stop TB. The declaration noted, among others, that TB kills two million people a year and that there are eight million new cases; that TB is an integral part of health cures; that there are effective cures; public awareness is inadequate; confronting TB requires cooperation between governments and society as a whole; TB control is an effective strategy for poverty alleviation; ensuring that human and financial resources are on a sustainable basis to meet the challenges of stopping TB; actively participating in a global partnership agreement to Stop Tuberculosis designed to foster ownership and accountability.

Since then Stop TB has become a viable program objective but TB has continued to spread and increase in 12 of top 20 countries since 1990. One reason is the lack of political commitment in some countries to the objectives of the Amsterdam Declaration and Stop TB. There is overreliance on the participation of external donors in three of the five high-burden countries studied (Bangladesh, Nigeria and Tanzania) and the quality of laboratories and the work load of health workers have suffered. The HIV/AIDS epidemic has created additional strains on the health infrastructure in all countries but Bangladesh, where HIV rates are low. The spread of HIV/AIDS in Africa has added a huge burden to already strained TB resources. Those with HIV are much more likely to contract TB than the general population. Resources to deal with this have not been generally forthcoming. Similarly, there has been limited international pressure to hold countries to their commitments made in the Amsterdam Declaration. Why else would Brazil, a country with middle-income status and in a region with a higher average human development index than either Africa or Asia, have such a high level of TB, which has come down only slowly? There is no high-level political commitment at the regional level in communities where TB levels have increased in recent years. In all top 20 countries, there is a tendency to relegate concern about TB to ministries of health. Partly this is because TB is a difficult disease – difficult to diagnose without a skin test and cured only with a prolonged drug protocol. Other ministries and regional governments also need to get involved.

This brings us to the next point – the awareness factor

In most of the top 20 high burden TB countries, the average level of education is not particularly high. Many families would have access to TV and radio but not to the Internet. This is compounded by the lack of media involvement in publicizing the threat of TB, ways to prevent exposure and appropriate testing. There are many false stories and rumors spread about TB – what it is, how it is spread and how it can be cured. There is little or no involvement by public information agencies in disseminating easy to understand material which would provide citizens with enough information to avoid getting TB or if TB is suspected, of where to get a test. New tests are now becoming available that give results in an hour or two. Dissemination of this material to the public could help to boost awareness and galvanize the public to increase their interest in being tested for TB. Anecdotal evidence suggests there is limited public understanding of TB which compromises their ability to make sound judgments about testing and treatment. In at least two of our five country panels, many people believe that TB has been eradicated. There is even less information and understanding about the possible coinfection of TB and HIV.

In this connection the media could become more involved with publicizing the TB epidemic and appropriate actions that should be taken. If governments would hire public relations firms to build up media interest in TB there would be more money in donations, greater public interest and awareness and less shame generated when people test positive and have to undergo treatment. The first priority would be to hold a press conference to upgrade the information of print, radio and TV media. Journalists complain that the information they receive is too technical and hard for the public to digest. At times, public health officials do not have public relations background and are also not used to being interviewed. All countries need at least one focal point where the media can go to get information and also a place where the government and NGOs can spread the word about the latest developments as well as the state of play with testing, treatment and eradication rates. Consider how polio and smallpox were eradicated – public awareness and a public health blitz. This could be carried out with traditional media as well as the burgeoning electronic media including cell phone and the Internet.

Stigma and discrimination

The stigma of coming down with a disease is hard to quantify. It seems that the views of society in the case of HIV/AIDS are pretty clear, although they have moderated over time. In the case of TB, it is hard for an outsider to understand why there would be a stigma attached. Is there a stigma attached to getting a cold or flu? Nevertheless, in developing countries there are broad cultural factors at work. The stigma attached creates a blockage in identification and treatment that inhibits the ability of health professionals to make progress in reducing the spread of the disease and puts more people at risk. Women, migrants and those in other high-risk groups are more likely to be stigmatized, particularly in regions where HIV infection rates are high. These feelings are particularly worrisome where knowledge about the causes, how it spreads and what treatments are available is limited. All the more reason for a more vigorous information campaigns as suggested in the previous section. Research by Public Health Watch suggests that women are particularly prone to feelings of prejudice and rejection as others fear that they will also become infected. Stereotypical attitudes of TB being a "man's disease" is common and women are very uncomfortable with the coughs that accompany the disease in its early stages. Furthermore, women generally also have more limited access to health providers and if the disease is diagnosed, the DOTS regime will require them to visit the clinic daily, exposing them to additional social opprobrium. TB spreads rapidly in crowded conditions – minority immigrants, prisoners, those in refugee camps and slums where population densities are high. Minorities are further handicapped because they do not speak the language well and would have difficulty understanding information on TB even if it were available.

TB and poverty

TB spreads in conditions where there is crowding, lack of sufficient air circulation and poor sanitation – all of which are found in urban slums and in poor villages in most high-risk countries. Furthermore, the hidden costs of TB treatment (trips to the clinic, a nutritious diet and possible lost earnings or cost of child care) often keep TB victims from making required visits to clinics or not returning at all. This cycle further exacerbates the spread of the disease within the community and the lack of treatment creates a further downward spiral of disease and loss of income. In Bangladesh it is estimated that the economic impact associated with TB and costs of treatment have pushed 30% of nonpoor patients below the poverty line. Extensive hidden costs of treatment also have a detrimental impact on the ability of patients to pay for treatment.

The fact that several countries (Sri Lanka and Brazil for example) have been able to raise living standards while undertaking significant reductions in poverty suggests that without such efforts the fight against TB will be slow and fragmented. Indonesia is an interesting case, where significant poverty reduction and a reduction in TB prevalence went hand in hand, until funding difficulties resulted in a temporary cessation of Global Fund assistance. This reinforces the need for sustained and reliable financing from outside sources to countries that have difficulty in ramping up their own contributions to the Stop TB effort.

Hidden cost of treatment

Typical DOTS requires taking daily medication for up to six months. This medication is ideally supervised by a health worker at a clinic. In many cases this might not be possible because of the distance from home to clinic and/or the cost of transportation as well as the cost of nutritional meals that should accompany the treatment and the cost of additional diagnostic tests. In Tanzania and Nigeria, states with the least accessible facilities are also among the poorest economically. For example, Zamfara state in northern Nigeria has ten DOTS centers to serve 3.6 million people while Ogun state in the south has more than ten times the number of DOTS centers (116) to serve more than a million fewer people (2.3 million). Patients have to spend hours away from work to visit the clinic and receive medication. Health centers can also be overwhelmed with patients and not have time to provide individual care. With a job and family obligations treatment at health centers is not an option for many patients. Furthermore, nutritional supplements are not ordinarily part of the health system and have to be met out of the patients' own budget. There is also limited support from civil society organizations, and this needs to be increased in the future if DOTS is to be successful as envisioned. What are the alternatives without more resources for health centers? They can be either self-administered drugs or supervision by a volunteer from the local village or town with some training in the treatment of TB.

The practicability of DOTS

The two cornerstones of DOTS are sputum microscopy and access to directly observed treatment. However, these are not always possible. The new technology discussed earlier, (Xpert MTB/RIF), makes the diagnosis of TB faster (an hour or two) and less demanding for the patient who normally has to wait a week or more for diagnosis. However, concomitant developments to reduce the length and regularity of supervision of drug therapy on a daily basis have not been possible. Full compliance with the DOTS protocol is not possible in some locations. This results in dropouts and possible spread of TB to others, including family members and friends. As an option many patients take the drugs themselves or come into a center once or twice a week. Another interesting development is the recent WHO guidelines that suggest an alternative to the daily dosage regime to three times a week. The following has been suggested in the WHO as an alternative to the once a day therapy.

> To quote the WHO
>
> Recommendation 2.1
> Wherever feasible, the optimal dosing frequency for new patients with pulmonary TB is daily throughout the course of therapy
>
> (Strong/High grade of evidence)
>
> There are two alternatives to Recommendation 2.1:
>
> Recommendation 2.1A

New patients with pulmonary TB may receive a daily intensive phase followed by a three times weekly continuation phase [$2HRZE/4(HR)^3$], provided that each dose is directly observed

(Conditional/High and moderate grade of evidence)

Recommendation 2.1B
Three times weekly dosing throughout therapy [$2(HRZE)^3/4(HR)^3$] may be used as another alternative to Recommendation 2.1, provided that every dose is directly observed and the patient is NOT living with HIV or living in an HIV-prevalent setting

(Conditional/High and moderate grade of evidence)

Source: WHO (2010, pp. 2–3)

In general, there is nothing in the WHO guidelines that indicates that reduction from daily to three times a week dosage will, in any way, compromise the success of the therapy in terms of relapse or failure rates. These new guidelines are good news, particularly where staff in treatment centers are under tremendous pressure to assist in the administration of DOTS to help patients. As noted in the mathematical model section, the protocol for treating TB differs where there are also cases of HIV involved. Furthermore, sputum tests alone are not always reliable if patients are HIV positive.

Community-based DOTS

Another alternative is to enlist the aid of community-based health workers, some of whom are volunteers and others that are paid. These efforts would go a long way in ensuring more reliable enforcement of DOTS regime. In any case, countries need to allocate more funds for community support for DOTS supervision. Some advocate using the model followed in the case of HIV, where case workers distribute ARV to patients. These same workers could also distribute TB drugs to those who have HIV and also to those who are only exhibiting TB symptoms.

As some country experiences demonstrate, this can be a highly successful program. As noted in the previous section, health workers and their patients are often overwhelmed by the DOTS protocol. Several countries (three of the five summarized here) have initiated community-based programs in collaboration with NGOs.

In Bangladesh, community health workers play an instrumental role in guaranteeing the effectiveness of DOTS. Local female community health workers (*shasto shebikas*) are trained to identify TB symptoms and refer patients to TB diagnostic centers in their communities. They also act as a liaison between the patient and the health center. Once the patient has been diagnosed, the health workers are given the appropriate drugs to give to the patient as outlined by the diagnostician at the health center including how long the drugs need to be taken and at what intervals (either once a day or three times a week). They also monitor the status of the patient. They receive a small fee for every patient cured. This system has resulted in high success rates at or above the 85% target level and these local community health workers also raise awareness about other health issues in the community, helping to reduce the stigma of TB as well as providing a link to general health information. It also forges better links with the governmental agencies to spearhead TB control and increases public confidence in its ability to guide the community to a healthy future. TB also needs further community support when there is a possibility of coinfection with HIV. This system has worked very effectively in Bangladesh and can serve as a prototype for DOTS programs in other countries where patients are poor, transportation is slow and unreliable and patients live a long way from the nearest health center. Without such case workers there is a good chance that many patients with not take the drugs as prescribed and run the risk of TB getting worse and perhaps mutate to a harder to treat version of the disease.

A program similar to the Bangladesh model has also been adopted in Tanzania, where success rates have risen dramatically and costs of administration have fallen as travel costs to and fro health centers have been eliminated. With minimal financial support the cure rate in one district increased from less than 50% to nearly 80% with budget savings because travel costs have been eliminated. Unfortunately, these programs have been terminated in Tanzania and the scope of the program has had to be scaled down since there is no financing for transportation or training of district health management teams. More needs to be done to extend the program, perhaps with assistance from NGOs.

In another experiment, in a village in Thailand health volunteers work with family members to distribute TB drugs and spread TB awareness in their communities. However, the program has failed to be completely effective since there is no compensation for these family members and, as one health worker said "We can't make them work for free all the time" (Public Health Watch, 2006, p. 267). For these kinds of community health programs to be scaled up to a national level, it requires the support of ministries of health with sufficient resources to pay village health workers. This would cut costs of travel to centers for treatment, increase the diagnosis rate, provide reliable delivery of drugs, reduce the stigma of having TB, enlist those who have been cured as advocates of DOTS therapy and cement relationships between the national health ministry and local communities. To extend such programs as these and scale them up to a national level for all the top 20 countries requires a serious effort on the part of the various governments as well as relevant NGOS in each country. However, there is no doubt that properly designed programs would improve the effectiveness of DOTS programs and at the same time be cost-effective.

Civil society engagement in TB policy making

In their book *Why Nations Fail*, Acemoglu and Robinson (2012) emphasize again and again the importance of developing inclusiveness in society. They are speaking primarily about the history of governance and the transformation of societies ruled by oligarchs and kings to those that embrace many different facets of society – merchants, bankers, traders, scholars and the like. In these more inclusive societies monopolies of any kind were discouraged and openness and competition were encouraged and flourished. In the context of TB policy, history shows that experts have always been in control. Medical practitioners and ministries of health have been in charge and their publications, including those of the World Health Organization, the World Bank and the Center for Disease Control in the US have put primary emphasis on the collection, dissemination, interpretation and refinement of statistics. These efforts are important in developing a database and establishing how countries have been dealing with the spread of TB and its coinfection with HIV/AIDS as well as disease-resistant strains. It is an ongoing challenge for these organizations to recognize and acknowledge the importance of a more inclusive approach to TB, which involves not only the medical community but also other sectors of society interested in diagnosis and treatment who can also aid in TB programs. This can be done by including those who might be impacted by the spread of TB, including the general public and those who might have TB and their families. Involving the wider community outside the medical community can lead to a greater understanding of the way TB is contracted and spread as well as how it is diagnosed. This is important in building greater understanding of the importance of the role and responsibility of the wider community in helping to formulate and implement TB policy. Without dialogue at the community level and the development of local media support for TB programs, there is a possible disconnect between the messages that WHO and other public health officials at the global level are trying to convey and the methodology and databases that are available to users. National officials often note discrepancies between national DOTS data and information reported by WHO. Public Health Watch of the Open Society Institute (2006) notes that

> As long as governments see the Amsterdam Declaration and other regional and international commitments as a useful way of attracting funding without incurring domestic responsibility, these commitments will not spur the desired broad public mobilization that is widely acknowledged to be a prerequisite for an effective, sustained TB control effort.
>
> (p. 32, TB Policy in Brazil)

Stop TB Partnership Working Group and the Global Fund have begun to work more closely with advocacy groups and to support social mobilization efforts. These efforts include the representation of people living with TB and with HIV/AIDS in decision-making structures. As part of the Global Plan to Stop TB, the following is a key element:

> Engage people with TB and affected communities to demand and contribute to effective care involving scaling up community TB care, creating demand through context-specific advocacy, communication and social mobilization and support development of a patient's charter for the tuberculosis community.
>
> (p. 32)

Yet, much more remains to be done. TB infection rates continue to rise in many countries and business as usual will not do. One way to sensitive communities and raise TB awareness would be to develop a series of pilot programs to see how best to enlist the support of local communities as well as their participation in identifying those who can be helped, and by so doing help their communities. And of course more resources have to be mobilized to extend the intensity of diagnosis and treatment programs as well as to enlist the support of volunteers and paid AIDS to help administer aspects of the DOTS program in people's homes and villages. This would encourage greater openness about TB, improve rates of diagnosis, help to reduce the stigma attached to having TB and, finally, cure more patients.

There is evidence in South Africa and other countries that the TB virus has spread to health professionals as well as to friends and family of those who are contagious. This is a lesson for all those working or living in an environment where TB is endemic and we should remember that in the early days of the TB epidemic in Europe, before the discovery of drugs to treat TB, the standard treatment was rest and relaxation in a quiet and somewhat isolated environment. This is all the more reason to take precautions against unneeded close contact with others in communities where TB is endemic.

3.13.7 New research findings and initiatives

Research into ways to respond to the global epidemic of TB, new strains of TB, including drug-resistant and intractable TB, along with HIV and the coinfection of the two has accelerated in the past decade. Xpert MTB/RIF, a test that can diagnose TB as well as the presence of rifampicin (a drug in the TB cocktail) resistance in 100 minutes, was discussed earlier. Furthermore, as mentioned earlier, work at the Vanderbilt Medical Center, led by Dr. Douglas Kernodle, reported a breakthrough that has the potential for revitalizing the ability of BCG to arrest the development of pulmonary TB.

Lienhardt et al. (2011) review progress on other drugs that can:

Improve diagnosis of drug susceptible and drug-resistant TB – MDR-TB and XDR-TB.

Shorten treatment of overt/contagious TB cases to less than two months.

Improve treatment of latent infected persons particularly in high-risk populations.

Provide mass vaccinations using a more effective vaccine than BCG.

Find more effective diagnostic tools for childhood TB.

None of these are yet available, but many are now in clinical trials and hopefully will be available in the next few years. One recent breakthrough, which is still in the clinical trial stage, suggests that a new combined drug regime could be effective in killing 99% of a patient's TB bacteria within two weeks (Reuters, 2012 and Diacon et al., 2012). If this new approach holds up to further scrutiny, it would be a game changer by reducing the treatment time so significantly and it would be effective in treating MDR-TB and HIV patients with TB.

Furthermore, a simple point of care diagnostic tool is needed that can diagnose all forms of TB, including both latent and contagious, including children and adults and those with other diseases such as HIV.

Once these diagnostic and treatment options have been adopted and refined, a massive information campaign and rollout will be needed to implement and quickly scale up health programs in countries where the epidemic has reached epic proportions. WHO will play a critical role in this phase, since it will be the focal point for which drugs are accepted, develop protocol for their use and serve as the overall controller/supervisor of the global coordination rollout and implementation effort. Health practitioners will also play a critical role as they serve to implement new drug programs on the ground.

It is important that the progress that is being made on these various research fronts is not dissipated for lack of interest or funding by the global community. Most of the 20 developing countries with the highest TB and HIV burdens now are dependent on the international donor community and this will continue in the future. Those in the Stop TB movement and the Global Partnership to Stop HIV/TB/Malaria have suggested that the large countries with a high overall TB burden (Brazil, Russia, India, China and South Africa, the so-called BRICS) could play a major role in this effort, particularly in research and development. At the first BRICS Health Ministers Summit in July 2011 in Beijing, these countries signed a declaration which recognized the need to establish priorities in research and development and called for innovation and transfer of technologies and innovation in a sustainable way (visit http://keionline.org/node/1183 and http://www.unaids.org/en/resources/presscentre/featurestories/2011/july/20110711bchinabrics/). It is also possible that other high-burden top 20 countries such as Nigeria, Tanzania, Kenya, Uganda and Indonesia could become involved.

3.13.8 Prioritizing resource allocation across countries

In *Disease Control Priorities in Developing Countries*, Jamison et al. (2006) suggest a hierarchy of approaches to HIV/AIDS. They develop four epidemic categories: Low level, Concentrated Epidemic, Generalized Low-level Epidemic and Generalized High-Level Epidemic. They propose a set of policies that are appropriate for each category, which address the needs of the respective population and which are cost-effective and well-focused. Here we propose a similar cascade of approaches for TB.

For countries outside the top 20, where the incidence of TB is low and the possibility of coinfection with HIV as well as MDR-TB and hard to treat TB are also low, the current DOTS approach suggested by WHO is appropriate.

For top 20 countries where new notifications are less than 100/100,000 (1%) and not trending up quickly a quasi-aggressive policy is appropriate. DOTS is followed and is supplemented with help from local and village volunteers or paid health personnel to make sure drugs are being taken. Monitoring of possible HIV-TB coinfection and multi drug-resistant tuberculosis (MDR-TB) is also recommended. Outreach and media approaches as well as the increased involvement of civil societies and NGOS should be ramped up. Merging of HIV/AIDS programs with TB programs should also be discussed. This would increase efficiency, allow for less duplication of effort and permit better surveillance of both diseases.

For the top 20 countries where coinfections with HIV and MDR-TB are a growing problems, a new and more vigorous and aggressive approach is needed.[2] This would entail a significant increase in budgets for media coverage, including radio, TV, print media, events featuring celebrities both local and foreign and a general attempt to bring TB to the awareness of everyone in the country. This is critical for those countries where the epidemic has taken a foothold and is a growing threat to the economy and society. Budgets have to be increased and appeals made to the international donor community. Coordination with HIV programs in these countries is essential as the two epidemics share many of the same challenges. Increased allocations from the Global Fund must be as well as contributions from other donors are needed. It has to be emphasized that TB can be eradicated if there is a political will to resolve the problem.

Role of external assistance

International donors have played a major role in program development, funding, technical support and research. The World Bank has several programs designed to support national efforts assisting in developing priorities and supporting the involvement of civil societies. A program for Southern African countries has been developed keeping in mind the unique challenges faced by this region (World Bank, 2010). This approach is aligned with the Africa Action Plan (AAP, 2005) and emphasizes leveraging of available financial and technical resources.

The Global Fund to Fight AIDS, Tuberculosis and Malaria (The Global Fund or GFATM) is an international financing organization that attracts resources to prevent and treat HIV, AIDS, tuberculosis and malaria. It is a public–private partnership that began operating in 2002 and has received support from many private foundations including the Gates Foundation. The Global Fund is the world's largest financier of anti-AIDS, TB and malaria programs and at the end of 2010 had approved funding of $21.7 billion that supported more than 600 programs in 150 countries.

It is a financing mechanism that leaves implementation to agencies in recipient countries. Grants are administered with the help of committees consisting of local stakeholder organizations in-country that include some or all of government, NGOs, the United Nations, faith-based and private sector participants.

The WHO is the directing and coordinating authority for health within the UN system. It is responsible for providing leadership on global health matters, shaping the health research agenda, setting norms and standards, articulating evidence-based policy options, providing technical support to countries and monitoring and assessing health trends. It has been instrumental in developing protocols for identification of HIV/AIDS and TB as well as treatment and care.

The United States spends over $300 million dollars annually to fight TB and HIV/AIDS worldwide. The United States Agency for International Development (USAID) is the lead US agency in global TB control and other industrial countries in the OECD.

Interface of TB diagnosis and control with human resource development

There are a few countries where incomes have risen and human development has improved to a point where TB incidence has fallen, even in the face of a weak TB program. In Brazil TB is not a strong priority and yet new TB cases have declined and case detection rates have gone up. Sri Lanka's program was mentioned earlier. Sri Lanka has a level of economic development comparable to that of India yet it has achieved a persistent decline in TB incidence along with a strong human development program.

By contrast, the global rankings of the top 20 TB countries reflect low HDI and Heritage Foundation Index scores (see Table 3.11). The majority of countries are in the low HDI category and with mostly political and economic regimes that are not free. This suggests that much more needs to be done to raise levels of health, education and political freedom in these countries. This would improve economic and social circumstances and would likely lower the incidence and spread of TB. The director of WHO, Mario Raviglione, said in a recent meeting in London

> Social protection issues are fundamental in TB control and that is why TB control has to go beyond working with National TB programs.
>
> (IRIN 2012)

Table 3.11 Heritage Foundation Index and HDI for selected countries

Country	Heritage index class	Heritage index	Human development index 2009	Human development index class
India	MU	123	134	M
China	MU	138	101	M
Indonesia	MU	115	124	M
Nigeria	MU	116	156	L
South Africa	MF	70	123	M
Bangladesh	MU	130	146	L
Ethiopia	MU	134	174	L
Pakistan	MU	122	145	L
Philippines	MU	107	112	M
Congo	MU	172	187	L
Russia	MU	144	66	H
Vietnam	MU	136	128	M
Kenya	MU	103	143	L
Brazil	MU	99	84	H
Tanzania	MU	119	152	L
Uganda	MF	78	161	L
Zimbabwe	R	178	173	L
Thailand	MF	60	103	M
Mozambique	MU	108	184	L
Myanmar	R	173	149	L
Cambodia	R	157	134	L

For heritage scores, class R is repressive, MU is mostly un-free, MF is mostly free.
For HDI, H is high human development, M is medium human development and L is low human development.
Sources: Heritage Foundation (2013) and UNDP (2013).

What does eradication of polio tell us about TB policy?

How did governments in India and Pakistan work to get rid of polio completely? It was through a high level of dedication and goal orientation. There was a high level of commitment for eradicating polio at all levels of society. The goal was ambitious and perhaps even audacious – the complete eradication of the disease. There were no halfway measures such as the various TB commitments of 80% compliance and 60% cure rates. Complete eradication was the goal. Furthermore, there was mobilization of stakeholders at all levels of society including politicians, policy makers, local officials and the man in the street. Many people visible in the community were in the media publicizing the campaign and there were ads in all the media blanketing the airwaves. Everywhere the push to vaccinate everyone was on from day until night. Vaccination of children was one of the major themes. There was a massive campaign to get all children vaccinated. There was even a "polio Sunday" when you could get polio drops for children. This was an effort that involved everyone up and down the social ladder and all stakeholders. There was massive support from NGOs such as the Rotary Club but no outside funding like we see for the current programs such as the Global Fund. Yet there was a group of committed people that continued to push the levels of response for polio until the last person was inoculated. It is true that TB is a bigger and more complicated epidemic and highly contagious. It requires more than inoculating everyone. Yet it can be done in every country and at every level of society. It requires dedication, sustained effort and hard work on the part of the entire community. Remember a child dies of TB every five minutes.

Is anything working?

Dye et al. (2009) has done an exhaustive analysis of TB incidence trends in a global sample of countries over a time interval from 1997 to 2006. A number of socioeconomic variables such as the human development index, infant mortality and access to improved sanitation were analyzed as potential factors contributing to changes in TB incidence. Health variables including budget spending on TB identification and control as well as the number of smear-positive cases were identified as an indication of the strength of the identification program. The study concluded that

> The striking observation in this study was that more than a decade after DOTS was first implemented, with varying levels of national coverage, only one direct measure of TB control intensity (detection of smear-positive cases) in a single region (Latin America and the Caribbean) was associated with a downward trend in TB incidence.
>
> (p. 686)

There are several possible reasons for this rather depressing result including lags between contracting the disease and identification of the virus, lack of complete data and slow implementation of the DOTS protocols globally. These factors are outlined more systematically in Box 3.2 and explain how recent trends are impacted by many other factors that vary globally.

> Recent trends in TB incidence are, by contrast, more strongly associated with biological, social and economic determinants that differ among countries and regions. The regional differences explain why

> only three general measures of development were dominant worldwide: the human development index, child mortality and access to improved sanitation.
>
> (p. 687)

In developing countries where the TB epidemic is seen to be getting worse, not better, we have to do several things.

First we have to find some countries or locations where the local TB case identification, detection and treatment are working to bring down incidence rates and raising cure rates. In India and Pakistan, 70–80% of first contact happens in the private sector and TB healthcare is highly variable and not at all homogenous in quality. Rather, it is a heterogeneous mix of qualified and unqualified providers within a variety of institutional settings. As a result, there are delays in case identification, erratic and unreliable treatment and therapy and unnecessary spending by patients. As a result, there are more cases of multidrug-resistant cases and a continued spread of infection.

However, one study, conducted by Khan et al. (2012) in Karachi, implemented a multifaceted approach to screening and case detection and compared results with an adjacent control area. The results of this study indicates that this approach, which involved lay people as screeners and mobile phone–based incentives for screeners and referral of patients with suspected TB to a private hospital that offered free TB care, yielded a significant increase in case notifications. It is difficult to pinpoint the primary reason for this better track record. It was probably a combination of the presence of a TB hospital with outreach to the community in the form of lay people and the blanket screening made possible by the use of cell phone. What we do know is all of these factors work, whether individually or in combination. The involvement of community resources has also been shown to provide a significant increase in case detection and more effective treatment in Bangladesh and Tanzania. In this connection, the use of modern computer technology can be implemented to improve record keeping and updating as well as using local community resources to add to the information registry of patients. As the TB and HIV epidemics have spread, the need to go beyond paper-based system has become paramount. The advantages of computer-based system can be further explored. There are unlimited upside opportunities to extend and adopt this technology in high-risk environments, both for TB and HIV.

Second, the enormity of the TB epidemic has to be brought to the attention of everyone from policy makers and civil society down to the general public and village headmen in the top 22 countries. International donors, celebrities and civil society can help. Village organizers and volunteers can help. In short, everyone in society can help. Public awareness has to be raised and campaigns begun at all levels of society, from the top government officials down to the village level. And local resources have to be raised and local ownership of the TB programs established. Foreign donors cannot be forever relied upon to provide the ongoing health sector infrastructure required to battle TB in the long run.

The Global Fund has to contribute more and raise more money. The fight against TB has a different set of challenges than the fight to cure HIV and malaria. Suffice it to say that the communicable nature of TB makes it a far greater threat to the general community than malaria, cholera or HIV.

The long-term drug burden of HIV is much greater, but the probability of spreading the infection is much smaller than TB. Furthermore, because the risk of further contamination with a more virulent form of the virus is high if the course of therapy is not successfully completed, the need for effective enforcement of the DOTS protocol is paramount. Someone with malaria, cholera or HIV is not a risk to the general community in the same extent that someone is who is carrying the active TB virus or the other two forms of the virus, which are even more virulent (MDR-TB and XDR-TB).

Box 3.2 Effectiveness of TB diagnosis and treatment programs

The proposition that TB diagnosis and treatment programs have not yet become the principal drivers of TB transmission and incidence will remain a hypothesis until four key assumptions can be tested. The first is that trends in case notifications reflect underlying trends in incidence. Some countries clearly had to be excluded from the analysis because their rising trends in case notification (for all forms of TB) obviously reflect improved case finding under DOTS rather than the underlying trend in incidence. Exclusions of this kind eliminate countries where improved case finding is associated with an increase, rather than the expected

Box 3.2 (Continued)

decrease, in reported cases. For the countries that were included in this analysis, the effect of treatment might not be discernible if a slow decline in TB incidence is masked by a moderate improvement in case detection.

The second assumption, essential in comparative analysis, is that there is measurable and meaningful variation among countries in incidence trends and their determinants. If TB control programmes were uniformly effective, their effectiveness would not be detectable in this analysis, but this seems unlikely because TB incidence is declining slowly and unevenly and because measures of the intensity of TB programme implementation vary greatly among countries. Moreover, our estimates of incidence trends are correlated with numerous biological, social and economic variables, which suggests that these trend estimates do reflect changes in incidence.

A greater potential problem is that the standard direct measures of TB programme performance – mainly case detection and treatment success – are not the best measures of factors that govern disease transmission and changes in incidence. The difficulties of estimating the total number of TB cases that arise each year – the denominator of the case detection rate as defined by WHO – have frequently been described . In addition, a high case detection rate does not necessarily imply rapid diagnosis; in principle, a large fraction of cases could be detected after long delays, once most infectious contacts in a community have already been made. In cohorts, outcomes are never known for patients who default, are transferred to other treatment centers without follow-up, or are never evaluated. This limits the usefulness of treatment success as a measure that should be inversely associated with infectiousness and transmission. Of 2.3 million patients in the 2005 global DOTS cohort, fewer than 10% had unknown treatment outcomes. However, treatment outcomes were not known for an estimated 1.5 million smear-positive, non-DOTS patients in 2005.

Third, transmission and the risk of infection may have been greatly reduced by more than a decade of DOTS implementation, but perhaps we have not yet seen the latter's full effect on incidence. In this study, incidence trends were measured as 10-year averages (1997–2006). Some countries did not have wide

DOTS coverage for at least the first half of this period and most were treating patients with combination chemotherapy, though not necessarily with the recommended regimens. The alternative explanation is that treatment programmes do not find patients soon enough to substantially reduce transmission.

Fourth, the effect of treating patients to reduce transmission could be offset by factors that increase the risk of developing active TB following infection. Tobacco smoking and diabetes are risk factors for TB, but in this analysis both were associated with declining TB incidence. It may be that these factors reflect social patterns that are linked to health, health services and economic development in ways that override their importance as risk factors for TB. In multivariate analysis, tobacco smoking among women was replaced by factors more closely tied to the real determinants of epidemic TB trends, such as GDP per capita in Central and Eastern Europe.

Verifying whether trends in case notifications accurately measure trends in incidence calls for detailed studies of the completeness and accuracy of national TB surveillance systems, preferably coupled with surveys of infection, prevalence and mortality.

Source: Dye et al. (2009)

Harries et al. (2010) has undertaken a review of the challenges facing healthcare practitioners in dealing with patient identification and treatment for HIV and TB. Identification and monitoring are the most important first steps. However, treatment is equally important. In the case of HIV, they have identified three stages of HIV that have to be monitored and followed up. First, HIV patients are diagnosed and treatment is suggested. Second, treatment is administered in the first four months of therapy. Third, treatment is needed over the long run. In the case of TB, the DOTS protocol is the recommended treatment. An information system to track all patients is critical to establishing who is taking medication and the dosage. If patients are not followed up and they leave the system, they could die, infect others or both. First of all the database is limited. The review looks at different programs in a few countries, primarily with respect to HIV but also with relevance to TB. Patients are lost for several reasons: (1) they are hard to contact because there is no reliable address or they move and there is no forwarding address, (2) samples and test results are lost, (3) missing patients are not tracked and (4) treatment and diagnosis occur in different locations. These problems are compounded when the only records are on paper, which is hard to transport.

Some of these difficulties can be circumvented with a system which begins by giving patients an identity card and number. The system would then keep records for all critical data pertaining to a patient including visits to health provider, contacts by health workers in their home village, laboratory tests and medication as well as continual updates of treatment status. Gaps in the flow of information would raise a flag to follow up missing patients and provide treatment. Failure to adopt such a feedback loop could be life threatening as well as risking the risk of further spread of the disease. An electronic medical record system (EMS) would facilitate and increase the efficiency of such a tracking system. Studies also demonstrate that a few developing countries have made significant progress in implementing EMS systems for both TB and HIV. In the case of TB, a system to track MDR-TB patients in Peru was able to reduce the time between submission of sample for laboratory analysis and referral back to health professionals – from an average of 60 days to 17 days. In South Africa cell phones are being used to assist in patient follow-up and to encourage patient compliance with TB treatment recommendations.

Future funding gap

In its *Global Tuberculosis Report* (2013), WHO reviews progress that has been made in diagnosis and treatment of TB. It highlights the new diagnostic tool for testing, which now includes drug-resistant TB – in less than two hours. This test is now available in 67 low- and middle-income countries. The report estimates that TB therapy has saved the lives of 20 million people over the past 17 years while treating over 50 million people who had TB. At this time there is a $3 billion a year shortfall in funding of TB diagnosis and treatment combined with a $1.4 billion shortfall in research funding. Ninety percent of current external funding is provided through the Global Fund to Fight AIDS, TB and Malaria. Without these needed funds programs would have to be cut back and the critical search to find a new TB vaccine could be slowed.

3.14 Statistical analysis

Using the top 21 high-burden TB countries classified by WHO in 2013, the results affirm that health interventions and the extent of per capita income and HDI play a very important role in curbing TB mortality

Table 3.12 Statistical analysis of TB mortality rate using GLS

C	95.807*
	(1.639)
DOTS	−0.014*
	(0.004)
HEALTHEXP	−4.676*
	(0.169)
GNIPC	−0.003*
	(0.000)
HDI	−52.016*
	(2.565)
R^2	0.996
No. of observations	74

Note: The method used generalized least squares regression, with standard errors in parentheses on top burden 21 TB countries identified. *denotes statistical significance at the 5% level.
TB mortality: Deaths due to tuberculosis among HIV-negative people (per 100,000 population).
DOTS: DOTS population coverage (%).
HEALTHEXP: Health expenditure, total (% of GDP).
GNIPC: GNI per capita, PPP (current international $).
HDI: Human Development Index.
Top 21 countries with high-burden TB classified by WHO include: Afghanistan, Bangladesh, Brazil, Cambodia, China, Democratic Republic of Congo, Ethiopia, India, Indonesia, Kenya, Mozambique, Myanmar, Nigeria, Pakistan, the Philippines, Russia, South Africa, Tanzania, Thailand, Uganda, Vietnam and Zimbabwe.

rates (Table 3.12). The degree of health expenditure, GNI per capita and HDI are highly negative in accordance to the literature. The greater the amount of health expenditure, the GNI per capita and HDI of the country will greatly lead to a reduction in TB mortality rates. Specific health intervention in TB in the form of DOTS coverage also contributes to the reduction of TB mortality rates in these top 21 high-burden TB countries, though not as significant as the other three indicators. It is also to be noted that the data on DOTS coverage is limited till the year 2007, and has restricted the sample size of the model.

4
Malaria

4.1 Introduction

On the surface, malaria looks like an easier target to control and eradicate than HIV-, TB- or cholera-type diseases. This is because malaria is borne by mosquitoes and should be easier to track and control than humans whose behavior is hard to predict and control and who are not subject to eradication using chemicals. However, upon further analysis, it is found that this is not the case. Malaria is a parasite and is spread by the anopheles mosquito. There are several kinds of anopheles and they live in different surroundings from one another. In a way it is like tracking down those people who are likely to have TB or HIV or who live in an environment where there are poor sanitation and/or cleanliness habits. However, doing this is much more difficult than locating pockets of TB, or cholera or HIV potential. Locating the clusters of different types of anopheles within a region as large as Sub-Saharan Africa is a monumental task. It is difficult to catch mosquitoes to see if they are carrying the malaria virus. Resources have not been devoted to tracing the different mosquito types, where they live and whether they bear the malaria virus. This is probably not too much of a problem since the vast majority of malaria cases are spread by the bite of the anopheles mosquito. There are several varieties of the anopheles but they are all capable of spreading the malaria virus.

The number of bites inflicted per person will also vary according to geographic elevation, climate and population density. There are several scientific studies that investigate these various factors and have begun to map a profile of malaria transmission intensity. This information is of use in plotting future strategy for mosquito control and patient treatment. For example, malaria rates could be high in one location or village and not in another that is close by, simply because the former is close to a mosquito-breeding ground.

Malaria has had a resurgence in recent years with higher population growth in threatened regions, poor diets and unsanitary living conditions and an increase in resistance to antimalarial drugs and to insecticides. It is estimated that there are five billion clinical episodes in areas where malaria is endemic and resulting in between one million and three million deaths each year. The wide range is due to the lack of reliable cause of death statistics and the possibility that death could come from other causes, particularly in poor regions of Africa where infant mortality is high. Malaria deaths are much more common among children. The *World Malaria Report* (2013) estimates that around 77% of global deaths from malaria occurred in children five years of age or younger. Although malaria is endemic in many developing countries, once someone has survived beyond the age of five the death rate from malaria subsides dramatically. There has been some decline in mortality since 2000 but not nearly as much as hoped for and in some cases rates have increased, particularly in Africa.

4.2 Burden of malaria

Globally, it is estimated that malaria was responsible for 1,124,000 deaths in 2000 with over 85% occurring in Africa (see Table 4.1). By 2012, total deaths from malaria have fallen but Africa now accounts close to 90% of total malaria deaths globally. WHO (2013e) estimates that 3.4 billion people were at risk from malaria out of which 1.2 billion people were at high risk. The high-risk population, with more than one case per 1000, were mainly in Africa (47%) and Southeast Asia (37%).

Furthermore, around 28% of all mortality among children under five of age resulted from malaria. Much of this evidence is subject to interpretation because it is often difficult to establish the exact cause of death, particularly where health records are not accurately kept and there may be more than one possible cause of death. Nevertheless, the global health burden of malaria is extremely high and focused on the very young.

WHO (2013e) reports that there has been global progress in tackling malaria between 2000 and 2012, where the scale up in malaria interventions has managed to avert an estimated 3.3 million deaths. About 90% of the deaths averted were of children under five years of age in Sub-Saharan Africa. Some 52 countries were likely to be on target to reduce their malaria case incidence rates by 75% by 2015. However, WHO also

Table 4.1 Malaria deaths, 2000 and 2012

	Deaths in thousands	
Region	**2000**	**2012**
World	1124	627
Africa	963	562
Region of Americas	1	0.8
Eastern Mediterranean	55	18
Europe	<1	0
Southeast Asia	95	42
Western Pacific	10	3.5

Sources: Jamison et al. (2006, Table 21.1, p. 415) and WHO (2013).

acknowledges that the progress in the identified 52 countries merely accounts for 4% of the burden of malaria and that there are high risk vulnerable groups in the high-epidemic countries.

Contributing to uncertainty as to the cause of death and actual mortality rates is the fact that the vast majority of deaths in Africa as well as other developing regions occur outside the formal health sector and the purview of the medical community. Furthermore, the civil registration system which records vital statistics is often understaffed and poorly managed. Verbal autopsies and interviews with relatives often form the basis for recorded cause of death. Because fever can be due to other diseases as well as malaria, the vital statistical record must be viewed as notional at best. Latest figures from WHO (2013e) report that there is a lack of reliable assessment of malaria trends in 41 endemic countries, including most high-burden countries.

A simple review of the incidence of fevers among young children suggests that each child has an average of around eight to ten fevers per year (see Jamison et al., 2006, p. 418). Many of these children could also suffer from anemia. There is also a risk of acquiring HIV because of exposure to contaminated blood when children are treated for severe malarial anemia. Furthermore, when HIV is present the risk of malaria doubles and the impact on pregnant women is also likely to increase the incidence of anemia.

4.3 Incidence of malaria

Incidence measures the number of new cases that develop among all those who are susceptible to that disease during a specific period of time. If the individual leaves a particular area, it could also be measured during the time period during which an individual is susceptible. WHO classifies malaria-endemic countries as high risk if the annual parasite index (API) exceeds one malaria case per thousand persons, low risk if the API is less than one malaria case per thousand persons or no risk for malaria. API is equivalent to the number of confirmed malaria cases during the year of the population under surveillance and multiplied by 1000. However, many cases are often undetected by routine disease recording systems. It is to be noted that the number of cases reported is thus adjusted to take into account for incompleteness in reporting systems, patients that seek treatment in the private sector, self-medicating or not receiving treatment at all and potential for overdiagnosis due to the lack of laboratory confirmation of cases. In Sub-Saharan Africa, in regions where malaria is highly endemic and virtually everyone has been infected many times, incidence do not convey much information because it is uniformly high. This is the situation that exists in a swath of countries across Central and Southern Africa. (see Figure 4.1)

Despite continuing efforts to identify, treat and control malaria, there has not been much progress in reducing the mortality rate in endemic countries. The type of intervention to treat the disease will depend upon the degree to which it is endemic in the country or a population. Note that the very high levels are located primarily in Africa and to a limited extent in South and Southeast Asia. These maps are an important source of detail about the potential for new and repeated infections. Areas of high malaria risk are thus considered most in need of control interventions by the government.

The spread of malaria as well as appropriate response and therapy will depend upon the intensity of the epidemic. We begin by reviewing some measures of the intensity of epidemics. The Entomological Inoculation Rate (EIR), in the case of anopheles mosquitoes, is the number of infected mosquito bites received per person per unit of time (usually per night). The EIR can be obtained in the field by direct mosquito collection. The EIR is the product of the number of human landings per night (a proxy for the number of bites and the proportion of infected mosquitoes out of all mosquitoes captured over the same period of time). The EIR provides a direct measure of malaria transmission and the risk of human exposure to infected mosquito bites. The key to reducing the EIR to levels where the incidence of the disease is reduced by medication (from over ten to less than ten) is to reduce the intensity of the infestation either by insect repellents, bed nets, spraying

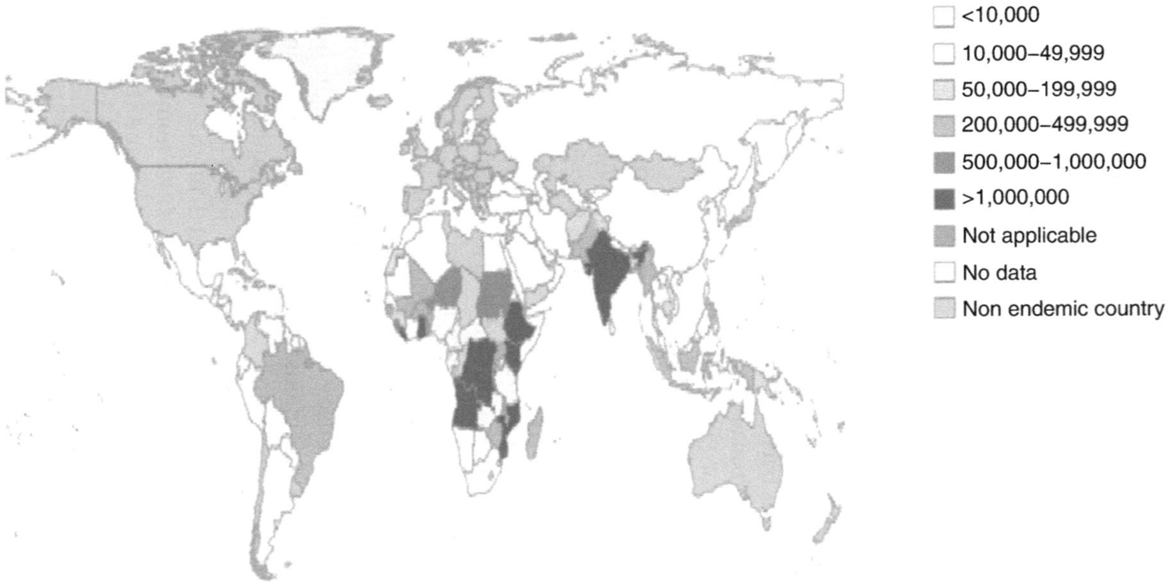

Figure 4.1 Reported cases of malaria, 2011
Source: WHO (2013).

of the walls of houses with dichlorodiphenyltrichloroethane (DDT) or by eradicating the breeding sites of the mosquitoes.

In addition to the EIR, scientists rely on the vectorial capacity (VC), which is the number of potentially infective contacts a person could have with the mosquitoes per unit time (Garrett-Jones, 1964). It takes into account of the number of bites per person per day, the feeding habits and life expectancy of the mosquito. This is a more indirect indication of malaria transmission as it measures the rate of *potentially* infective contact. Where mosquito infestations are seasonal in nature some of the population is not protected all the time. This means that in areas with moderate to low levels of mosquito infestation there is the possibility of epidemics that will produce high morbidity and mortality since these populations have limited or no immunity. In areas of stable and high transmission such as Sub-Saharan Africa, little is known about the impact of early treatment on malaria transmission aside from the fact that with a high EIR a reduction in the transmission intensity (how many bites) is unlikely to affect the incidence of the disease. All we have is the result of a few clinical trials which show the overall impact in Zanzibar (Bhattarai et al., 2007).

4.4 Causes

In tropical Africa, one human bite per infected mosquito can occur every day or several times a day and people are infected throughout their life. Morbidity and mortality during infancy and early childhood are high. Those who survive develop some immunity and by the time the person reaches adulthood most malaria infections have few if any symptoms. This environment where mosquito infestation is year around and survivors to adulthood are asymptomatic is called *stable malaria* (see Jamison et al., 2006). In environments where transmission is low and/or erratic full immunity is not acquired and symptoms of malaria including fever, fatigue and sweats can occur at all ages. This is termed *unstable malaria*. A tourist visiting a country where malaria is endemic can come down with malaria and can experience these symptoms periodically throughout life.

In certain malaria environment, epidemic conditions can arise when there are changes in geographic, economic or social conditions, or such as unseasonably heavy rains following drought, or unexpected changes in temperature, or movement of people into a region with little or no malaria. Malaria can also arise in urban environments. Discussion of epidemic conditions is discussed further in the section. See also Snow and Omumbo (2006, Chapter 14).

4.4.1 Agricultural and industrial activities and malaria infestations

As agriculture has expanded in Africa and in the mosquito-intensive areas of Sub-Saharan Africa, mosquito infestation is on the rise. There are several reasons for this. First, crop production on previously virgin forest land has increased the probability that mosquitoes will breed on these lands. The anopheles *gambiae* is attracted to open pools of stagnant but clear water and these become much more abundant during the rainy season when the forest canopy is gone. Further, new towns and irrigation projects will result in influx of population and the chances of infection rise. The increase in mosquito resistance to insecticides over time also complicates the treatment of new strains of malaria that arise as a result.

4.4.2 Urbanization

While malaria remains primarily a phenomenon of rural areas, there has been some spreading to urban areas, particularly in the suburbs and shanty towns that have sprung up outside major cities. In Sub-Saharan Africa, a combination of rapid growth, squalid living conditions, poor health and sanitation and the presence of pools of stagnant water have been a fertile breeding ground for mosquitoes.

4.4.3 Episodic periods of malaria infection in Africa

Another factor in the spread of malaria could be related to geography and variations in other environmental variables. Malaria epidemics in Africa occur in several countries primarily in highlands where there are seasonal variations in mosquito infestations as well as variations in altitude, temperature and rainfall. Generally models of high mosquito infestation would involve differences in altitude, temperate, rainfall and time of year (seasonal variation). However, no one has been able to develop a general model that can predict well when an epidemic is likely to occur.

There are varying conditions in semiarid regions where there are short intervals of rain and changes in temperature that can provide good breeding ground for mosquitoes. In semiarid locations, epidemics are observed when moisture levels are higher than normal as a result of higher rainfall. Abeku (2007) notes that a major epidemic in northeastern Kenya from January to May 1998 was the result of an abnormally high rainfall during November and December the previous year (see also Brown et al., 1998). For these climatic conditions, heavy rainfall during few months could lead to a higher transmission risk of malaria sometime later.

In highland areas it is difficult to predict when the conditions are going to be most favorable for a potential epidemic. Most of the epidemics affecting highland regions of Africa occur over a short annual mosquito-breeding season, which results in higher levels of malaria transmission. These levels are observed against an annual cycle of insect infestation, making high infestation periods difficult to predict beforehand. Because it is difficult to predict in advance when conditions are going to be ripe for a pronounced upswing in mosquito infestation, the policy to address the epidemic in highland areas has to be flexible and reaction speedy.

Therefore, greater emphasis has to be put on preparation. Because of the variability in the chances of getting malaria, many of the highland residents will not have been exposed to malaria. In these situations it may be better to rely on surveillance and take appropriate action if an outbreak seems likely. As noted earlier, geographical factors as well as temperature and rainfall frequency and quantity are important. Valley bottoms are more likely to have higher concentrations of mosquitoes as are areas that are adjacent to stagnant water or where water is used for industrial purposes such as brick making.

Rainfall and temperature variations are being used to predict the transmission of malaria to human hosts. In hindsight it seems that major epidemics in Ethiopia were preceded by a month or more of high minimum temperature and in Zimbabwe by a severe epidemic in the following year. Studies are also ongoing in Uganda and Kenya to further clarify the variables and mechanisms that have been causing epidemics (see Abeku, 2007, p. 683) and to develop appropriate policy responses.

Historical records of the past few decades suggest that variations in malaria deaths in Tanzania and Kenya may be related to possible episodic variations (see Figure 4.2). Further investigation of country statistics is needed to confirm this suspicion, particularly in view of the absence of data for Kenya for the years 2007–2009, the dramatic drop-off in deaths in Kenya for 2011–2012 and the abrupt increase in deaths in Tanzania in 2003.

Even with some idea of the variables involved, early detection of a significant increase in transmission is required to contain the spread of the epidemic. There are a variety of tools that can be used to monitor

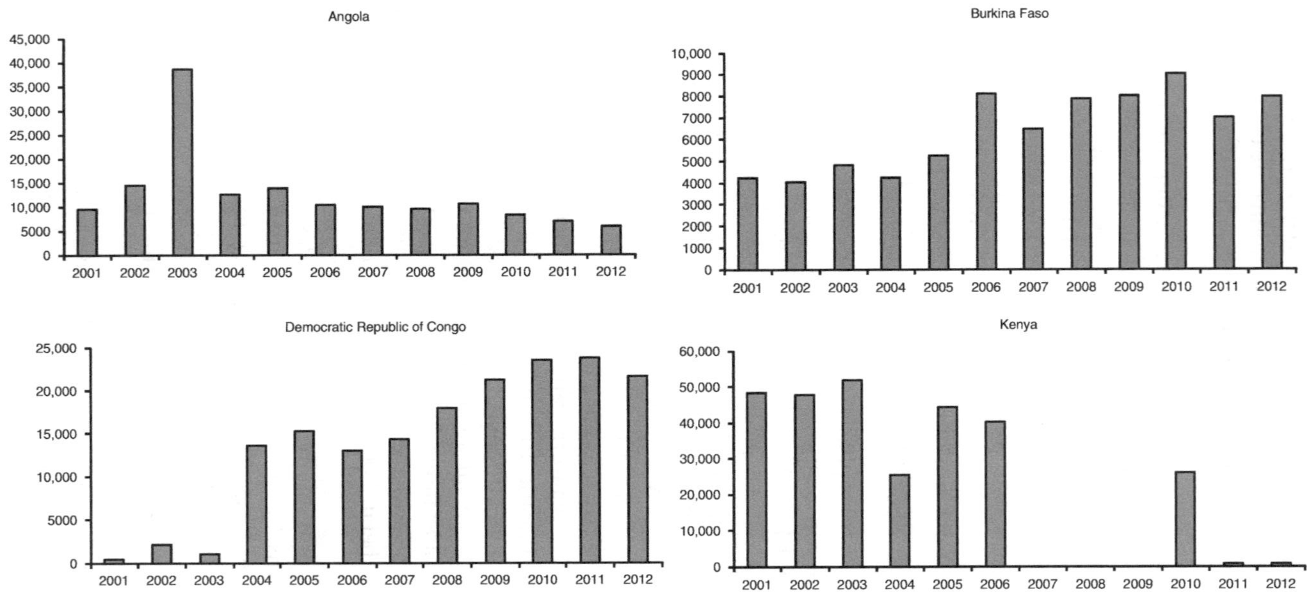

Figure 4.2 Reported malaria deaths in Africa, 2000–2012
Source: WHO (2013e), Annex 6D.

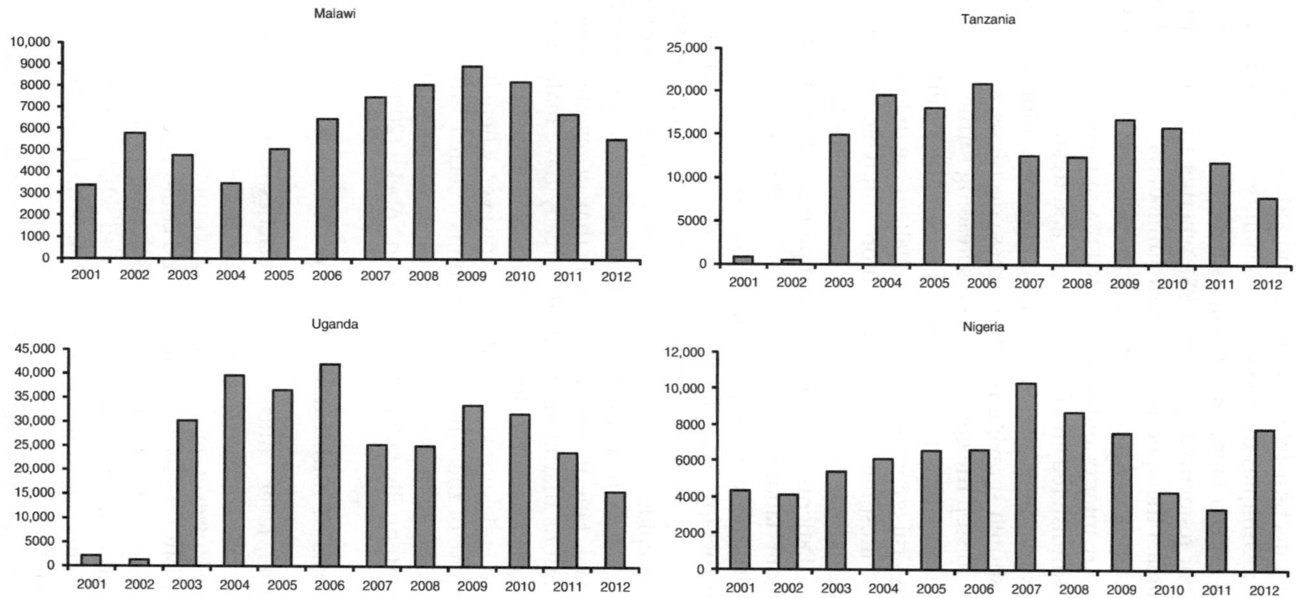

Figure 4.2 (Continued)

the spread of infection by sampling in individual villages and applying statistical techniques to assess the probability of an epidemic. Once a threshold has been breached, decisions have to be made whether to ramp up indoor residential spraying (IRS), whether to give everyone in the affected area a therapeutic shot of an antimalarial drug (called mass drug administration or MDA) or only to those who have been diagnosed with malaria. Are infants and adults treated the same way? And how are drugs to be administered and further testing and treatment to be carried out in a timely manner? Is MDA to be used in combination with IRS and how intense should spraying be? All of these decisions will have to be made quickly to stop the epidemic from spreading further.

All of these questions present challenges for the health authorities where the physical environment is more challenging in locations where the pattern of mosquito infestation is more unpredictable. If an epidemic is declared based on preliminary samples, then there are two basic choices. Patients with malaria symptoms can be treated either with or without laboratory confirmation of malaria. The treatment can be artemisinin-based drug therapy or a less expensive artesunate-amodiaquine therapy. This can be combined with IRS and DDT. How many houses are sprayed will depend upon the local conditions and the severity of the epidemic. A second option is to treat everyone in the epidemic location with an antimalarial drug such as schizontocidal and gametocytocidal. One important caveat is that in regions where there are few indications that many residents already have malaria or where historically there have been few epidemics of malaria, care should be taken not to overdiagnose the epidemic. However, where it is suspected that a large share of the subject population is infected "MDA with relatively inexpensive ACT drugs distributed once or repeated within 1 to 2 weeks can substantially reduce transmission" Abeku (2007, p. 685).

4.5 Diagnosis of malaria and interventions

As noted earlier, fever, chills, sweats, headaches, muscle pains, nausea and vomiting are the first few symptoms that a person is suffering from malaria. However, any one of these symptoms or a combination of these is not always specific to malaria and could be caused by another infection or tainted food. Therefore, a clinical diagnosis is required to ascertain whether the patient is infected and what treatment is appropriate. While clinical diagnosis is inexpensive and can be an effective method for detecting malaria and ruling out other causes, clinicians are often prone to misdiagnosing malarial infection, particularly in locations where there have been many cases of malaria in the past. Misdiagnosis can lead to unnecessary prescription of malaria medications, which is costly and would not help if the patient is suffering from another disease or malady. Nevertheless, anyone with a fever who has malarial symptoms should be treated within 24 hours of the onset of symptoms.

Aside from treating the symptoms, microscopy is the most popular method of detecting malaria infection and is usually available in better-equipped clinics, although there are gaps in many African countries. This technique, which requires the use of a microscope by a trained technician, is inexpensive and serves to confirm the initial clinical diagnosis. It also provides the clinician with important treatment information by identifying which parasite is responsible for the infection and what drug treatment is appropriate. Aside from the microscope, microscopy is relatively inexpensive at less than $0.50 a slide and is a standard technique used for diagnosing other diseases including tuberculosis. There are a number of factors that could compromise the diagnosis (poor slide preparation, bad chemical and inaccurate reading of the results), but a good clinic will usually provide accurate diagnoses.

Nevertheless, in many cases diagnosis and treatment will be made without any laboratory analysis. In countries including Ethiopia, Burundi, Eritrea, Rwanda, Kenya and Tanzania and less so in Mozambique, Zambia, Uganda, Botswana and Zimbabwe, there has been documented resistance to some antimalarial drugs such as chloroquine (see Table 4.2) and Sulfadoxine-Pyrimethamine. An alternative multiple

Table 4.2 Chloroquine treatment failure in Africa, 1997–2002

% Failure (Median)	Country
60–80	Ethiopia, Burundi and Eritrea
40–60	Rwanda, Kenya, Tanzania, Gabon and Republic of Congo
20–40	Mozambique, Zambia, Uganda, Botswana, Chad, Cameroon, Democratic Republic of Congo, Ghana, Liberia, Mauritania, Guinea and Benin
0–20	Zimbabwe, Niger, Cote d'Ivoire, Tongo, Burkina Faso, Senegal, Mali, Sierra Leonne, Gambia and Nigeria

Source: Adapted from Jamison et al. (2006, Figure 21.2, p. 420).

combination of artemisinin and other drugs (artemisinin combination therapy ACT) is now recommended by the World Health Organization.

4.5.1 ACT

Clinical trials in several African countries suggest that giving the drug artemisinin (known as artemisinin combinational therapy (ACT)) to infants during the first year of life (up to three doses in that year) is an effective way to reduce malaria incidence in them. Trials were carried out in Ghana, Nigeria and Congo within the context of a home management program to control malaria. The program was designed to reach families in rural areas that were not well served by the formal healthcare network. Ajayi et al. (2008) reported on the effectiveness of ACT based on three study sites in Sub-Saharan Africa. The three countries where malaria was hyperendemic were Ghana, Nigeria and the Congo. The results demonstrated the cost-effectiveness and ability of ACT to control malaria in a home management environment.

4.5.2 Sulfadoxine-Pyrimethamine (SP)

Sulfadoxine-Pyrimethamine (SP) is an alternate treatment for infants and pregnant mothers. As with ACT, a therapeutic dose at predefined time intervals is given regardless of the infection status of the patient. A thorough review of the effectiveness of SP is provided by Carneiro et al. (2010). Based on the results from considering the number of infants and young children treated, Carneiro et al. estimate that this SP therapy could prevent approximately 3–5% of childhood cases of clinical malaria, where the intensity of transmission is high (i.e., EIR exceeds 100 infective bites per person per year).

WHO has currently also recommended that parasite-based diagnosis or new rapid diagnostic tests should be used in all cases of suspected malaria, with the possible exception of children in high-prevalence areas. This is because many drugs including ACT are being prescribed without any indication of malaria, except for fever. Further, the widespread use of drugs for which resistance had grown and/or which have proved to be relatively ineffective such as SP and chloroquine are also being used rather indiscriminately. ACT is now the drug of choice. However, dosage and costs will vary depending on the drug combination and frequency of use.

Effectiveness of treatment will depend to some extent upon the cost of drugs in the country and the effectiveness of the health system. Jamison et al. studied three different regions and levels of malarial transmission in Africa. In Southern Africa (South Africa and other contiguous countries), the Americas and Southeast Asia, where healthcare is reasonably reliable and of acceptable quality, prompt care and intervention reduced the period of infectivity, reduced transmission and lowered mortality.

In the future home-based malarial treatment, more effective public sector procurement and supply chains, and reducing private sector pricing should make ACTs more accessible for Sub-Saharan African children, who bear the brunt of the burden of the malarial disease. However, delays are still being experienced in delivery of ACT throughout Africa. Much of the funding for ACT has been made available from the Global Fund for TB, HIV and Malaria. However, implementation of programs with ACT as their lynchpin treatment option has slowed in the past few years. This is because the Global Fund for TB, HIV and Malaria has suspended funding of its drug subsidy program in 2012. Financing of malaria programs was less than half of the estimated US$5.1 billion required globally while local government spending rose at an annual rate of only 4% between 2005 and 2012. This resulted in a global resource gap of US$2.6 billion needed for malaria control (WHO, 2013e). This has dramatically slowed the implementation of ACT accessibility because the drug is so expensive and beyond the reach of many health ministries in Africa. There were good reasons to suspend the support including misappropriation and misuse of funds which resulted in wastage and inefficiency (see Doucleff (2012)). A new funding model by the Global Fund has been implemented for the years 2014–2016, where countries will be assigned a certain level of funds based on their burden of malaria and ability to pay for malaria control. Funding for malaria program will be approximately 32% of the total amount of funds disbursed by the Global Fund. Countries will also need to present commitment for investment in malaria control before they can secure the financing. It has been found that countries that display greater commitment have shown greater success in reducing malaria case incidence. For instance, countries that spend more than US$5 per capita per year on malaria programs (Argentina, Azerbaijan, Costa Rica, Malaysia, Mexico, Suriname and Turkey) had just 0.6% of estimated cases and 0.3% of deaths in 2012 due to malaria.

In fact we were unable to find much evidence for the effectiveness of ACT to reduce infant mortality in children who had been exposed to the malaria virus in countries with severe infestation. In one very powerful study reported for Zanzibar by Bhattarai et al. (2007), it was found that malaria-related admissions, blood transfusions and malaria-attributed mortality decreased significantly by 77%, 67% and 75%, respectively, between 2002 and 2005 in children under five as a result of artemisinin-based combination therapy. This is a welcome result and needs to be followed up with other studies in countries where infant mortality rates remain high and ACT is being used.

Aside from this study, there are only a few clinical trials reported in the literature. In one set of clinical trials in Côte d'Ivoire, two artemisinin-based combinations were effective in reducing fevers and the malaria parasite (Toure et al., 2009). In another study, randomized trials comparing four different ACTs at ten sites in seven African countries – Burkina Faso, Gabon, Mozambique, Nigeria, Rwanda, Uganda and Zambia – were carried out (Hitt, 2010). Participating in the trial with clinical malaria were 4114 children between 6 and 59 months of age. Patients were randomized to four different ACT combinations with little difference in the effectiveness. All were able to demonstrate some success in preventing infections for six weeks instead of four, reducing the average number of infections per infant and suggesting that children might develop only one or two infections during a rainy season rather than three or four. This would reduce the risk of complications as well as the cost of treatment. The study did not establish a judgment or draw conclusions about the rate of infant mortality decline that might arise from these treatments.

Recently rapid diagnostic tests (RDTs) for malaria have been developed and are a viable alternative to laboratory tests in remote areas where the potential to extend accurate malaria diagnosis to areas where microscopy services are not available, such as in remote locations or after regular laboratory hours. These tests are also being used to supplant more cumbersome and costly laboratory procedures in some locations. Rapid malaria diagnostic tests have been developed in the lateral flow format. These tests use finger-stick or venous blood, take only 10–15 minutes, and do not require a laboratory. Even nonclinical staff can easily learn to perform the test and interpret the results. As rapid diagnostic tests are adopted more widely, they will permit greater flexibility in the testing and diagnostic procedures for malaria and should help to bring down the rate of infection for infants and children who can be diagnosed and treated on the spot by roving health technicians. If universal testing of all suspected malaria cases were implemented, this could dramatically cut down the need for ACT treatment in Africa by as much as 60% (WHO, 2013e).

Some malaria treatment programs require testing of patients after treatment to confirm that parasites have been cleared. Only one RDTs test is suitable for treatment monitoring. For more details refer to http://www.rapid-diagnostics.org/rti-malaria-diag.htm.

4.6 Targets for malaria control

International targets were established for an action plan (Global Malaria Action Plan or GMAP) in 2011. They were (a) to reduce global malaria deaths to near zero by the end of 2015, (b) reduce global malaria cases by 75% from 2000 levels by the end of 2015 and (c) eliminate malaria by the end of 2015 in ten new countries since 2008 including in the European region.

As we enter 2014, it does not look like the first two objectives are anywhere close to being met in Africa – see Table 4.3. In 2012, 483,000 children under five years of age fell ill and died of malaria. Hence, it means that one child dies of malaria almost every minute, when malaria is entirely preventable and treatable. Millions of people lack access to diagnosis and treatment, particularly in countries with fragile health systems.

Despite some progress in tackling malaria over the past few years, out of 40 African countries, the trend in malaria deaths is down only in 23 countries, while it has increased in the remaining 17 countries. The rise in malaria death rates is especially so in high-burden countries of Democratic Republic of Congo and Uganda where the annual deaths due to malaria were easily above 15,000 in 2012. The number of malaria cases is down only in eight out of the 40 selected African countries. More detailed time series for the high-burden malaria countries shown in Figure 4.2 reveal that malaria cases are up in seven out eight countries.

4.6.1 Indoor residual spraying (IRS) and insecticide-treated bed nets (ITN)

What is being done to protect against malaria in Africa where the epidemic is claiming over 100,000 lives every year in the high-burden countries as displayed in Table 4.3? Aside from treating infants and expectant mothers with ACT, which is proving to be quite effective, there are two additional approaches. The first is to spray the walls of residences with an insecticide, usually DDT. This is called indoor residual spray (IRS). These sprayings can last up to six months. A small percentage of households in Africa have been protected in this way. Much of the emphasis on IRS has been focused in Latin America and parts of Asia, particularly Sri Lanka in the early 1960s and Central and South America in the late 1950s to early 1970s. After World War II, the

Table 4.3 Malaria cases and deaths in Africa, 2012

	Country	Population million	Cases of malaria 2012	Malaria death 2012	Trend in malaria cases[1]	Trend in malaria deaths[1]
1	Angola	20.8	1,496,834	5736	Up	Down since 2003
2	Benin	10.1	1,151,038	2261	Down but up in 2012	Up
3	Botswana	2.0	308	3	Down	Down from 2006
4	Burkina Faso	16.5	6,089,101	7963	Up	Up
5	Burundi	9.8	2,151,076	2263	Up	Up since 2007
6	Cameroon	21.7	313,315	3209		Down since 2008
7	Central African Republic	4.5	451,012	1442		Up
8	Chad	12.4	590,786	1539	Up since 2004	Volatile. Up since 2009
9	Congo	4.3	117,640	623	Flat	Up
10	Côte d'Ivoire	19.8	2,168,215	1534	Sharply up	Up
11	Democratic Republic of Congo	65.7	6,263,607	21,601	Sharply up since 2006	Up since 2003
12	Djibouti	0.9	Na	Na	Down since 2009	Sharply down since 2006
13	Equatorial Guinea	0.7	15,169	77	Up but down since 2010	Up
14	Eritrea	6.1	42,178	30	Up	Down
15	Ethiopia	91.7	3,876,745	1621	Up since 2008	Down since 2004
16	Gabon	1.6	137,695	134	Up since 2009	Down
17	Gambia	1.8	116353	289	Up since 2008	Erratic. Down since 2007
18	Ghana	25.4	8,774,516	2855	Up	Down since 2007
19	Guinea	11.4	1,220,574	979	Up	Up since 2008
20	Guinea Bissau	1.7	50,381	370	Up since 2009	Down
21	Kenya	43.2	5,788,381	26,017(2010)	Up	Down since 2006

22	Liberia	4.2	1,407,455	1725	Up since 2005	Sharply up in 2008/9 then down
23	Madagascar	22.3	359,420	552	Up since 2006	Down since 2003
24	Malawi	15.9	3,659,565	5516	Up (2011–2012)	Up but with a slight decline in last two years
25	Mali	14.9	2,171,739	1894	Up (2010–2012)	Up but with slight decline in last years
26	Mauritania	3.8	165,834	106	Up since 2008	Erratic.
27	Mozambique	25.2	1,813,984	2818	Up sharply since 2009	Down
28	Namibia	2.3	3163	4	Down since 2006	Down since 2001
29	Niger	17.2	3,525,112	2825	Up since 2006	Up since 2006
30	Nigeria	168.8	2,087,068	7734	Up sharply since 2009	Down since 2007 with slight rise in 2012.
31	Rwanda	11.5	483,470	459	Up slightly since 2008	Down since 2001
32	Senegal	13.7	366,912	649	Up since 2006	Down since 2007
33	Sierra Leone	6.0	1,537,322	3611	Up since 2006	Up since 2005 with slight dip since 2010
34	South Africa	52.4	6846	72	Down	Down
35	Swaziland	1.2	626	7	Down	Down
36	Togo	6.6	6,642,928	1197	Up	Down since 2008
37	Uganda	36.3	10,338,093	15,632	Up with dip in 2011	Up since 2007
38	Tanzania	46.4	2,972,186	7820	Down slightly	Down since 2006
39	Zambia	13.9	4,695,400	3705		Down
40	Zimbabwe	13.0	276,963	351	Up	Down

Note: [1]Time period of 2000–2012 and depending on the availability of data.
Source: WHO (2013e), Annex 6A, Annex 6D and country profiles.

World Health Organization used DDT to spray homes with spectacular results. Malaria incidence and malaria-related mortality reductions were achieved, especially in India and Sri Lanka. Spraying was accompanied with the widespread use of chloroquine, which proved to be an effective antimalarial drug. The program was so effective that by the mid-1960s, malaria incidence in India and Sri Lanka was so low as to be almost undetectable (see Carter and Mendis, 2002). The widespread use of DDT in agriculture was abandoned when it was found to have detrimental effects on the ability of bird shells to thicken. However, indoor spraying has continued at a modest pace in recent years. In Africa it was estimated that by 2012 about 15% of households would be protected. See Table 4.4 for information on the extent of protection through ITN and IRS in Africa. To augment IRS, insecticides are also being used to spray breeding sites. Larviciding is not as effective as IRS and is more effective when it is applied in areas where there are well-identified breeding grounds. It has been used effectively in some urban areas, industrial sites and refugee camps. Also, it has to be applied more frequently than IRS (see Najera and Zain, 2002).

The second and most widely used method for control of malaria is to supply insecticide-treated bed nets (ITN) to households. Long-lasting bed nets are now being distributed throughout Africa and the WHO estimates that about half the families in Africa have at least one of these bed nets per household. The goal is to provide one for every two persons by 2015. Data for the eight countries with the highest incidence of malaria deaths in Table 4.5 show that the percentage of children sleeping under bed nets has not reached 50% in seven of the top eight high-burden countries by 2011, although there has been significant progress since 2008. The *World Malaria Report* presents a somewhat rosier picture, particularly for the future. It mentions only households with at least one bed net at around 50% of households and that the number of bed nets procured between 2008 and 2010 were sufficient to cover 75% of the 800 million persons at risk. This shows that there are lots of bed nets being delivered but does not account for who is sleeping under them. Information on the number of children under five years of age in the countries where they are most at risk (see Table 4.6) are most critical as these are where the fatality rates are highest in high-incidence countries.

How effective are the ITNs? Based on the results of over 20 studies in Africa and Asia by Breman et al. (2006), malaria episodes of ITNs users were reduced by 50% and 29% protection against severe malaria. ITNs reduced child mortality by 18% in five sites in Sub-Saharan Africa. To evaluate these results it is important to note that in most of these countries malaria is endemic and those using nets have, in all likelihood,

Table 4.4 Insecticide-treated net (ITN) and indoor residual spraying (IRS) in Africa, 2000–2012

Country	Percentage sleeping under ITN	Households with at least one ITN percentage of households	Protected with IRS percentage of households	ITN trend	IRS trend
Angola	5(2007)	20(2007)	2(2010)	None	Flat from 2005
Benin	5(2006)	20(2006)	5	None	Flat from 2005
Botswana	No info	No info	18	No info	Flat from 2005
Burkina Faso	No info	60%	No info	Up from 20	No info
Burundi	No info	5	2	None	Down from 2005
Cameroon	No info	15(2006)	No info	No info	No info
Central African Republic	20(2007)	No info	No info	Up from 15	No info
Chad		No info	No info	No info	No info
Congo	2(2005)	3(2005)	No info	No info	No info
Côte d'Ivoire	2(2005)	2(2005)	No info	No info	No info
Democratic Republic of Congo	1(2007)	60(2009)	No info	No info	No info
Djibouti		15(2006)	No info	Down	No info
Equatorial Guinea		60(2008)	50		Up
Eritrea	No info	70(2008)	3 Trend	No info	Flat
Ethiopia		60(2007)	60	Up	Flat from 2008
Gabon	No info	No info	No info	No info	No info
Gambia	No info	50(2009)	40	Flat from 2006	Sharply down
Ghana	10(2008)	50(2009)	1	Up from 2006	Flat
Guinea	No info	20		No info	No info
Guinea Bissau	No info	40(2006)	No info	No info	No info

Table 4.4 (Continued)

Country	Percentage sleeping under ITN	Households with at least one ITN percentage of households	Protected with IRS percentage of households	ITN trend	IRS trend
Kenya	30(2008)	50(2008)	3		Down from 2007
Liberia	20(2009)	40(2008)	10	Flat from 2008	Up from 2009
Madagascar	30	50	40		Up gradually
Malawi	5(2004)	30(2006)	10		Up since 2008
Mali	50(2008)	85(2008)	1	Up from 2006	Flat
Mauritania	0	2	No info	No info	
Mozambique		0	30		Flat
Namibia	3	50(2009)	4	Up	Flat
Niger	2(2006)	40(2008)	0	Flat	No info
Nigeria	2(2007)	3(3007)	No info	No info	No info
Rwanda	40(2008)	50(2008	No info	Flat	No info
Senegal	20(2008)	60(2008)	3(2007–2009)	Up	Flat
Sierra Leone	15(2008)	60(2007)	2(2010)	Down since 2007 slightly up	Up since 2009
South Africa	No info	No info	100(2010)	No info	Up since 2008
Swaziland	2(2007)	No info	No info	No info	No info
Togo	No info	65(2009)	No info	Up since 2006	No info
Uganda	20(2009)	50(2009)	5(2009)	Up since 2005	Up slightly
Tanzania	No info	40(2007)	10(2009)	No info	Up since 2007
Zambia	20(2007)	60(2008)	50(2010)	Up from 2002	Up from 2000
Zimbabwe	3(2008)	5(2006)	50(2010)	No info	Up from 2008

Sources: WHO (2012) and WHO (2013e), country profiles.

Table 4.5 Children aged five or younger sleeping under insecticide-treated bed nets in top eight affected African countries

Country	2000	2001	2002	2003	2004	2005	2006	2007	2008	2009	2010	2011
Kenya	2.9			4.6						46.7		
Democratic Republic of Congo		0.7						5.8			38.1	
Uganda		0.2					9.7			32.8		42.8
Burkina Faso				1.9			9.6				47.4	
Tanzania					10.0	16.0			25.7		63.6	
Nigeria				1.2					5.5		29.1	
Angola		2.3						17.7				25.9
Malawi	2.9				14.8		24.7				39.4	

Source: World Bank (2013).

Table 4.6 Bed net distribution and usage in top eight affected African countries

Country	Nets distributed annually		Percentage of homes with		Percentage of children under five		Percentage pregnant women	
	LLIN[1] + ITN recently (million)		1 or more ITN		Sleeping under ITN the previous night		Sleeping under a ITN	
	2008–2010	2010–2012	2006–2008	2010–2012	2007	2008–2012	2007	2008–2012
Kenya	1.2–2.8	0.4–1.2	48–56	63–67	39–47	43–61		47–51
Democratic Republic of Congo	0.6–11.7	0.3–18.6	9	52–59	6			
Uganda	0.9–7.4	0.7–7.4	14–26	50–64	8–21	32–48	9–23	43–55
Burkina Faso	0.7–6.9	0.2–6.9	15–45	50–54	6–24	45–47		38–46
Tanzania	3.7–14.0	0.2–14.5		65–92		25–70		22–74
Nigeria	0.7–19.3	14.4–18.9	8	37–43	6	5–29		5–34
Angola	1–1.7	0.5–1.7	26–29	20–44	17–19	24–29	15–26	24–28
Malawi	1.0–2.5	1.5–6.7	34–56	49–56	21–43	37–56		34–51

Sources: WHO (2011a), Annex table and WHO (2013e, Annexes 4 and 5).
Note: [1]Long-lasting insecticidal net (LLIN) is designed to remain effective for multiple years without retreatment.

already developed immunity to malaria. So it is difficult to evaluate the 50% and 29% figures. The 18% reduction in childhood malaria seems a small improvement given the significant expenditure on ITNs. Nevertheless, several studies in China, Tanzania and Vietnam as well as new initiatives in Eritrea, Malawi, Togo and Zambia are scaling up with higher coverage. See Box 4.1 on Zambia's malaria program.

Box 4.1 Zambia's malaria program

Key statistics

- Of all people who die of malaria in Zambia, 50% or more are children under five years of age;
- 50% of under five hospital admissions are due to malaria;
- Malaria accounts for 20% of maternal deaths.

Background

Though Zambia has made strides in malaria prevention and control in the last five years, malaria still kills more children under the age of five than any other disease or illness. Malaria affects more than four million Zambians annually, accounting for approximately 30% of outpatient visits and resulting in almost 8000 deaths each year. This figure has come down to less than 5000 by 2010. Under five-year-old children and pregnant women are the most vulnerable, especially those living in more remote and impoverished areas, with 35–50% of under-five mortality and 20% of maternal mortality attributable to malaria.

Combating malaria is vitally important in the battle to save young lives and protect children from losing their mothers.

Malaria is both preventable and treatable, but it is a complicated disease whose prevention and control requires multiple interventions. Preventing malaria requires creating a malaria-free environment, which means spraying the inner walls of populated structures (homes, schools, hospitals, businesses and other institutions) with insecticides and always sleeping under insecticide-treated nets (ITNs). Other measures include environmental control to prevent the development of mosquito-breeding grounds.

For those whom prevention measures fail, prompt and effective treatment is imperative. Treatment begins with recognizing the symptoms of malaria, seeking treatment immediately at the

Box 4.1 (Continued)

onset of illness, and having access to community or facility-based healthcare workers who have the knowledge to treat malaria at its various stages.

Source: UNICEF (2013a).

Jamison et al. (2006, Chapter 21) have reviewed the cost-effectiveness of both of these control methods – ITN and IRS – and conclude that both are cost-effective when used separately. What happens when they are used together or when some houses have one and others the other? The details are provided by Yakob, Dunning and Yan (2011). They conclude that the most effective strategy is to treat as many houses as possible with bed nets and the remainder with IRS. *It is not recommended to use both together*. They act antagonistically. This recommendation comes after a rigorous testing experience of treating houses with combinations of IRS and INT in a controlled setting. Hopefully WHO and country officials will take note. It is also interesting to note that IRS has not been used in any of the countries with an epidemic of malaria as judged by the number of cases or deaths per annum.

An analysis of the effectiveness of bed nets was conducted by Choi et al. (1995). They analyzed field trials from ten studies and their results suggested that insecticide-impregnated bed nets are effective in preventing malaria with an effectiveness rate of approximately 50%. However, the effectiveness has yet to be proven in the field in countries where the bed nets are now being used. For the countries with malaria epidemics where mortality statistics are reported in Figure 4.2, the observed change in mortality rates is not fully in line with expectations given the reported effectiveness of the bed nets. They have, in fact, risen for some countries, particularly between 2006 and 2010. Comparisons of malaria deaths in the countries where comparable data are available show that the death rate increased from 113,505 to 120,504 between 2006 and 2010.

Additional research or perhaps more experience with the use of these nets is needed to reconcile these seemingly contradictory results, which might also have arisen as a result of sampling errors. A study of the effectiveness in India suggests that field trial results are less optimistic than controlled experiments.

One puzzling phenomenon observed is the way these bed nets are being distributed in some countries in Africa. Take Nigeria for example, a country where there are over two million cases of malaria and approximately 8000 deaths annually, most of them being children. (Nigeria is one of the top high-burden malaria countries in the world. In Nigeria they are now distributing two bed nets per family. What does that lead to? You guessed it – a gross misallocation of bed nets. WHO estimates that 30% of households get more bed nets than needed and 43% of households received fewer bet nets than needed. Only 27% of households received the ideal number of nets. Was there any trading going on? There is no evidence that the 30% traded with some of the 43%. So there were wasted bed nets and excess demand for bed nets. What an inefficient program and a waste of resources. The *World Malaria Report* also notes that costs for spraying are positively related to the number of people protected by the program. However the challenge is to ensure that the key vulnerable groups have access to ITNs and use it rightfully to full capacity.

When it comes to cost, WHO is doing a good job. It calculates the cost of replacing ITNs in relation to their useable life. If new nets last five instead of three years, nearly $4 billion could be saved in replacement costs. At the same time there could be greater insecticide resistance toward the end of the expected life span which has to be taken into account. In getting the best price for nets per year, expected coverage rather than cost per net should be the criteria for bidding.

It is noted in the *World Malaria report* that IRS comprises a significant share of malaria control expenditures and costs decline with the size of the program. Another consideration is the cost of the insecticides. It mentions that one type of insecticide (pyrethroids) should be avoided where net coverage is high, probably as a result of the antagonistic interaction with the bed net insecticide. More details for individual country programs are needed to make judgments about the relative cost and efficiency of IRS and ITN in different country settings. In countries or locations where infestations have a wide year to year variance, a different strategy is called for vis-à-vis locations where infestations are more predictable (see Section 4.4.3 on episodic periods of malaria infestation in Africa).

There has been a lot of variation in the number of malaria deaths over time. From a simple visual inspection of the data in Figure 4.2 and Table 4.7, it is hard to tell much about the factors influencing these movements. What we do know is that the number of deaths has fallen in the last few years in Kenya, Tanzania, Nigeria and Zambia. In Malawi,

Table 4.7 Malaria in most affected African countries

Country	Malaria deaths, 2012	Trend in deaths from malaria	Trend in cases of malaria	Household percentage with one or more bed net, 2012	Percentage of households with enough ITNs for individuals who slept in the house the previous night, 2012
Kenya	26,017(2010)	Down	Up	67	27
Democratic Republic of Congo	21,601	Up	Up	59	
Uganda	15,632	Up	Up	64	26
Burkina Faso	7963	Up	Up	50	17
Tanzania	7812	Down	Down	92	52
Nigeria	7734	Down since 2007	Up	43	14
Angola	5736	Down	Up	44	6
Malawi	5516	Up	Up	49	18

Note: These figures were interpolated from graphs in the report – better information may be available.
Sources: WHO (2012) and WHO (2013e).

it fell dramatically and then rose before falling again these past few years. Without further detailed county analysis, it is difficult to understand the underlying reasons for these patterns. One problem is that the country appendix tables in the *World Malaria Report* for 2012 are not consistent with the figures reported in Table 4.3. The WHO (2012) appendix tables show a smooth trend in malaria deaths compared with the volatile series in Figure 4.2. For example, in Tanzania the appendix tables show deaths per 100,000 falling slowly from 2006 to 2010 from around 90 per 100,000 to 75 per 100,000 population. Given a total population of 45 million, this works out to around 3300 deaths in 2010. Figure 4.2 shows 15,819 malaria deaths in Tanzania in 2010. There has to be a way to resolve these differences before we can go forward. In Kenya too the differences are dramatic. In the appendix tables the death rate was around 100 per 1000,000 population, falling slowly from 2006 to 2010. However, the rate fell dramatically to around two per 100,000 in 2011. With a population of 41 million, this translates to a drop of 4000 fatalities from malaria to 200 fatalities in a few years. This inconsistency in figures may also be due to the methodology of the model for which malaria deaths are estimated. One instance given by WHO was that of the reported decline in the estimated mortality deaths between 2011 and 2012 and this is partly due to the model that is used to estimate malaria deaths in children under five years of age in Africa. The model uses ITN coverage to adjust the proportion of all deaths that are attributed to malaria (reported in the Country Profiles) and ITN coverage has flattened in 2011 due to the cut in funding for malaria control.

One message from this simple analysis is that there is little evidence of an impact of bed net ownership either on deaths or cases of malaria in the recent record. Each of the eight countries has anywhere from 43% to 92% of households with at least one bed net but these bed nets are not used by all members of the households (see Table 4.7, last column). Furthermore, we do not know who is sleeping under these bed nets. It should be the children but Table 4.6 suggests that not all bed nets were being used by children five or under. Furthermore, none of these countries has a significant spraying program. And, of all the countries in Africa only a few have any significant spraying program.

4.7 Overall impact of programs to reduce incidence of malaria

To evaluate the impact of all the programs designed to reduce the incidence and mortality of malaria, UNICEF has constructed three maps of Africa with an estimated number of lives saved (see Figure 4.3). This is

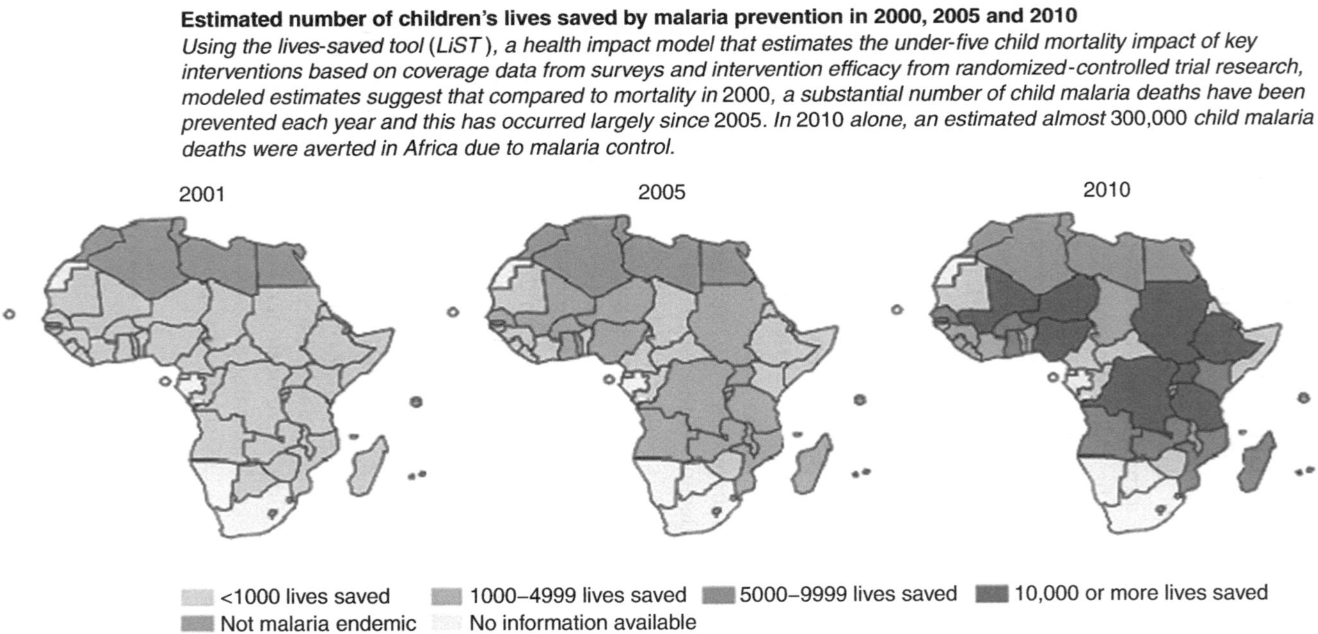

Figure 4.3 Estimated number of children's lives saved by malaria prevention, 2000, 2005 and 2010
Source: WHO, UNICEF, UNDP and the World Bank (2011).

very good public relation and is certainly evidence of the overall success of malaria reduction in Africa. However, it does not give much detail about which program was responsible for how many lives saved and in which countries. Because all of these programs (bed nets, spraying and ACT) are relatively new, we are still at the evaluation stage. The effectiveness will have to be judged as they are evaluated over time. So far, as indicated in the analysis of mortality in the epidemic countries, there has been limited evidence of a decline in mortality.

4.7.1 Locations

Looking at malaria in the other regions, there are no countries with a significant number of deaths that can match any of the top 20 countries in Africa.

4.7.2 ACT

Another approach is to recognize that many adults in Africa already have malaria and that more effort should be put into treating infants and their mothers. Table 4.3 records the number of malaria cases in African countries, with several reporting over 2 million cases. Most experts contend that these numbers are an under estimate of the actual number of cases since it does not capture people who had malaria but did not seek care at health facilities. The actual numbers could be three times larger. If these are indeed under estimates and recognizing that the biggest threat of malaria is for the young who have by far the highest mortality, more effort should be put on keeping infants from getting malaria.

In general, we can also look at the antimalarial drugs that are given to all patients. The ACT record for the eight countries with the highest death rates is generally good with the exception of Nigeria (see Table 4.8). In almost all cases, ACT is the drug of choice. Testing proportions of suspected cases is still above 50% in most countries. The use of ACT can be easily extended to other countries and the use of artemisinin therapy can also be used in other rural and urban environments either in a home management or more formal healthcare system. Of course the programs will need to be evaluated as they are extended to different environments.

4.7.3 SP

The authors were unable to estimate the number of deaths avoided by SP therapy. EIR of more than 100 is likely in countries where malaria is endemic and case rates as well as mortality are high. So far there is very

Table 4.8 Proportions of patients treated with antimalarial drugs

Country	Proportions of patients treated with ACT or other antimalarial drug								ACT is free for all ages in public sector	Children under five years of age with fever who received treatment with any antimalarial drug
	2005	2006	2007	2008	2009	2010	2011	2012		
Kenya	18	100				100	100	100	Yes	24(2008)
Democratic Republic of Congo		5	10	23	58	61	89	68	Yes since 2006	29.8(2007)
Tanzania			100	100	100	100	100	100	Yes	58.2(2005)
Burkina Faso				40	68	100	100	100	No	48(2006)
Uganda		100	100	62	100		100	100	Yes since 2006	61.3(2006)
Malawi	100	100		90	100	100	100	100	Yes since 2007	23.9(2006)
Angola		44	50	60	90	74	100	99	Yes since 2006	27.9(2006)
Nigeria			16*	23*	21*	20	16	27	Yes since 2009	33.3(2008)
Treatment very good I didn't record testing proportions – they are lower but above 50%									Over 50% in most cases	

Note: *ACT only.
Source: WHO (2013e) country profile and World Bank (2013).

few evidence reported in the literature regarding the effectiveness of SP in reducing infant mortality.

4.7.4 IRS and ITN

Turning to the evidence on the use of bed nets and residual spraying, it seems that many more people (and children) are still being infected in the high-mortality countries and probably also in the rest of Africa. Malaria cases and deaths have not changed much over the past five years despite greater number of bed nets in the high-mortality countries. IRS coverage has declined and implementation is not clear for most programs. Over the years, there has been an increase in insecticide resistance and this will threaten the effectiveness of both ITN and IRS. The cost of IRS may also increase due to an increase in insecticide resistance and thus the need to change to a more expensive insecticide (WHO, 2013e).

Because malaria is often difficult to diagnose, it is possible that many cases are not being detected and this is another reason why the case rate has not been falling in all the high-mortality countries. The fault is not with treatment, which is nearly universal with the preferred antimalarial drug. Better protocol for identifying patients as well as the age profile of those who are dying is needed particularly in high mortality countries. The relationship between cases, treatment and mortality needs to be studied in greater detail. The study for Orissa in India pointed out that there are probably strong nonlinearities in the effectiveness of bed nets so that a threshold effect is an important factor in evaluating effectiveness. When ITN coverage is low (less than 25%), effectiveness is minimal, whereas coverage of 50% or more has much stronger impacts as well as positive externalities on other residences where bed nets were not being used. As noted earlier, greater emphasis has to be put on treating infants. More studies need to be carried out to verify this inference and also to check who is sleeping under a bed net. It is not enough to count the number of bed nets and people and draw the conclusion that when they are close to equal, there is blanket coverage of all residents. The case of Nigeria is a case in point.

It should also be noted that the high malaria incidence countries are among the poorest in the world. Table 4.9 shows human development indices (HDI) and the average years of schooling for the selected countries. HDIs are all above 140 and two above 180, in the lowest 3% of countries globally. The average education level is also low. For two countries the average numbers of years completed is below four years and for the remainder, except Kenya (7), Tanzania (5.1) and Nigeria (5.2), it is

Table 4.9 Human development index (HDI) and average years of education for countries with most global deaths from malaria 2012

Country	HDI	Average years of education
Kenya	145	7.0
Democratic Republic of Congo	186	3.5
Tanzania	152	5.1
Burkina Faso	183	1.3
Uganda	161	4.7
Malawi	170	4.2
Angola	148	4.7
Nigeria	153	5.2

Source: UNDP (2013).

below five years. The ability of the average villager to understand how to use bed nets and the implications of not sleeping under a bed net every night might be difficult to understand and follow since many can read and write only at an elementary level. To test the interaction between these kinds of social indicators and the incidence of malaria requires more in-depth analysis of the culture in high-incidence countries and the best way to implement methods of control and treatment.

4.7.5 Locating the breeding ground

Locating the breeding ground is another initiative suggested by Abeku (2007), something that has been missing from most of the literature on malaria. *Anopheles gambiae,* one of the primary vectors of malaria in Africa, breeds in numerous small pools of water that form due to rainfall. The larvae develop within a few days and are able to escape from the water before it dries out. As a result it is difficult, if not impossible, to predict when and where the breeding sites will form, and to find and treat them before the adult mosquitoes emerge. Therefore, larval mosquito control for the prevention of malaria in Africa has not been attempted on a large scale. It may, however, be appropriate at specific settings such as urban environments or desert fringe areas where habitats are more stable and predictable. WHO has recommended larval control as appropriate only at areas where the larval habitats are "few, fixed and findable." Otherwise a more ecologically damaging strategy would be to spray in a more indiscriminate manner in hopes of locating breeding sites based on intuition and some crude scientific evidence. So far this has not been a strategy that has been seriously proposed or followed.

4.8 Action points for future policy directions for malaria

Artemisinin has been suggested as a therapy for infants and young children who are the most likely to die of malaria in many countries in Central and Southern Africa, where the infestation of mosquitoes is extremely high. So far there have been few clinical trials looking at the effectiveness of artemisinin, and whether artemisinin is more effective when used in combination with policies that improve diet and reduce anemia. How the trials could be used to influence policies for malaria reduction among infants and young children as well as their mothers would be welcome and would help to fill in gaps in knowledge about ways in which infant deaths from malaria can be reduced.

The Global Fund to combat HIV/AIDS, TB and Malaria has recently cut off its subsidies for artemisinin. Artemisinin is more expensive than many other drugs that have been suggested to address malaria in infants and children such as SP and chloroquine. We recommend that alternative sources of funding be sought to replace these funds and efforts should also be made to tighten the controls on how drugs are prescribed and dispensed to cut waste.

In the countries of Africa where malaria is endemic and most adults have already built up immunity, it makes more sense to target households with infants and their mothers for the distribution of bed nets and spraying of household surfaces with DDT or other insecticides. The clinical trials do not appear to record the number of infant deaths saved by either of these programs. More clinical trials are needed to assess which program is more effective in averting infant deaths (up to four years of age) and how effective they have been when used in conjunction with artemisinin or other antimalarial drugs.

Decision rules have to be developed to assess whether to distribute bed nets to everyone who lives in villages and urban locations where malaria is mild and varies over time with the possibility of periodic epidemics. Where to draw the line? It does not seem effective to distribute bed nets to all households without ensuring that infants and mothers should be served first. Furthermore, there is no compelling reason why adults should sleep under bed nets aside from the fact that they would not be bothered by mosquito bites while they are sleeping. In situations where malaria is of epidemic proportion and adults have already built up immunity, bed net use is recommended for comfort more than a way to avoid contracting malaria.

WHO in consultation with other international agencies and country health officials in Sub-Saharan Africa should develop guidelines regarding who should receive and use bed nets, when spraying should occur and when to spray. It is important to have different guidelines for different countries and different epidemiology in different countries and different times of year.

4.9 Statistical analysis

We have conducted an analysis of the causes of malarial mortality for the top 30 countries with reported malaria deaths in the world. The results of this analysis are displayed in Table 4.10. Estimated mortality from malaria was the dependent variable with several explanatory variables. Of these bed net usage was a highly significant explanatory variable. Data was unavailable for the use of spraying as an alternative to

Table 4.10 Statistical analysis of malaria mortality using GLS

Constant	−5385.289*
	(2356.944)
Bed nets	−101.599*
	(15.999)
Anti-malarial drugs	−48.943
	(25.914)
HEALTHEXP	−247.784*
	(88.540)
GNIPC	−7.42E-09*
	(0.000)
HDI	41,898.780*
	(4642.862)
R^2	0.734
No. of observations	43

Note: The method used generalized least squares regression, with standard errors in parentheses on top 30 countries with reported malaria deaths. * denotes statistical significance at the 5% level.
Indicators used:
Malaria deaths: Reported malaria deaths (WHO, 2012).
Bed nets: Use of insecticide-treated bed nets (percentage of under five population).
Antimalarial drugs: Children with fever receiving antimalarial drugs (percentage of children under five years of with fever).
HEALTHEXP: Health expenditure, total (percentage of GDP).
GNIPC: GNI per capita, PPP (current international $).
HDI: Human Development Index.
Note: Top 30 countries with reported malaria deaths include: Democratic Republic of Congo, Burkina Faso, Angola, Malawi, Uganda, Zambia, Cameroon, Sierra Leone, Nigeria, Ghana, Mozambique, Niger, Burundi, Mali, Benin, Côte d'Ivoire, Togo, Chad, Ethiopia, Congo Central African Republic, India, Guinea, Kenya, Sudan, Myanmar, Guinea Bissau, Zimbabwe, Gambia and Papua New Guinea.

bed nets. The other explanatory variables, namely health expenditures, human development index, and gross national per capita income, were also significant, though HDI exhibits a perverse sign.

Looking at the top 30 high-burden malaria death case countries, Table 4.10 shows a strong case for insecticide-treated bed nets, health expenditure and GNI per capita in reducing death rates due to malaria. The use of insecticide-treated bed nets (percentage of under five population) is highly negative and significant in curbing malaria mortality rates. The other specific malaria health intervention in the form of antimalarial drugs for children under the age of five years with fever is weakly significant. So it provides support for more extended usage of such health intervention for malaria, especially for the provision of insecticide-treated bed nets to the most vulnerable groups. The level of health expenditure and GNI per capita is also critical to curbing malaria mortality rates. HDI is also significant, though it exhibits a perverse positive sign. This could be due to correlations between GNI per capita and the HDI indicators. We reran the model without these two indicators

Table 4.11 Statistical analysis of malaria mortality using GLS (without GNI per capita and HDI)

Constant	14,269.050*
	(1268.178)
Bed nets	−86.165*
	(13.866)
Anti-malarial drugs	−93.239*
	(13.109)
HEALTHEXP	−604.583*
	(50.313)
R^2	0.737
No. of observations	55

Note: The method used generalized least squares regression, with standard errors in parentheses on top 30 countries with reported malaria deaths. * denotes statistical significance at the 5% level.
Indicators used:
Malaria deaths: Reported malaria deaths (WHO, 2012).
Bed nets: Use of insecticide-treated bed nets (percentage of under five population).
Antimalarial drugs: Children with fever receiving antimalarial drugs (percentage of children under five years of with fever).
HEALTHEXP: Health expenditure, total (% of GDP).
Note: Top 30 countries with reported malaria deaths include: Democratic Republic of Congo, Burkina Faso, Angola, Malawi, Uganda, Zambia, Cameroon, Sierra Leone, Nigeria, Ghana, Mozambique, Niger, Burundi, Mali, Benin, Côte d'Ivoire, Togo, Chad, Ethiopia, Congo, Central African Republic, India, Guinea, Kenya, Sudan, Myanmar, Guinea Bissau, Zimbabwe, Gambia and Papua New Guinea.

to examine the relationship between malaria mortality rates and the respective health interventions.

After the removal of GNI per capita and HDI from the model, we examine the importance of the respective health interventions on malaria mortality rates (Table 4.11). Empirical results affirm the importance of insecticide-treated bed nets and health expenditure in general in the control of malaria death rates. The significance of antimalarial drugs has risen sharply and appears to be highly significant in curbing malaria mortality rates. A caveat is to be noted – the documentation of usage of insecticide-treated bed nets and antimalarial drugs was first available in the year 2000 and not frequently reported annually. Thus, the data for malaria health-specific intervention is only available for the sample countries for approximately three to four years over the entire period of the sample years 1999–2010. This thus restricts the sample size and the number of observations that we had in the running of the model. Over time, there should be greater data on such antimalarial interventions and should be able to provide greater statistical case for such intervention. Hence, the current model is able to demonstrate the importance of health intervention on malaria mortality rate and the urgent need for government action.

5

Diarrhea and Other Water-Borne Diseases

5.1 Introduction

Global estimates of the incidence of diarrheal diseases suggest that there has been little if any progress in reducing the overall morbidity of these diseases. The authoritative handbook of diseases in developing countries (*Disease Control Priorities in Developing Countries*, edited by Jamison et al., 2006) goes so far as to say that

> the estimated median incidence of diarrheal disease in children under 5 in developing countries has not changed much since the early 1990s.
>
> (p. 373)

The report goes on to say that

> incidence rates in Sub-Saharan Africa and Latin America are clearly greater than in Asia or the Western Pacific... Incidence continues to show a peak in infants age 6 to 11 months dropping steadily thereafter.
>
> (p. 373)

Walker et al. (2013) conducted a study on the incidence of diarrhea in low- and middle-income countries and estimated that it has declined very slowly from 3.4 episodes per child year in 1990 to 2.9 episodes per child year in 2010. The most vulnerable group, infants aged between 6 to 11 months, could suffer up to 4.5 episodes per year in 2010. There is a pressing need for government intervention for diarrheal diseases, especially given the heavy burden on the health of each child due to multiple episodes per year in low- and middle-income countries.

Despite little progress in cutting the incidence of diarrheal diseases, there has been a significant decline in infant mortality, most likely as a result of modern medical case management of childhood cases. There are several related developments that have impacted on infant mortality as a result of methods to control diarrhea.

1. Better and more widespread information is being given to mothers about the need for rehydration therapy as diarrheal symptoms arise. This has been coordinated with better and more accurate information on how to prepare rehydration fluids at home.
2. This has been supplemented by the increased availability of hydration solutions that can be prepared at home or that are now widely available from local health practitioners and drug stores.
3. Recommendations have been strongly made to continue breastfeeding and have discouraged the use of prepared formulas such as similac that are mixed with water. Since the water may be contaminated, it would make the diarrhea worse.
4. Advising mothers to provide some complementary foods in addition to mother's milk during diarrheal episodes and as a normal practice after the episode has ended.
5. Advise mothers to repeat the suggested feeding and rehydration protocol during subsequent episodes of diarrhea.

The strategy suggested in item 1, of recommending oral rehydration therapy (ORT) for all infants suffering from diarrhea, has resulted in significant reductions in mortality around the globe. Country case studies in Philippines, Brazil, Egypt and Mexico reported that the use of ORT went from near zero in the early 1980s to 33, 35, 50 and 81% a decade later in their countries respectively. This resulted in a sharp decline in episodes of diarrhea, which led to a fall in child deaths and hospital admissions. The evidence also suggests that even relatively low rates of ORT had a beneficial impact on infant mortality.

Nevertheless, many of the background conditions responsible for high rates of diarrheal diseases, such as poor housing, overcrowding, lack of refrigeration, open sewers, cohabitation with domestic animals, open defecation, unsanitary conditions and lack of access to clean water, continue to persist in many developing countries in Asia, Africa and Latin America. As a result, the mortality rate from diarrheal diseases will remain much higher than that in industrial countries for a long time in the future. Major changes in housing, sewage, safe water and sanitation will have to be made before the epidemic is brought under control. Diarrheal diseases remain among the top five preventable killers of children under five in developing countries. However, the infant mortality rate has fallen and continues to fall and that is a good sign.

The WHO (2013f) estimates that almost one billion people lack access to an improved supply of water. There are 1.7 billion cases of diarrheal diseases and 260 million people are infected with schistosomiasis annually. Most of the illnesses and deaths occur in developing countries in Asia, Africa and Latin America. Many of these grim statistics could be avoided by simple sanitation and water safety measures along with the development of clean water resources and prompt treatment of cholera and diarrhea symptoms. Despite the efforts to reduce mortality by the use of ORT suggested earlier, the death toll could reach 30–40 million between 2012 and 2020. The lack of safe water and proper sanitation lie at the heart of this ongoing human tragedy. This combines with poor personal hygiene and tainted food to create a disease chain that affects all age groups, particularly young children and infants. Increasingly, untreated wastewater that is being used to irrigate crops is also of concern as it increases the chances of contaminated food supplies.

In 2002 Peter Gleick estimated that between 34 and 76 million people will perish from water-related diseases by 2020. Using the midpoint of this range, it comes to around three million deaths per year between 2002 and 2020. Gleick argues that better water quality is one of the most serious public health challenges and one which has received less attention, particularly in view of the enormous benefits in terms of cost-effectiveness. This is analyzed in greater depth as we show later. There are four categories of diarrheal diseases: *water-borne diseases*, which include ingesting contaminated bacteria or viruses, including cholera, typhoid, dysentery and other diarrheal diseases; *water-washed diseases* caused by poor personal hygiene such as tick- and lice-borne diseases, skin and eye contact with contaminated water and trachoma; *water-based diseases* caused by parasites in water including schistosomiasis and other helminths; and *water-related diseases* including malaria and yellow fever.

The world's most prolific killers are *water-borne diseases* such as diarrheal disease from bacteria like typhoid, cholera, *Escherichia coli, Salmonella* and many others. Diarrhea is caused by unsanitary personal hygiene and contaminated water. Because over a billion people do not have safe water access and more than double that number lack access to basic sanitation, diarrhea has reached epidemic proportions in many countries.

Treating drinking water is the best way to reduce the incidence of water-borne diseases. Better sewage treatment and disposal combined with universal access to latrines or other methods of disposing human waste as well as discouraging open defecation are easy and cost-effective ways of providing clean water. A coordinated program of personal hygiene and education at the village level along with use of soap for hand washing, installation of latrines and water purification and judicious use of chlorine to purify drinking water can save millions of lives and increase labor productivity as well as uplift well-being of citizens. Tube wells and water purification methods can be augmented by new technology using a water purifying straw. At a cost of a dollar or two a year one straw can provide an individual with safe drinking water for a year. Of course distribution and education would further raise the cost but it is something to be considered for developing countries as an alternative to purification schemes that would be much more costly.

5.2 Diarrhea

Diarrhea remains one of the major causes of mortality for children under five years of age. The burden of diarrheal diseases bears heavily on infants in lower- and middle-income developing countries. The mortality toll from diarrhea is shown in Table 5.1. The number of childhood deaths was estimated by WHO at around 12 million per annum in 1990, which fell to around seven million in 2011 while maternal deaths fell from around half a million in 1990 to under 300,000 in 2010, helped by the spread of oral rehydration. Diarrhea is transmitted by the oral transmission of fecal matter by hand, water, soil, from animals or from food. Children in these countries have higher rates of diarrhea as a result of a variety of factors. These generally include poor sanitation and unsafe

Table 5.1 Burden of diarrhea per year in children aged 0–4 years, by WHO region, 2010

	Incidence*	Total deaths ('000)
African region	3.3	353.3
American region	3.2	11.0
Eastern Mediterranean region	2.9	96.6
European region	2.8	6.3
Southeast Asian region	2.4	227.7
Western Pacific region	2.2	16.9
World	2.7	711.8

Note: *Incidence = Episodes per child per year.
Source: Walker et al. (2013, Table 5.1).

water, poor personal hygiene, widespread practices of open defecation, malnutrition and poor diets lacking in vitamin A and zinc and the presence of animals in food preparation areas. Children in poorer areas also have a lack of access to health care and oral rehydration therapy when they fall ill with diarrhea symptoms. In Bangladesh alone diarrhea kills over 100,000 children under five annually and is the cause of death of one in four deaths of under five children. Morbidity rates are much higher. Globally, an estimated 65 million episodes occur yearly among children under five years of age and three to four episodes a year per child. Of the estimated 1.8 million lives lost from diarrheal diseases each year, over 80% are children under the age of five.

Improvements in the delivery of public health combined with the support of entire communities have made a big difference in increasing life expectancy and reducing morbidity from diarrheal diseases, and these programs are highly effective at low cost. As discussed earlier, wider use of rehydration therapy is essential to reduce the high rates of morbidity and mortality among children as a result of chronic or even epidemic cases of dysentery and diarrhea. More can be done by adopting simple measures to improve water quality. Chlorine is the most widely used method of water purification. It can be delivered in bulk to villages or made available at water collection points with recommended dosage included. Other methods of purification include sand filtration and use of solar radiation. However, they are not used in many locations.

Several countries have adopted better sanitation and public health practices, which have reduced the incidence of water-related diseases. In Bangladesh, better sanitation practices, which now cover 80% of the population from close to zero in 1970, have resulted in a sharp decline in the incidence of diarrhea. Where diarrhea still occurs, oral rehydration therapy is an effective tool in reducing the intensity of the episode and preventing the possibility of death. The key to success as with any of these programs is political commitment. Analysis by Keusch et al. (2006) suggests that

> in the face of HIV and the attention being given to tuberculosis and malaria, coordinated efforts to build safe water and sanitation capacity at the local level, one village at a time, that are sufficient to significantly influence the burden of illness are unlikely – even though many more infants and children die each year of preventable and treatable diarrhea than of HIV/AIDS.
>
> (p. 384)

It should also be noted that the cost-effectiveness of many diarrhea abatement programs is generally quite high and low-cost solutions are available. More resources need to be devoted to treating diarrhea and provide clean water to communities in poor countries if the lives of thousands more children are not to be lost without a fight.

5.3 Diagnosis

Diarrhea can take many forms although it is generally characterized by water and persistent bowel movements and can be fatal as a result of dehydration if not treated quickly. WHO defines diarrhea as the passage of three or more loose or liquid stools per day (or more frequent passage than is normal for the individual). It is to be noted that frequent passing of formed stools and the passing of loose, "pasty" stools by breast-fed babies is not diarrhea. Technically, three major types of diarrhea are observed. The first is acute water diarrhea, which without treatment results in rapid dehydration and can lead to death if not treated. The second is persistent diarrhea where the stool is not so watery but which lasts for two weeks or longer and is characterized by poor absorption of nutrients and is accompanied by malnutrition. While persistent diarrhea is not as common as watery diarrhea, it is responsible for a disproportionally large number of deaths. According to one study it has a mortality rate which is three times as large as episodes that are shorter in duration. In Bangladesh, for example, persistent diarrhea associated with severe malnutrition was responsible for nearly half of all diarrheal deaths and the relative risk for death among malnourished infants with persistent diarrhea was about 17 times greater than infants with mild malnutrition (Fauveau et al., 1992). The third is bloody diarrhea, which is a sign of problems caused by inflammation of the intestine and is not usually associated with mild dehydration. Bloody diarrhea is often confused with dysentery, which is also characterized by abdominal cramps and straining to pass stools. Both diarrhea and dysentery result in bloody stools and abdominal inflammation. Diarrhea and dysentery are exacerbated by malnutrition and generally poor health. It is estimated that about half of diarrheal deaths in infants and children result from a combination of malnutrition and dehydration and are compounded by a lack of proper medical treatment and care in the home.

5.4 Morbidity and mortality

The incidence of bouts of diarrhea peaks at the age of 6–11 months and may be related to the child being weaned and more exposed to unclean food and water rather than mothers' milk. There are more cases of diarrhea in Sub-Saharan Africa and Latin America compared to Asia, although there is a lack of systematic compilation of data that can confirm this impression. Furthermore, time series data are also scarce and/or unreliable so that inferences are difficult to make. As suggested in the introduction, many experts suggest that morbidity has not changed much over time in developing countries. Keusch et al. (2006) note some shifts in the age distribution toward more cases in the six months to one year interval but the median diarrheal incidence has not moved much since the early 1990s. Incidence rates in Latin America and Sub-Saharan Africa are higher than in Asia and the Western Pacific.

Identification of the different kinds of diarrhea is scarce although there is some indication that the principal cause of bloody diarrhea, *Shigella*, is responsible for over 100 million episodes each year (see Kotloff et al., 1999). According to the Global Enteric Multicenter Study (GEMS), a three year case-control study of childhood diarrheal diseases conducted at seven sites in Africa and Asia, Kotloff et al. (2013) reports that just four pathogens were responsible for the majority of moderate-to-severe diarrhea cases suffered by the children in the clinical study. Researchers tested stool samples from children diagnosed with moderate-to-severe diarrhea cases to determine the fraction of cases attributed to each pathogen for the selected countries (Gambia, Mali, Mozambique, Kenya, India, Bangladesh and Pakistan). These included: (1) *rotavirus*, which was the leading cause among infants suffering from diarrhea; (2) *cryptosporidium*, which was the second leading cause among infants (a pathogen previously not expected to be a major contributor); (3) *Shigella*, which was the leading cause among children aged five years and below; and (4) *Enterotoxigenic E. coli* in at least one age group for each site. Children suffering from a single episode of moderate to severe diarrhea can suffer an 8.5 fold increase in the risk of death in the subsequent two months as compared to control children in the study (GEMS Fact Sheet, 2013).

There is better information available regarding mortality through vital statistics records compiled by health departments in most countries. These data show that there has been a decline in infant mortality and much of this has been a result of lower levels of infant deaths as a result of closer attention to dehydration caused by diarrhea (see Victoria et al., 2000). The five protocols suggested in the introduction to this chapter are largely responsible for this trend. Data from a variety of countries reviewed provide strong evidence that ORT is working to reduce mortality rates in many countries and rates of use of ORT are generally reasonably high (see Table 5.2).

Table 5.2 All persons receiving oral rehydration salts (in percent), 2007–2012

Country	Percent
Afghanistan	53
Albania	54
Armenia	33
Bangladesh	78
Bolivia	35
Burkina Faso	21
Cambodia	34
Central African Republic	16
Chad	13
Georgia	40
Kenya	39
Lebanon	44
Madagascar	17
Mongolia	38
Mozambique	55
Niger	34
Peru	32
Philippines	47
Senegal	22
Sri Lanka	50
Turkmenistan	40
Zambia	60
Zimbabwe	21

Source: UNICEF (2013, Table 3).

ORT is not effective against *Shigella* and therapy for *Shigella* and dysentery-type diseases is quite different from ORT as *Shigella* has to be treated with antimicrobials. Unfortunately, bloody diarrhea is not tracked separately by most countries so it is difficult to obtain any time series estimates of the progress that is being made to control and treat *Shigella*. Kotloff et al. (1999) estimated that 600,000 deaths per year are caused by *Shigella* among children under five, which is somewhere between a quarter and a third of all the estimated number of global childhood deaths from diarrhea. Clearly, more needs to be done to identify the different types of diarrhea and to make sure that *Shigella* is treated differently from watery diarrhea and incorporate our understanding that complications from a poor diet can be a contributing factor to *Shigella* and mortality, which arises from lack of treatment and other complicating factors. Kotloff et al. (2013) also stress the need for interventions to target the pathogens (rotavirus,

Shigella, Cryptosporidium, typical enteropathogenic *E. coli*), which substantially reduce the burden of moderate-to-severe diarrhea. There is an existing vaccine for *rotavirus,* but few intervention tools for the second leading cause of infant mortality, *Cryptosporidium.* In order to prevent diarrheal diseases and improve health outcomes, there is a pressing need to expand the access of existing health interventions and promote new intervention tools where needed.

5.5 Long-term impact of diarrheal disease on cognitive function

The impact of diarrheal disease on those who survive to adulthood has not been systematically assessed with scientific precision. The main reason is that the incidence and frequency of diarrhea in childhood has not been analyzed. Furthermore, diarrhea is only one of the health risks that arise among poor children in developing countries. Generally, poor health, diets lacking in vitamins, sufficient calories and protein also contribute to a risky health profile for adults. We do know that early childhood malnutrition from any cause has the potential of reducing physical fitness and work productivity as an adult but to identify specific causes would require more detailed information on childhood histories, which are not currently available on a widespread basis. There are a few scientific studies that throw additional light on the impact of diarrhea on health outcomes of adults who suffered from severe diarrhea as children. Niehaus et al. (2002) looked at a cohort of 47 children in a poor urban community in Brazil. They concluded that test scores were 25–65% lower in children with an early history of persistent diarrhea and that there was also a significant inverse correlation between early diarrheal episodes and cognitive and intellectual capacity in later years.

However, another meta-study by Fischer Walker et al. (2013) did not find a significant relationship between diarrhea and cognition. However, they did find a significant relationship between stunting and cognition. Furthermore, there were weak links between stunting and diarrhea. As a result of their meta-analysis of several studies, the authors concluded that "While diarrhea may not directly impact cognitive impairment, the links between diarrhea and stunting, and stunting and cognition are clear and provide additional rationale for accelerating interventions to reduce diarrhea." They further concluded that

> Our understanding of the complex relationships among diarrhea, nutritional status, poverty, care seeking, and developmental

> stimulation in the home would benefit greatly from additional studies explicitly designed to consider the role of each of these factors individually and more importantly to consider the mediating effects of one factor on another. (p. 5)

From this limited survey, it is clear that much more work has to be done to untangle the web of factors that have resulted in a failure to reduce the overall pattern of diarrheal episodes on a global scale. Progress in reducing mortality has been made and that is to be applauded. However, the environment that causes repeated cases over time also needs to be addressed in a systematic way, even though the challenges are many and the way ahead in some countries is still unclear.

5.6 Prevention

The most obvious ways to prevent diarrhea are also the most powerful. Better sanitation, including hand washing with soap, careful food preparation, use of latrines and toilets, avoiding open defecation, boiling water for cooking, and chlorinating (or life straw) drinking water, will make great inroads in preventing diarrhea. These factors together have collectively been shown to cut child mortality by as much as 55% and perhaps even more. Estimates suggest that the number of deaths because of poor water quality could be reduced to 50% if water supplies were cleaned.

If a safe water source is nearby, the cost of collection is low. If it is far away, care has to be taken so that the water collected remains clean. Water collection can be expensive in terms of time spent but it can pay dividends in terms of sustaining good health. A chlorine faucet at a well provides good water quality for a low price. Globally, it is estimated that good water can reduce cases of diarrhea by up to 50%. However, studies have shown that water is a less likely vehicle for diarrhea than food and that controlling flies and hand washing can reduce it by a further 23% and 40–50%, respectively (see Jamison et al., 2006, p. 783). There is also a significant reduction in child mortality by as much as 65% in some cases as a result of better food preparation and personal cleanliness. A safe water supply and good sanitation (latrines and no open defecation) can work together to reduce the incidence of diarrhea. There may be some interdependent influence on children's health but most of the evidence suggests that they act somewhat independently to reduce the chance of contamination of the food and water supply. Prevention of open defecation also prevents the contamination of children's play areas and the common yard areas. Evidence suggests that despite efforts to improve health and sanitation, the incidence of diarrheal episodes continues to be very high among infants in most developing countries.

Other preventative measures have also been suggested and are now being more widely adopted in developing countries. In addition to the five points mentioned in the introduction, breast-feeding up to at least six months of age is recommended even if the child has diarrhea. Upon a review of 18 studies from developing countries, Lamberti et al. (2011) report that not breast-feeding was associated with a 165% increase in diarrhea incidence for young infants aged five months and less. Not breast-feeding was also associated with a 32% increase in diarrhea incidence and 47% increase in diarrhea-related mortality of infants 6–11 months of age. Cholera and measles vaccinations have also had a salutary impact on childhood diarrhea although the impact has been negligible since these vaccination programs have not been adopted by many countries. If the mother has HIV, the infant should still be breast-fed for the first 6 to 12 months but the mother should be on ART. This prevents the transmission of the virus to the infant and cures the diarrhea as well. The use of vaccines against rotavirus, which is one of the most common causes of childhood diarrhea deaths, can also substantially reduce the disease burden of diarrhea. Munos, Walker and Black (2010) estimated that the use of these vaccines could reduce close to two-third of very severe rotavirus infections and could approximately halve rotavirus-related hospital admission in young children.

5.7 Control and treatment

When a child has diarrhea, there is almost always a risk of dehydration and oral rehydration therapy (ORT) is recommended by WHO and health ministries in developing countries. Many countries around the world have adopted ORT therapy (see Table 5.2) and this is the major reason why mortality rates have declined in the past few decades. In a review of 205 studies, mainly from developing countries, Munos, Walker and Black (2010) reported that use of oral rehydration solution (ORS) reduced diarrhea-specific mortality by close to 70% and rates of treatment failure by 0.2%. Zinc supplements used with ORS to treat children with diarrhea also help to reduce mortality rates in children aged five years and below. However, according to the *Countdown to 2015*, only one-third of children are receiving access to ORS for diarrhea in countries with high burden of maternal and/or child mortality. Note, however, that on average ORS was used more often when family

Table 5.3 Under five year olds with diarrhea receiving oral rehydration salts (in percentage), 2007–2012

Country	Poorest 20% of population	Richest 20% of population
Algeria	15	19
Azerbaijan	3	36
Bangladesh	81	82
Burkina Faso	13	31
Burundi	35	42
Cambodia	32	34
Cameroon	5	34
Congo	13	18
Central Africa Republic	11	28
Chad	5	29
Colombia	47	61
Egypt	34	23
Ethiopia	18	45
Equatorial Guinea	24	37
Côte d'Ivoire	6	12
Gambia	43	32
Ghana	45	34
Guinea	18	59
Guinea Bissau	16	37
Honduras	56	47
India	19	43
Indonesia	32	27
Jordan	18	30
Kenya	40	37
Liberia	41	64
Madagascar	12	29
Malawi	67	73
Mali	8	29
Mauritania	10	34
Morocco	18	25
Mozambique	40	50
Namibia	50	59
Nepal	39	36
Nicaragua	53	64
Niger	14	32
Nigeria	15	53
Pakistan	41	44

Peru	27	42
Philippines	37	55
Rwanda	22	37
Senegal	21	31
Sudan	21	16
Sierra Leone	75	70
Somalia	7	31
Turkmenistan	45	30
Uganda	43	45
Tanzania	41	38
Yemen	31	37
Zambia	61	61
Zimbabwe	18	28
Average	29	44

Source: UNICEF (2013, Table 13).

incomes were in the top 20% as opposed to the lower 20% (see Table 5.3).

Some countries have been able to mount effective oral rehydration therapy programs even in the face of continued high rates of diarrhea in the population. By some estimates diarrhea was responsible for at least half of infant deaths in Egypt in the late 1970s (Levine and the What Works Working Group, with Molly Kinder, 2004) and the infant mortality rate was one out of ten live births. In the early 1980s, a nationwide program of ORT was begun with the help of USAID. It had an ambitious set of objectives, including increasing ORT understanding and awareness, increasing the number of severe diarrhea cases treated with ORT and reducing diarrhea mortality in children. To achieve these objectives, it developed a program for Egypt with four main components.

First was product branding and design. This included a smaller serving container (200 mL rather than a full liter), a recognizable brand name "gaffaf," meaning drought in Arabic. The name helped to establish a link between the symptoms of diarrheal dehydration and the oral therapy. The logo of a mother feeding a baby became the most recognized product label in Egypt.

Second was production and distribution. A tracking system was established to forecast demand and keep a supply of ORT product available. A parastatial company was one of the main suppliers and sold through public sector stores. Subsidies were provided by UNICEF and a national foundation. There was competition from private sector providers of antidiarrheal drugs, which were not as effective as ORT. To create financial incentives for pharmacies to promote the ORT product, the national foundation provided pharmacies with free measuring cups which they then sold to customers along with the ORT product.

Third, a social marketing and mass media campaign was mounted, aimed at mothers of children under three years of age as well as health professionals and pharmacists. Media reporters were also involved and journalists filed stories on the benefits of ORT. The message was simple – there were dangerous and possible fatal effects of diarrhea and there was a cheap and easy way to treat it. The campaign coincided with a rapid growth in TV ownership, up to 90% of households in 1984 up from just 38% in 1980. TV spots were designed to appeal particularly to poorer audiences. A popular soap opera star was recruited as a spokesperson. There were also billboards, magazine ads and posters in clinics and pharmacies. The campaign reached many mothers and sales of the ORT product, called oral rehydration salts (ORS) and also called Rehydran, increased rapidly.

Fourth, training of health workers was undertaken to accurately diagnosis diarrhea and dehydration and to teach mothers how to use ORT. Audiovisual materials were prepared and distributed and a number of rehydration centers were established in clinics and hospitals. Between 1984 and 1990, 14,000 practicing nurses and 10,000 doctors underwent the training course. Medical and nursing schools also added rehydration and ORT to their academic programs. The training stressed the importance of breast-feeding, that ORT should be the primary tool to manage cases of diarrhea, the importance of good hygiene and that the use of antidiarrheal drugs should be limited.

The impact of the ten-year program was dramatic. Virtually all mothers were aware of ORT and ORS by 1986 and use of ORS was widespread. Civil records showed that infant diarrhea mortality fell 82% between 1982 and 1987 and there were comparable but smaller declines in overall infant and child mortality (36% and 43%, respectively). Other data from surveys suggest that the overall impact was even more dramatic. Levine and the What Works Working Group with Molly Kinder (2004) estimated that 300,000 childhood deaths were averted between 1982 and 1989. Nevertheless, there are challenges remaining in Egypt. The private sector has been slower to adopt ORT and private doctors see the bulk of patients (close to 75% of all cases). Furthermore, the market for antidiarrheal drugs other than ORT remains large and this presents an ongoing challenge for ORT. Furthermore, ORT has generally been more successful in treating poorer families than well-off families (34% versus

23%) and its coverage is still low compared with other countries (see Table 5.3).

Turning to another success story, ORT was also adopted on a widespread scale in Bangladesh. A much larger population (100 million versus ten million in Egypt) and a much lower per capita income required a different approach based on door-to-door interviews and training of mothers in the use of ORT. Originally the program relied on a pinch and scoop method (*lobon-gur*) of a pinch of salt, a fistful of sugar and a liter of water. Commercial packets are now available. In the decade from 1980 to 1990, 13 million mothers were taught to make ORT mixtures in their homes. ORT usage in Bangladesh is now around 80%, one of the highest in the world. For the richest 20% of the income distribution, the rate of ORT adoption from 2007 till 2012 was 82% and comparable for the poorest 20% of the income distribution at 81%, according to latest figures from UN Children's Fund (see Table 5.3). Coordinated program at the village level can make a big difference. In Bangladesh, a community-led total sanitation program (CLTS) involves ending open defecation by the entire community. This was augmented by a program to install and maintain latrines combined with lessons in personal hygiene. These lessons in personal hygiene have reinforced the efforts to train mothers in the use of ORT. To assess the success of the ORT program, over 9000 households in 90 villages were revisited in a follow-up and pharmacies, health workers and village doctors were also interviewed a second time. Many of the mothers in the original ORT program were very young during the house-to-house campaign. The follow-up found that ORT is still being used effectively and the knowledge has been passed on to others in the interim. Drug sellers and villagers now recommend ORT much more frequently than before the massive campaign to train mothers in the use of ORT was implemented. In the future, use of ORT can be improved further by augmenting it with food and vitamin supplements to improve the health of both mothers and children (see Chowdhury et al., 1997).

One important result is that both Bangladesh and Egypt experienced a rapid decline in infant mortality during the 1980s and early 1990s. In Bangladesh, the infant mortality rate (IMR) fell from 130 per 1000 live births in 1980 to 86 in 1993 (33% decline), while in Egypt the rate fell from 113 to 54 over the same period (52% decline). In two more advanced developing countries, Costa Rica and Sri Lanka, where ORT is also available and where the incidence of diarrhea is lower, the decline in infant mortality over the same period was equally dramatic – the IMR in Costa Rica fell from 22 to 14 (36%) and in Sri Lanka from 37 to 22 (41%). However, because they started from a much higher threshold, the total number of deaths avoided was much higher in Bangladesh and Egypt.

It should be noted that many countries, both poor and middle income, also had declines in infant mortality over this period. Mali, for example, one of the poorest countries in Africa had an ORS of only 17% and low levels of sanitation, yet had a decline in infant mortality comparable to Bangladesh albeit starting at much higher levels – 154 to 98 (36% decline).

In Niger, also one of the poorest countries in the world, infant mortality did not fall at all between 1980 and 1989. It was 134 in both years and even increased in some intervening years. However, in the decade from 1998 to 2008 it fell by 32% while child mortality (zero to five years) fell by 43% between 1998 and 2009. In addition to diarrhea, health programs also gave high priority to achieving universal access to primary health care for women and children with a focus on avoiding deaths from malaria, pneumonia, measles and diarrhea. The government also built more health centers and upgraded staff training. The government also strengthened the distribution system for essential commodities. Amouzou et al. (2012) noted that

> Government of Niger achieved great reductions in child mortality by responding forcefully to opportunities and constraints in their context. They created a conducive policy environment focused on high-impact interventions, and operationalized those policies in ways that improved financial access to services (by eliminating user fees for children and pregnant women) and improving geographic access to services. Niger – with lower levels of resources and at least equal environmental challenges relative to neighboring countries – has sprinted toward universal primary health-care coverage and higher rates of child survival. This case study shows the value of taking a broad approach to understanding country-level programming for women and children, and producing information that can be used in Niger and other settings to reduce unnecessary deaths. Niger is an unusual context, and has produced remarkable results for child survival that can set the bar for other countries in the region and worldwide (p.9).

The lesson for the experiences of Niger, Egypt and Bangladesh is that even poorer countries can achieve significant reductions in infant mortality with minimal levels of ORS, sanitation and water availability, although the level of infant mortality is many times higher than countries with better health and sanitation facilities. To achieve further reduction in infant mortality will require wider use of ORS/ORT and extension of the health and nutrition programs to reach a larger share of the population at risk. The fact remains that many countries have not made similar progress. We look at some of these countries and suggest what they can do to emulate the successful experiences of Niger, Bangladesh and Egypt in a subsequent section.

Before doing so we turn to the general issue of infant and maternal care in countries that have not been able to make much progress in reducing infant mortality and mother's mortality. One would think that South Africa, with the highest per capita income in the Sub-Saharan Africa, would be a good example of a country where progress has been made in reducing both mother and infant's mortality. This is not the case. According to the *Guardian* (12 August 2011), maternal mortality has increased from 150 deaths per 100,000 live births in 1998 to 625 in 2007. HIV played a role in many of these deaths according to government reports. However, the failure to reduce maternal mortality goes beyond the impact of HIV/AIDS. Botswana and Swaziland have similar HIV infection rates but much lower maternal and infant mortality. There were numerous cases of substandard care, abuse of maternity patients by health workers, generally poor quality care, financial and administrative inefficiencies and lack of accountability. The state has failed to provide oversight and accountability for abusive staff and failures to achieve an improvement. Abuses were most egregious in the Eastern Cape province. In some instances health workers demanded bribes to assist women in labor.

Several causes have been cited for the failure of the health system to deliver quality care to infants and their mothers in the country in Sub-Saharan Africa with the highest per capita income and a sophisticated medical system where most women deliver babies in clean hospitals. Poorly trained and overworked hospital staff is one reason given for the lack of care and neglect. The number of midwives is much lower than the WHO standard. Another reason is the carryover of attitudes that prevailed for generations during the time of apartheid. One black woman who is suing the hospital where she gave birth said "You wonder, because so many black people were fighting for empowerment (during the battles against apartheid). Now that we've got it we are abusing each other." And apartheid had a debilitating effect on education, which has adversely affected the quality of trained midwives and their attitudes as well. It will take more time and further discussions within the health services sector and the medical profession to reestablish a system where trust and care are paramount. It must also be realized that the scars left by apartheid are not easily or quickly healed.

Lesotho is one of the smallest countries in Africa and its mountainous terrain makes it difficult to treat communicable diseases effectively with a limited budget. It is landlocked and completely surrounded by South Africa. It is geographically one of the highest countries in the world. The entire country is about 6000 feet. It has made slow progress in reducing infant and mother's mortality. This is complicated by the fact that Lesotho also has one of the highest rates of HIV infection in the world. Several programs have been put in place to upgrade the level of training for health professionals and to reduce the transmission of HIV from mother to child. Infant mortality has trended down somewhat in the past two decades to the range of 60–70 deaths per 100,000 births. However, under five mortality has continued to trend upward. The World Bank estimates that over 70% of HIV-positive pregnant women receive ARV treatment to reduce the chance of mother-to-child transmission and knowledge of how HIV can be spread from mother to child has increased dramatically from an estimated 42% in 2004 to 71% in 2008. Nevertheless, the health budget is small and Lesotho still has a low GDP per capita of $1664 and its human development index is only 160, in the lowest 10% of all countries. Its high HIV incidence, low income and human development index as well as its geographic location constrain its progress toward achieving Millennium Development Goals 4 and 5, which are discussed in the next section.

Bangladesh has adopted a village-based strategy to stop open defecation and begin a process of building latrines and sewage treatment facilities. These ideas have been spearheaded by several community action groups. A study analyzed 53 local governments that were declared free of open defecation several years ago. Surveys of 3000 households were conducted and indicated that around 90% of households in these villages under the direction of local governments have sustained use of a latrine system. However, hygiene was not as high as desired. Nevertheless, the study did find that there had been a shift in social customs away from open defecation to the use of latrines in many villages. Furthermore, the study found ongoing sanitation practices reinforce latrine use and that chemical and other sanitation products are widely used and available. Several videos available on YouTube also show that the process of shifting toward use of latrines has been a bottom-up process and that there has been no pressure from outside the village although there were usually some outside advisers involved. Rather, local pride and support of the use of latrines and better health practices has provided the stimulus. Often one village member has offered to build a latrine and others have subsequently followed. This is the kind of process that has been working in a variety of circumstances where social engineering objectives have been initiated in microenvironments. After a good experience, whether it is sanitation or adoption of high-yielding varieties of rice or other food crops, others in surrounding areas or even in other more remote locations have adopted the new practice. There is usually no subsidy and the process is usually begun with a visit from visitors who ask a series of leading questions about where the village housing is located, where the roadways and shops are. All of this is delineated by different colors of soil – there are never any paved roads. After this and having gained the villagers' attention, the villagers are asked to identify where they defecate. There are many words for defecate in every language and these are used appropriately in context. Some villagers will be asked to put a small pile of different colored soil where they defecate and this will be repeated by many villagers. Then everyone sits around and someone or many will say how disgusting this is. Comments like "we are all eating shit" or "we are eating each other's" shit are common. And then someone or several people will say something must be done about this and the suggestion to build a latrine or toilet will be made. And so the process starts with people taking a little money from their own pocket to build a simple latrine. Without external assistance, this process is being repeated all over the world. Kar and Chambers (2008) of the Institute for Development Studies estimate that the number has gone from a few when the program started in Bangladesh in 1999 to 20 million villages in Africa and Asia with also some in Latin America.

5.8 Millennium Development Goals

The Millennium Development Goals 4 and 5 specify several objectives for reducing child and maternal death, respectively by 2015. Child deaths are targeted to fall by 67% between 1990 and 2015 while maternal deaths are to fall by 75% over the same period. At the beginning of 2013, the global community was not on track to achieve either of these goals. Progress on achieving Goals 4 and 5 was slow between 1990 and 2005. There has been some acceleration in commitment recently with initiatives by the UN strategy for child and women's health in 2005 and the African Union Summit on Maternal and Child Health. In 2012, there were several additional initiatives including a Child Survival Call to Action in Washington, DC, a Summit in London on Family Planning and conferences in Oslo, Norway and Nigeria. See Goodluck and Stoltenberg (2013) for further details.

There have also been strong programs developed in a number of countries including India, Nepal, Ethiopia, Malawi and Rwanda. In Nigeria, a Save One Million Lives initiative has been launched and Sweden, Norway, the United Kingdom and the Gates Foundation have developed programs for contraceptive implants. Still, Ethiopia and Rwanda have not made sufficient progress in attaining Goal 4. Niger, which had the highest rate of infant mortality of 311 per thousand in the world in 1990, was still able to achieve an annual rate of reduction of 3.9% for infant mortality, just below 15 countries that were making sufficient progress. Only 23 countries (or 30% of countries being followed) are on track to achieve the target level of infant mortality reduction by 2015, while 38 are making insufficient progress and 13 are making no progress (see Table 5.4). Only two are in Africa and none in Sub-Saharan Africa.

What are the reasons for these failures? A lack of funding combined with a lack of understanding of the variety of interrelated factors responsible for infant mortality is largely responsible. The countries where there has been no progress are at the very bottom 10% of the human development index and those making insufficient progress are also low on the HDI. In these countries there is a systemic failure to deliver even a minimal level of acceptable health service to the community (see Table 5.4). In order to make more progress, greater commitment of both the local health officials and the international community are needed with particular emphasis on improving personal hygiene, availability of clean water and proper sanitation. Without emphasis on all of these aspects of public health, infant mortality is unlikely to decline rapidly. At the same time the examples of Niger, Bangladesh and Egypt show that per capita income does not necessarily have to be high to have a successful program that reduces infant mortality. See Box 5.1 for factors contributing to the success cases for Thailand, Kyrgyzstan and Tamil Nadu.

Table 5.4 HDI and health indicators for selected countries

	Under-five mortality rate (average annual rate of reduction, %)	Infant mortality rate	Health expenditure, public (% of GDP)	Physicians (per 1000 people)	Nurses and midwives (per 1000 people)	HDI
	1990–2010	2012	2010	2010	2010	2012
Afghanistan	1.7	71.0	2.35	0.19	0.07	175
Angola	2.1	99.5	2.06	–	–	148
Azerbaijan	3.5	30.8	1.17	3.78	8.34	82
Benin	2.2	58.5	2.22	0.06	0.77	166
Botswana	1.0	41.0	3.32	0.34	2.84	119
Burkina Faso	0.8	65.8	4.08	0.05	0.57	183
Burundi	1.3	66.9	3.18	–	–	178
Cameroon	0.0	61.1	1.52	–	–	150
Central African Republic	0.2	90.7	1.94	–	–	180
Chad	0.9	89.4	1.01	–	–	184
Comoros	1.9	57.7	3.03	–	–	169
Democratic Republic of Congo	0.3	99.9	2.12	–	–	186
Congo	1.1	62.2	1.39	0.10	0.82	142
Côte d'Ivoire	1.0	76.2	1.52	0.14	0.48	168
Djibouti	1.5	65.7	5.39	0.23	0.80	164
Equatorial Guinea	2.3	72.2	2.43	–	–	136
Ethiopia	2.8	46.5	2.56	0.02	0.24	173
Gabon	1.1	42.4	1.82	–	–	106
Gambia	2.6	49.2	2.48	0.04	0.57	165
Ghana	2.5	48.6	3.02	0.09	1.05	135
Guinea	2.8	65.2	2.01	0.10	0.04	178
Guinea Bissau	1.7	80.8	2.31	0.05	0.55	176
Haiti	−0.4	56.5	2.74	–	–	161
India	3.0	43.8	1.06	0.65	1.00	136
Kenya	0.8	48.7	1.76	0.18*	0.79*	145
Lesotho	0.2	74.2	8.11	–	–	158
Mali	1.8	79.6	2.82	0.08	0.43	182

Table 5.4 (Continued)

	Under-five mortality rate (average annual rate of reduction, %)	Infant mortality rate	Health expenditure, public (% of GDP)	Physicians (per 1000 people)	Nurses and midwives (per 1000 people)	HDI
	1990–2010	2012	2010	2010	2010	2012
Mauritania	0.6	64.8	4.03	0.13	0.67	155
Mozambique	2.4	63.1	3.32	0.03	0.34	185
Myanmar	2.6	41.1	0.24	0.50	0.86	149
Niger	3.9	62.8	2.38	0.02	0.14	186
Nigeria	2.0	77.8	1.71	0.40	1.61	153
Pakistan	1.8	69.3	0.79	0.81	0.56	146
Papua New Guinea	1.9	48.4	3.09	0.05	0.46	156
Rwanda	2.9	38.8	5.72	0.06	0.69	167
Sao Tome and Principe	0.8	38.0	2.65	–	–	144
Senegal	3.1	45.2	3.28	0.06	0.42	154
Sierra Leone	2.3	117.4	3.19	0.02	0.17	177
Somalia	0.0	90.8	–	0.04	0.11	–
South Africa	0.3	33.3	4.05	0.76*	–	121
Sudan	1.0	49.3	1.99	0.28	0.84	171
Swaziland	1.0	55.7	5.54	–	–	141
Tajikistan	3.1	49.0	1.59	2.10	5.30	125
Tanzania	3.6	37.7	2.82	0.01	0.24	152
Togo	1.8	62.0	3.42	0.05	0.27	159
Turkmenistan	2.8	44.8	1.50	2.39	4.42	102
Uganda	2.8	45.4	2.12	0.12	1.31	161
Uzbekistan	2.0	34.4	2.73	2.54	10.68	114
Yemen, Rep.	2.5	46.3	1.17	0.20	0.68	160
Zambia	2.5	56.4	3.63	0.07	0.78	163
Zimbabwe	–0.1	55.7	–	–	–	172

Note: *Data for the year 2011.
Sources: World Bank (2013) and UNDP (2013).

Box 5.1 Success Experiences of Thailand, Kyrgyzstan and Tamil Nadu

Thailand has made impressive achievements in health outcomes over the past few decades, and has adopted country-specific targets known as MDG Plus after meeting the MDG goals. Infant mortality has fallen from 68 per 1000 live births in 1970 to approximately 11 deaths per 1000 live births in 2012. Such a decline in infant mortality is among the fastest in low- and middle-income countries. Life expectancy has also improved though limited by spread of AIDS. One of the contributing factors behind Thailand's success includes high priority given to health and its continuity in successive national plans despite changes in political leadership over time. Such continuity in health policy and plans implemented allowed for the strengthening of rural health care and expanded coverage of maternal and child care services. Another factor is the strengthening of the capacity of health institutions and healthcare workers and tapping onto the public–private partnerships at the district levels and informal groups such as the Rural Doctors Society of Thailand. A bonding system was introduced that required newly qualified doctors to spend three years in public health facilities, mostly in rural areas. The government also worked to increase the number and the quality of nurses through establishing its own nursing and midwifery colleges. After serving four years of mandatory rural health services, the technical nurses could undertake additional training to attain a bachelor's degree to further upgrade themselves. This helped to increase the supply of healthcare services needed in rural districts. By 2001, Thailand has also consolidated the previously fragmented health systems to achieve near universal health coverage. Sustained investments were made in rural infrastructure and education for women also helped to support the improvements in health. Lastly, Thailand was able to shape health systems according to their specific context and needs, with extensive piloting and evaluation of policies.

Kyrgyzstan is one of the poorest of the 15 Soviet Republics. Since independence, the government has faced substantial challenges to provide a well-functioning health system. Yet the government has managed to achieve improvements in health outcomes as compared to its more prosperous neighbors. There have been

Box 5.1 (Continued)

significant reductions in infant mortality and under-five mortality. With the funds from international assistance, Kyrgyzstan has undertaken health reforms since 1996. Given the near collapse of the inherited health system, the country's first President established health care as a priority and the setting of laws underpinning the health reforms and the civil state which survived two revolutions. The passing of three major laws over four years was critical for the move towards compulsory health insurance and universal coverage. Deliberate care was taken to ensure coherence of health reforms by creating a stable bureaucracy and reducing political influence over appointments. This allowed for institution memory and avoided repeating of mistakes. Institutional and staff capacity was strengthened. A total of 42% of the existing hospitals were closed between 2000 and 2003 while community health centers were upgraded to meet the demand for health services instead. Primary care doctors under the Soviet system were retrained as general family practitioners and were supported by a network of nurses, midwives and better-trained mid-level health workers. Given its mountainous terrain resulting in insufficient coverage of health services in certain areas, Kyrgyzstan tapped on village health committees and volunteers to provide healthcare services to such vulnerable groups. The state also provided benefits packages for vulnerable population and subsidies for essential medicines. Major investment was made to strengthen the accountability and transparency in the allocation of resources within the health system.

Tamil Nadu, India's seventh most populous state, has also made great strides in reducing maternal mortality and infant mortality. Between 1980 and 2006, maternal mortality has fallen from 319 deaths per 100,000 live births to 111 deaths. Infant mortality also fell by 60% as compared with 45% for the nation. The government has expanded healthcare coverage with 90% of deliveries being attended by a skilled birth attendance and 81% of infants full immunized. There are four contributing factors. First, it was one of the first Indian states to implement a large-scale multipurpose worker (village nurse) scheme in 1980. To become a village nurse, the women needed to have at least ten years of schooling and to undergo one and half year of training. The scheme has been scaled up to deliver integrated primary care in rural areas currently. Like Bangladesh, there was an increase in the scope of the activities of community health workers in Tamil Nadu. Such activities included primary care and referrals during home visits, which enhanced the level of integration between health programmes, and contributed to the progress in maternal and child health. Like Thailand, newly graduate doctors were also posted to rural areas and it was deemed as a qualifying stage in their professional development.

Second, Tamil Nadu also implemented a large network of primary healthcare centers, with about 1500 primary health centers, each serving about 30,000 people on average, and a further 8680 subcenters were available by 2005. Performance of the centers is monitored monthly. A system of compulsory monitoring and audit of maternal deaths in both public and private sectors was also adopted. This allowed the government to identify systemic weakness and local health officers were given the authority to develop context specific appropriate solutions. Solutions that were found to be effective were later replicated in other districts. Tamil Nadu also actively pursued public–private partnerships to expand capacity in the health sector to respond to diverse needs of users. Preventive maternal and child health care were provided by the public sector whilst the private sector undertakes 80% of outpatient visits and 60% of admissions. Public–private engagement is common in contracting out clinical and laboratory services and information campaigns. Third, there was a rapid scale-up in immunization schedules with assistance from UNICEF, Rotary Club, and the Christian Medical College in Vellore. Lastly, the government replaced the former drug procurement and distribution system with the autonomous Tamil Nadu Medical Services Corporation in 1995, so as to ensure access to reliable supply of essential drugs whilst cutting down on funds misappropriation. Beyond the reforms in the health sector, the government has actively promoted female empowerment and investment in infrastructure, in particular electricity and clean water and this has significantly contributed to the advancements in health outcomes.

Source: Balabanova et al. (2013)

In many countries the number of infant deaths is still unacceptably high based on standards for middle-income or high-income countries, in many cases one in ten live births. However, even in some of these countries, there has been measurable progress toward achieving the Millennium Development Goal 4. For example, in Liberia, where the infant mortality rate was 227 per 1000 live births in 1990, the rate had fallen to just over 100 deaths per live births, a rapid rate of 4% per annum. This enabled Liberia to maintain its rate of progress at a satisfactory level to achieve its goal by 2015. Malawi is another example of a similar decline in infant mortality and at even a higher rate of decline of 4.4% per year. And there is the example of Niger mentioned earlier. There are, however, few other countries that have been able to bring down mortality rates from very high levels. The successful countries have higher HDI levels and generally lower levels of infant mortality in the range of 30–50 per 1000 live births by 2010.

What this analysis suggests is that even greater efforts have to be made by the international donor community to address the general health infrastructure in those countries which have sufficient national incentives, domestic resource and infrastructure to be able to effectively support an additional infusion of resources. In the cases of those countries having made insufficient progress, study teams could be mounted to study in what ways they can be assisted to increase the chance of infant and maternal survival.

Turning to maternal mortality, only nine countries are on track to achieve Goal 5 compared with 23 that are on track to achieve Goal 4. Eight of these countries (Bangladesh, Cambodia, China, Egypt, Eritrea, Lao PDR, Nepal and Vietnam) are also on track to achieve Goal 4. Note that none of these countries is in Africa. There are nine countries where there has been no progress, they are all in Africa and none has had any reduction in maternal mortality. All but one has had an increase in maternal mortality.

There are a variety of reasons why mothers die in childbirth or shortly thereafter. The major reasons for high rates of maternal death are poor access to health and medical services. WHO records show that almost all maternal deaths occur in developing countries. More than half occur in Sub-Saharan Africa and almost a third in South Asia.

WHO records also indicate that the maternal mortality ratio in developing countries is 15 times as high in developing countries as it is in developed countries (240 versus 16 per 100,000 live births). Eighteen countries have maternal mortality rates of over 500 per 100,000 live births and they are all in Sub-Saharan Africa (refer to Table 5.5). There

Table 5.5 Maternal mortality ratio (modeled estimate, per 100,000 live births)

Country	1990	2000	2010
Chad	920	1100	1100
Somalia	890	1000	1000
Central African Republic	930	1000	890
Sierra Leone	1300	1300	890
Burundi	1100	1000	800
Guinea Bissau	1100	970	790
Liberia	1200	1300	770
Sudan	1000	870	730
Cameroon	670	730	690
Nigeria	1100	970	630
Lesotho	520	690	620
Guinea	1200	970	610
Niger	1200	870	590
Zimbabwe	450	640	570
Congo	420	540	560
Democratic Republic of Congo	930	770	540
Mali	1100	740	540
Mauritania	760	630	510

Source: World Bank (2013).

are higher rates of maternal mortality in rural areas and for women with lower family income.

WHO notes that globally the risk of maternal mortality is highest for adolescent girls under 15 years of age and that complications in pregnancy and childbirth are the leading cause of death among adolescent girls in most developing countries. Another reason for high mortality is that the number of children born per mother is much higher in developing countries and this raises their risk of death during and after pregnancy. WHO estimates that the probability that a 15 year old woman will die from maternal causes is around 25 times higher than in developed countries (one in 3800 versus one in 150). Maternal deaths arise from severe bleeding after childbirth, infections, eclampsia and unsafe abortions. The presence of diseases such as HIV/AIDs and malaria can also be possible factors. In a developed country, the vast majority of these causes could be effectively treated. In summary Sub-Saharan Africa suffers from the highest levels of infant mortality and maternal mortality. With a few exceptions, none of the countries in Africa will achieve the Goals 4 and 5 spelled out in the Millennium development agenda. The poorest countries will make little or no progress by 2015 unless a massive effort is made to build up health and sanitation services.

Lozano et al. (2011) concludes that

> Under-5 deaths have continued to decline, reaching 7.2 million in 2011. Comparing rates of decline from 1990 to 2000 with 2000 to 2011 shows that 106 countries have accelerated declines in the child mortality rate in the past decade. Maternal mortality has also continued to decline from 409,100 (uncertainty interval 382,900 to 437,900) in 1990 to 273,500 (256,300 to 291,700) deaths in 2011. We estimate that 56,100 maternal deaths in 2011 were HIV-related deaths during pregnancy. Based on recent trends in developing countries, 31 countries will achieve MDG 4, 13 countries MDG 5, and nine countries will achieve both.
>
> (p. 1139)

However, the authors conclude that even though progress on reducing maternal and child mortality in most countries is accelerating, most developing countries will take many years past 2015 to achieve the targets of the MDGs 4 and 5. Similarly, although there continues to be progress on maternal mortality, the pace is slow, without any overall evidence of acceleration. Immediate concerted action is needed for a large number of countries to achieve MDG 4 and MDG 5.

This summary is more optimistic than our analysis of the data already discussed. In any event more resources have to be devoted to reducing infant and mothers' mortality. It remains to be seen if it can be successfully carried out.

Looking beyond, the 2015 deadline set for the MDGs, WHO and UNICEF has recently launched the integrated Global Action Plan for the prevention and control of pneumonia and diarrhea in 2013. These two diseases tend to have overlapping risk factors such as those related to poverty, undernutrition and poor hygiene and are the two leading causes for under-five mortality. The Action Plan has set targets that are significantly higher than the current levels. It proposes to end preventable childhood deaths due to pneumonia and diarrhea by 2025. It also aims to have 90% of children to have access to antibiotics for pneumonia and oral rehydration salts for diarrhea, up from current levels of 31% and 35%, respectively. All children are to have access to improved sanitation and safe drinking water, from 63% and 89%, respectively. There are also plans to have 90% coverage of new vaccines against pneumococcal bacteria and rotavirus. The Action Plan was launched together with a new *Lancet* series on childhood pneumonia and diarrhea. Bhutta et al. (2013) estimated using the Lives Saved Tools that the scaling-up of health interventions by 80% in the 75 countdown countries could avert 95% and 67% of deaths in young children less than five years due to diarrhea and pneumonia, respectively. They estimated the financial cost of ending preventable deaths from childhood diarrhea and pneumonia by 2025 to be $6.715 billion. The current level of health spending would need to be increase by $3 billion.

5.9 Statistical analysis

To analyze further the causes of infant deaths from diarrhea, we developed a regression model where the incidence of diarrhea deaths is a function of the extent of sanitation, the availability of clean water, the share of health spending in the government budget, gross national income per capita, the human development index and the extent of use of oral hydration for infants.

5.9.1 Determinants of diarrhea deaths for infants

We looked at the determinants of diarrhea deaths for infants under five years old using a database of 30 developing countries with highest distribution of causes of death due to diarrhea. These results are presented in Table 5.6. The model was a pooled time series model and was estimated using generalized least squares. There were only 38 observations because data for several pertinent variables were available for a limited time interval and this constrained the sample size.

In general, the results shown in Table 5.6 provide a strong case for the usage of diarrhea treatment (children under the age of five receiving oral rehydration and continued feeding). The levels of per capita income and HDI also strongly affect diarrhea death rates, and with the expected *a priori* signs. Access to safe water is also significantly negative. Health expenditure in general is rather insignificant in the diarrhea model. Access to sanitation is significant though with a perverse positive sign. The pooled model is again constrained by the availability of ORS data since the frequency of the data is on an annual basis and limited to specific available years, thus leading to a small sample size.

In order to relax the constraints that the ORS data have in terms of data availability, we reran the same model without the ORS indicator and the GNI per capita to reduce the possible correlation between GNI per capita and HDI. This has allowed for an increase in the sample size. The compact model reaffirms the importance of access to safe water, health expenditure and HDI to the reduction of diarrhea death

Table 5.6 Statistical analysis of infant mortality due to diarrhea

C	20.988*
	(1.060)
SANITATION	0.041*
	(0.009)
H_2O	−0.023*
	(0.012)
ORS	−0.059*
	(0.010)
HEALTHEXP	−0.033
	(0.052)
GNIPC	−0.001*
	(0.000)
HDI	−10.441*
	(2.409)
R^2	0.934
No. of observations	38

Note: The method used generalized least squares with standard errors in parentheses on top burden 30 countries identified. *denotes statistical significance at the 5% level.
Diarrhea deaths: Distribution of causes of death among children aged < 5 years (%) due to diarrhea.
SANITATION: Improved sanitation facilities (% of population with access).
H_2O: Improved water source (% of population with access).
ORS: Diarrhea treatment (% of children under five receiving oral rehydration and continued feeding).
HEALTHEXP: Health expenditure, total (% of GDP).
GNIPC: GNI per capita, PPP (current international $).
HDI: Human Development Index.
Note: Top 30 countries with highest distribution of causes of death due to diarrhea include: Afghanistan, Angola, Belize, Benin, Burkina Faso, Burundi, Cameroon, Central African Republic, Chad, Democratic Republic of Congo, Djibouti, Eritrea, Ethiopia, Guinea, Guinea Bissau, India, Lao PDR, Madagascar, Mali, Mauritania, Niger, Nigeria, Pakistan, Panama, Rwanda, Sao Tome and Principe, Sierra Leone, Somalia, Sudan and Yemen, Rep.

rates (Table 5.7). The sign of the improvement in sanitation facilities is perverse though.

In general, the results of the models are encouraging and point toward the importance of greater heath interventions. Owing to some of the health measures being implemented recently, there are some constraints on the availability of data. More data are needed so as to improve the

Table 5.7 Statistical analysis of infant mortality due to diarrhea disease (without GNI per capita and ORS)

C	22.85*
	(0.43)
SANITATION	0.08*
	(0.01)
H_2O	−0.06*
	(0.01)
HEALTHEXP	−0.14*
	(0.02)
HDI	−19.80*
	(1.17)
R^2	0.724
No. of observations	189

Note: The method used generalized least squares with standard errors in parentheses on top burden 30 countries identified. *denotes statistical significance at the 5% level.
Diarrhea deaths: Distribution of causes of death among children aged <5 years (%) – diarrhea.
SANITATION: Improved sanitation facilities (% of population with access).
H_2O: Improved water source (% of population with access).
HEALTHEXP: Health expenditure, total (% of GDP).
HDI: Human Development Index.
Note: Top 30 countries with highest distribution of causes of death due to diarrhea include: Afghanistan, Angola, Belize, Benin, Burkina Faso, Burundi, Cameroon, Central African Republic, Chad, Democratic Republic of Congo, Djibouti, Eritrea, Ethiopia, Guinea, Guinea Bissau, India, Lao PDR, Madagascar, Mali, Mauritania, Niger, Nigeria, Pakistan, Panama, Rwanda, Sao Tome and Principe, Sierra Leone, Somalia, Sudan and Yemen, Rep.

sample size and to further assess the determinants of mortality rates of such diseases.

We expanded the model to analyze the importance of the extent of Vitamin A distribution and it was also statistically significant. For oral rehydration, these results reinforce the findings of many of the country studies reviewed earlier. The significance of Vitamin A therapy is an important finding and highlights the need to distribute Vitamin A to families with infants. We were unable to assemble a reliable database for the extent of open defection. However, it is not unlikely that sanitation and open defecation are correlated. Projects to improve the level of sanitation and enhance the availability of safe water should be ramped up. There are many other reasons for moving forward with these projects including increasing life expectancy and well-being for the general population. Some of these results were presented earlier when the determinants of life expectancy were discussed in chapter 1. There is a critical need to reduce infant mortality due to diarrheal diseases as well as to curb the spread of the HIV/AIDS, TB and malaria epidemics. In addition, governments can also re-look the ways in which health expenditure can be better utilized to bring about quality health outcomes for developing countries.

Notes

2 HIV/AIDS

1. The RV144 study in Thailand was the first HIV vaccine trial to show some effectiveness in preventing HIV infection. See http://www.nejm.org/doi/full/10.1056/NEJMoa0908492 for more details.
2. According to WHO (2013a), the average HIV prevalence among female sex workers was highest in Sub-Saharan Africa (37%), followed by Eastern Europe (11%), Latin America and the Caribbean (6%), Asia (5%) and the Middle East and North Africa (2%).
3. HIV therapy should be started several weeks after initiation of TB so as to reduce the risk of immune reconstitution syndrome.
4. It is to be noted that there are different tests available in Europe and United States. Some look at certain bands that are more prevalent in the specific continent. The WHO currently approves of the HIV testing done in Africa. These are not subpar tests but just different test methods from the United States and its interpretation of results.
5. However, it is to be noted there are constraints on the database for the data on ART coverage. Data on ART coverage for those with living with advanced HIV is only available in recent years such as 2009 and 2011.

3 Tuberculosis

1. Includes Burkino Faso and Malawi, which are not among the top 20 countries with the highest TB incidence.
2. There are a few small countries in Southern Africa that have similar TB and HIV profiles as the targeted countries with high rates of coinfection that fit in this category that are not in the top 20 list (Botswana, Lesotho, Namibia and Swaziland). These counties are analyzed in a recent World Bank report.

Bibliography

Abeku, T. 2007. Response to malaria epidemics in Africa. *Emerging Infectious Diseases*, 13(5): 681–866.

Acemoglu, Daron and James A. Robinson. 2012. *Why nations fail: The origins of power, prosperity, and poverty*. New York: Crown Publishers.

Ajayi, Ikeoluwapo O., Edmund N. Browne, Fred Bateganya, Denis Yar, Christian Happi, Catherine O. Falade... Franco Pagnoni. 2008. Effectiveness of artemisinin-based combination therapy used in the context of home management of malaria: A report from three study sites in sub-Saharan Africa. *Malaria Journal*, 7: 190.

Amouzou, A., Oumarou Habi, Khaled Bensaïd and the Niger Countdown Case Study Working Group. 2012. Reduction in child mortality in Niger: a Countdown to 2015 country case study. *Lancet*, 380: 1169–1178.

Anand, A. Date, Marco Vitoria, Reuben Granich, Mazuwa Banda, Mayada Youssef Fox and Charlie Gilks. 2010. Implementation of co-trimoxazole prophylasia and isoniazid preventive for people living with HIV. *Bulletin of the World Health Organization*, 88(4): 253–259.

Arnold, Carrie. 2012. At-home HIV test poses dilemmas and opportunities. *Lancet*, 380(9847): 1045–1046.

AVERT. 2013. HIV and AIDS in Zambia. http://www.avert.org/aids-zambia.htm.

AVERT. 2013a. HIV and AIDS in South Africa. http://www.avert.org/aidssouthafrica.htm.

AVERT. 2013b. Universal access to HIV treatment. http://www.avert.org/universal-access-hiv-treatment.htm.

Balabanova, Dina, Anne Mills, Lesong Conteh, Baktygul Akkazieva, Hailom Banteyerga, Umakant Dash, ... Martin McKee. 2013. Good health at low cost 25 years on: Lessons for the future of health systems strengthening. *Lancet*, 381(9883): 2118–2133.

Baral, S.D., T. Poteat, S. Strömdahl, A.L. Wirtz, T.E. Guadamuz and C. Beyrer. 2013. Worldwide burden of HIV in transgender women: A systematic review and meta-analysis. *Lancet Infectious Diseases*, 13(3): 214–222.

Bellan, Steve, Kathryn J. Fiorella, Dessalegn Y. Melesse, Wayne M. Getz, Brian G. Williams and Jonathan Dushoff. 2013. Extra-couple HIV transmission in sub-Saharan Africa: A mathematical modelling study of survey data. *Lancet*, 381(9877): 1561–1569.

Bhargava, A., D.T. Jamison, L.J. Lau and C.J.L. Murray. 2001. Modeling the effects of health on economic growth. *Journal of Health Economics*, 20(2001): 423–440.

Bhattarai, A., A.S. Ali, S.P. Kachur, A. Mårtensson, A.K. Abbas, R. Khatib, A.W. Al-Mafazy... A. Björkman. 2007. Impact of artemisinin-based combination therapy and insecticide-treated nets on malaria burden in Zanzibar. *PLoS Med*, 4(11): e309.

Bhutta, Zulfiqar A., Jai K. Das, Neff Walker, Arjumand Rizvi, Harry Campbell, Igor Rudan and Robert E. Black. 2013. Childhood pneumonia and diarrhea

2: Interventions to address deaths from childhood pneumonia and diarrhea equitably: What works and at what cost? *Lancet*, 381: 1417–1429.

Bloom, D., D. Canning and J. Sevilla. 2004. The effect of health on economic growth: A production function approach. *World Development*, 32(1): 1–13.

Bloomberg. 2012. Anti-AIDS pill out of sex-worker reach in push for cure. http://www.bloomberg.com/news/2012-07-15/anti-aids-pill-out-of-sex-worker-reach-in-push-for-cure.html.

Boehme, C.C., M.P. Nicol, P. Nabeta, J.S. Michael, E. Gotuzzo, R. Tahirli, M.T. Gler, ... D. Alland, ... Perkins. 2011. Feasibility, diagnostic accuracy, and effectiveness of decentralised use of the Xpert MTB/RIF test for diagnosis of tuberculosis and multidrug resistance: A multicentre implementation study. *Lancet*, 377(9776): 1495–1505.

Bpharm, Murtada Sesay, Charles Gilks and Marco Vitoìria and WHO. 2006. *Guidelines on co-trimoxazole prophylaxis for HIV-related infections among children, adolescents and adults in resource-limited settings: Recommendations for a public health approach*. Geneva: WHO.

Branson, B.M. 2003. Point of care rapid test for HIV antibodies. *The Journal of Laboratory Medicine*, 27(7/8): 288–299.

Breman, Joel G., Anne Mills, Robert W. Snow, Jo-Ann Mulligan, Christian Lengeler, Kamini Mendis... Ogobara K. Doumbo. 2006. Conquering Malaria. In Dean T. Jamison, Joel G. Breman, Anthony R. Measham, George Alleyne, Mariam Claeson, David B. Evans, Prabhat Jha, Anne Mills and Philip Musgrove, eds., *Disease control priorities in developing countries* (pp. 413–432). Washington, DC: World Bank.

Brown, V., Issak M. Abdir, M. Rossi, P. Barboza and A. Paugam. 1998. Epidemic of malaria in north-eastern Kenya. *Lancet*, 352(9137): 1356–1357.

Carneiro, Ilona, Lucy Smith, Amanda Ross, Arantxa Roca-Feltrer, Brian Greenwood, Joanna Armstrong Schellenberg, Thomas Smith and David Schellenberg. 2010. Intermittent preventive treatment for malaria in infants: A decision-support tool for Sub-Saharan Africa. *Bulletin of the World Health Organization*, 88: 807–814.

Carter, Richard and Kamini N. Mendis. 2002. Evolutionary and historical aspects of the burden of malaria. *Clinical Microbiological Review*, 15(4): 564–594.

Choi, H.W., J.G. Breman, S.M. Teutsch, S. Liu, A.W. Hightower and J.D. Sexton. 1995. The effectiveness of insecticide-impregnated bed nets in reducing cases of malaria infection: A meta-analysis of published results. *American Journal of Tropical Medicine and Hygiene*, 52(5): 377–382.

Chowdhury, A.M., F. Karim, S.K. Sarkar, R.A. Cash and A. Bhuiya. 1997. The status of ORT (oral rehydration therapy) in Bangladesh: How widely is it used? *Health Policy Plan*, 12(1): 58–66.

Churchyard, Gavin J. and Lois J. Eldred. 2008. The 3I's satellite symposium: Reducing the risk of tuberculosis in HIV-infected individuals, 4th South African AIDS conference, 31 March, Durban, South Africa. *The Southern African Journal of HIV Medicine*, Summer 2008.

Cohen, D.A., Shin-Y. Wu and T.A. Farley. 2005. Cost-effective allocation of government funds to prevent HIV infection. *Health Affairs*, 24(4): 915–926.

Corbett, Elizabeth L., Catherine J. Watt, Neff Walker, Dermot Maher, Brian G. Williams, Mario C. Raviglione and Christopher Dye. 2003. The growing burden of tuberculosis: global trends and interactions with the HIV epidemic. *Archives of Internal Medicine*, 163(9): 1009–1021.

Currie, C.S.M., B.G. Williams, Russell C.H. Cheng and C. Dye. 2003. Tuberculosis epidemics driven by HIV: Is prevention better than cure? *AIDS*, 17: 2501–2508.

Currie, C.S.M., K. Floyd, B.G. Williams and C. Dye. 2005. Affordability and cost-effectiveness of strategies to control tuberculosis in countries with high HIV prevalence. *BMC Public Health*, 5(1): 130.

Diacon, Andreas H., Rodney Dawson, Florian von Groote-Bidlingmaier, Gregory Symons, Amour Venter, Peter R. Donald, Christo van Niekerk...Melvin K. Spigelman. 2012. 14-day bactericidal activity of PA-824, bedaquiline, pyrazinamide, and moxifloxacin combinations: A randomised trial. *Lancet*, 380(9846): 986–993.

Doucleff, Michaleen. 2012. Global Fund moves to discontinue project subsidizing malaria drugs. *National Public Radio*, 16 November 2012. http://www.npr.org/blogs/health/2012/11/15/165231445/global-fund-moves-to-discontinue-project-subsidizing-malaria-drugs.

Dowling, J.M. and C.F. Yap. 2013. *Happiness and poverty in developing countries: A global perspective*. New York: Palgrave Macmillan.

Dye, C. and Katherine Floyd. 2006. Tuberculosis. In Dean T. Jamison, Joel G. Breman, Anthony R. Measham, George Alleyne, Mariam Claeson, David B. Evans, Prabhat Jha, Anne Mills and Philip Musgrove, eds., *Disease control priorities in developing countries* (pp. 289–310). Washington, DC: World Bank.

Dye, C., K. Lönnroth, E. Jaramillo, B.G. Williams and M. Raviglione. 2009. Trends in tuberculosis incidence and their determinants in 134 countries. *Bulletin of World Health Organization*, 87: 683–691.

Easterlin, Richard A. 1996. *Growth triumphant: The twenty-first century in historical perspective*. Ann Arbor, MI: University of Michigan Press.

Easterlin, Richard A. and Laura Angelescu. 2012. Modern economic growth: Cross-sectional and time series evidence. In Kenneth C. Land, ed., *Handbook of social indicators and quality of life research* (pp.113–136). New York and London: Springer.

Economist. 8, Sept 2012. Bad blood. http://www.economist.com/node/21562241

Ettehad, Dena, H. Simon Schaaf, James A. Seddon, Graham S. Cooke and Nathan Ford. 2012. Treatment outcomes for children with multidrug-resistant tuberculosis: A systematic review and meta-analysis. *The Lancet Infectious Diseases*, 12(6): 449–456.

Fairall, Lara, Max O. Bachmann, Carl Lombard, Venessa Timmerman, Kerry Uebel, Merrick Zwarenstein...Eric Bateman. 2012. Task shifting of antiretroviral treatment from doctors to primary-care nurses in South Africa (STRETCH): A pragmatic, parallel, cluster-randomized trial. *Lancet*, 380(9845): 889–898.

Fauveau, V., F.J. Henry, A. Briend, M. Yunus and J. Chakraborty. 1992. Persistent diarrhea as a cause of childhood mortality in rural Bangladesh. *Acta Paediatrica Supplement*, 381: 12–14.

Fischer, Walker C.L., L. Lamberti, L. Adair, R.L. Guerrant, A.G. Lescano, R. Martorell,...Robert E. Black. 2012. Does childhood diarrhea influence cognition beyond the diarrhea-stunting pathway? *PLoS ONE*, 7(10): e47908. doi: 10.1371/journal.pone.0047908.

Fox News. 2012. Researchers to test monthly vaginal ring for HIV prevention. http://www.foxnews.com/health/2012/07/25/researchers-to-test-monthly-vaginal-ring-for-hiv-prevention/#ixzz24svSAvJY.

Garrett-Jones, C. 1964. The Human blood index of malaria vectors in relation to epidemiological assessment. *Bulletin of World Health Organization*, 30: 241–261.

Gilks, C.F., S. Crowley, R. Ekpini, S. Gove, J. Perriens, Y. Souteyrand, D. Sutherland, M. Vitoria, T. Guerma and K. De Cock. 2006. The WHO public-health approach to antiretroviral treatment against HIV in resource-limited settings. *Lancet*, 368(9534): 505–510.

Gleick, Peter. 2002. *Dirty-water: Estimated deaths from water-related diseases 2000–2020*. Oakland, CA: Pacific Institute for Studies in Development, Environment, and Security.

Global Enteric Multicenter Study (GEMS). 2013. GEMS Factsheet. University of Maryland, School of Medicine. http://medschool.umaryland.edu/GEMS/

Golub, Jonathan E., Jacquie Astemborski, Mohammed Ahmed, Wendy Cronin, Shruti H. Mehta, Gregory D. Kirk, David Vlahov and Richard E. Chaisson. 2008. Long-term effectiveness of diagnosing and treating latent tuberculosis infection in a cohort of HIV-infected and at risk injection drug users. *Journal of Acquired Immune Deficiency Syndromes*, 49(5): 532–537.

Goodluck, Ebele Jonathan and Jens Stoltenberg. 2013. A tipping point for change: Saving millions of additional lives in 2013 and beyond. *Lancet*, 381(9864): 350–352.

Government of India. 2013. *Health and family welfare statistics in India*. India: Statistics Division, Ministry of Health and Family Welfare, Government of India.

Guardian. 12 August 2011. South Africa's maternal mortality rate increases fourfold. http://www.theguardian.com/global-development/2011/aug/12/south-africa-maternal-mortality-health.

Halstead, S.B., Julia A. Walsh, Kenneth S. Warren and Rockefeller Foundation, eds. 1985. *Good health at low cost: Proceedings of a conference held at the Bellagio conference center, Bellagio, Italy, 29 April–3 May 1985*. New York: The Rockefeller Foundation.

Harries, A.D., Dermot Maher and Stephen Graham. 2004. *TB/HIV: A clinical manual*. Geneva: WHO. http://www.who.int/tb/publications/who_htm_tb_2004_329/en/index.html.

Harries, A. D., Rony Zachariah, Elizabeth L. Corbett, Stephen D. Lawn, Ezio T. Santos-Filho, Rhehab Chimzizi, ... Kevin M De Cock. 2010. The HIV-associated tuberculosis epidemic—when will we act? *Lancet*, 375(9729): 1906–1919.

Harvard School of Public Health News. 2012. New test for tuberculosis could improve treatment, prevent deaths in Southern Africa. http://www.hsph.harvard.edu/news/press-releases/tuberculosis-test-improve-treatment-southern-africa/.

Heritage Foundation. 2013. http://www.heritage.org/index/

Heymann, S.J. 1993. Modeling the efficacy of prophylactic and curative for preventing the spread of tuberculosis in Africa. *Transactions of the Royal Society of Medical Hygiene*, 87(4): 406–411.

Hitt, Emma. 2010. Artemisinin-based treatment effective for malaria in African children. Paper presented at American Society of Tropical Medicine and Hygiene (ASTMH) 59th Annual Meeting, 4 November 2010. http://www.medscape.com/viewarticle/732115.

Howard, Andrea A. and Wafaa M. El-Sadr. 2010. Integration of tuberculosis and HIV services in Sub-Saharan Africa: Lessons learned. *Clinical Infectious Diseases*, 50(S3): S238–S244.

Human Rights Watch. 2011. South Africa: Failing maternity care. http://www.hrw.org/news/2011/08/08/south-africa-failing-maternity-care.

Hutton, G., K. Wyss and Y. N'Diekhor. 2003. Prioritization of prevention activities to combat the spread of HIV/AIDS in resource-constrained settings: A cost-effectiveness analysis from Chad, Central Africa. *International Journal of Health Planning and Management*, 18(2): 117–136.

IRIN Humanitarian News and Analysis. 2012. Health: Spending your way out of TB infection. http://www.irinnews.org/report/94889/health-spending-your-way-out-of-tb-infection.

Jamison, Dean T., Joel G. Breman, Anthony R. Measham, George Alleyne, Mariam Claeson, David B. Evans, Prabhat Jha, Anne Mills and Philip Musgrove. 2006. *Disease control priorities in developing countries.* Washington, DC: World Bank.

Jamison, D.T., L.J. Lau and J. Wang. 2005. Health's contribution to economic growth in an environment of partially endogenous technical progress. In G. Lopez-Casasnovas, B. Rivera and L. Currais, eds., *Health and economic growth: Findings and policy implications* (pp. 67–91). Cambridge, MA: MIT Press.

Kar, K. and R. Chambers. 2008. Handbook on community-led total sanitation. London: UK. Plan and Institute of Development Studies, University of Sussex. http://www.communityledtotalsanitation.org/resource/handbook-community-led-total-sanitation.

Keusch, Gerald T., Olivier Fontaine, Alok Bhargava, Cynthia Boschi-Pinto, A. Zulfiqar, Eduardo Gotuzzo Bhutta, Eduardo Gotuzzo,... Ramanan Laxminarayan. 2006. Diarrheal disease. In Dean T. Jamison, Joel G. Breman, Anthony R. Measham, George Alleyne, Mariam Claeson, David B. Evans, Prabhat Jha, Anne Mills and Philip Musgrove, eds., *Disease control priorities in developing countries* (pp. 371–388). Washington, DC: World Bank.

Khan, J.A, Saira Khowaja, Faisal S Khan, Fahad Qazi, Ismat Lotia, Ali Habib,... Salmaan Keshavjee. 2012. Engaging the private sector to increase tuberculosis case detection: an impact evaluation study. *Lancet Infectious Diseases*, 12(8): 608–616. http://www.thelancet.com/journalslaninf/article/PIIS1473-3099(12)70116-0/fulltext.

Kirwan, Daniela E. and Robert H. Gilman. 2013. Same-day diagnosis and treatment of tuberculosis. *The Lancet Infectious Diseases*, 13(2): 102–104.

Knowledge Ecology International. 2011. BRICS Health ministers' meeting – Beijing declaration. http://keionline.org/node/1183.

Kotloff, Karen L., James P. Nataro, William C. Blackwelder, Dilruba Nasrin, Tamer H. Farag, Sandra Panchalingam... Myron M. Levine. 1999. Global burden of shigella infections: Implications for vaccine development and implementation of control strategies. *Bulletin of the World Health Organization*, 77: 651–666.

Kotloff, Karen L., James P. Nataro, William C. Blackwelder, Dilruba Nasrin, Tamer H. Farag, Sandra Panchalingam, ... Myron M. Levine. 2013. Burden and aetiology of diarrheal disease in infants and young children in developing countries (the Global Enteric Multicenter Study, GEMS): A prospective, case-control study. *Lancet,* 382: 209–22.

Lamberti L., C.F. Walker, A. Noiman, C. Victora and R. Black. 2011. Breast-feeding and the risk for diarrhea morbidity and mortality. *BioMed Central Public Health,* 11(3): S15.

Lawn, S.D. and G. Churchyard. 2009. Epidemiology of HIV-associated tuberculosis. *Current Opinion in HIV and AIDS,* 4(4): 325–333.

Levine, Ruth and The What Works Working Group, with Molly Kinder. 2004. *Millions saved, proven successes in global health, preventing diarrheal deaths in Egypt,* Chapter 7. Washington, DC: Center for Global Development.

Lienhardt, C., M. Espinal, M. Pai, D. Maher and M.C. Raviglione. 2011. What research is needed to stop TB? Introducing the TB research movement. *PLoS Med,* 8(11): e1001135.

Lopez, Alan D., Colin D. Mathers, Majid Ezzati, Dean T. Jamison and Christopher J.L. Murray, eds. 2006. *Global burden of disease and risk factors.* New York: Oxford University Press; Washington, DC: World Bank.

Lozano, R., H. Wang, K.J. Foreman, J.K. Rajaratnam, M. Naghavi, J.R. Marcus, L. Dwyer-Lindgren, ... C.J. Murray. 2011. Progress towards millennium development goals 4 and 5 on maternal and child mortality: An updated systematic analysis. *Lancet,* 378(9797): 1139–1165. doi: 10.1016/S0140-6736(11)61337-8.

Lutalo, Ibrahim M., Gisela Schneider, Marcia R. Weaver, Jessica H. Oyugi, Lydia Mpanga Sebuyira, Richard Kaye, Frank Lule, Elizabeth Namagala, W. Michael Scheld, Keith P.W.J. McAdam and Merle A. Sande. 2009. Training needs assessment for clinicians at antiretroviral therapy clinics: Evidence from a national survey in Uganda. *Human Resources for Health,* 7: 76. http://www.human-resources-health.com/content/7/1/76.

Mallal, S.A., M. John, C.B. Moore, I.R. James and E.J. McKinnon. 2000. Contribution of nucleoside analogue reverse transcriptase inhibitors to subcutaneous fat wasting in patients with HIV infection. *AIDS,* 14(10): 1309–1316.

McKee, Martin, Anne Mills and Rockefeller Foundation, eds. 2011. *Good health at low cost: 25 years on; what makes a successful health care system.* New York: Rockefeller Foundation.

Menzies, Nicholas A., Ted Cohen, Hsien-Ho Lin, Megan Murray and Joshua A. Salomon. 2012. Population health impact and cost-effectiveness of tuberculosis diagnosis with Xpert MTB/RIF: A dynamic simulation and economic evaluation. *PLoS Med,* 9(11): e1001347.

Mullins, James. 2012. China registers success with TB–diabetes screening initiative. *Lancet,* 380(9842): 635–636.

Munos, M.K., C.L.F. Walker and R.E. Black. 2010. The effect of rotavirus vaccine on diarrhea mortality. *International Journal of Epidemiol,* 39(1): i56–i62.

Murray, Christopher J.L. and Joshua A. Salomon. 1998. Modeling the impact of global tuberculosis control strategies. *Proceedings of the National Academy of Science of the United States of America,* 95(23): 13881–13886.

Najera, J.A. and M. Zain. 2002. *Malaria vector control: Decision making criteria and procedures for judicious use of insecticides.* Communicable disease control, prevention and eradication WHO Pesticide Evaluation Scheme (WHOPES). WHO/CDS/WHOPES/2002.5. Geneva: WHO.

Nathanson, Eva, Paul Nunn, Mukund Uplekar, Katherine Floyd, Ernesto Jaramillo, Knut Lönnroth...Mario Raviglione. 2010. MDR tuberculosis – critical steps for prevention and control. *New England Journal of Medicine*, 363: 1050–1058.

Niehaus, Mark D., Sean R. Moore, Peter D. Patrick, Lori L. Derr, Breyette Lorntz, Aldo A. Lima and Richard L. Guerrant. 2002. Early childhood diarrhea is associated with diminished cognitive functions 4 to 7 years later in children in a Northeast Brazilian Shantytown. *American Journal of Tropical Medicine and Hygiene*, 66(5): 590–593.

Offianan A. Toure, Louis K. Penali, Jean-Didier Yapi, Berenger A. Ako, Walamtchin Toure, Kali Djerea, Genevieve O. Gomez and Oyewole Makaila. 2009. A comparative, randomized clinical trial of artemisinin /naphtoquine twice daily one day *versus* artemether/lumefantrine six doses regimen in children and adults with uncomplicated falciparum malaria in Côte d'Ivoire. *Malaria Journal*, 8: 148. doi: 10.1186/1475-2875-8-148.

Office of the United States Global AIDS Coordinator. 2012. *PEPFAR blueprint: Creating an AIDS-free generation*. Washington, DC: U.S. Dept. of State.

Palella, F.J., Jr., M. Deloria-Knoll, J.S. Chmiel, A.C. Moorman, K.C. Wood, A.E. Greenberg, S.D. Holmberg and HIV outpatient study investigators. 2003. Survival benefit of initiating antiretroviral therapy in HIV-infected persons in different CD4+ cell strata. *Annals of Internal Medicine*, 138(8): 620–626.

Public Health Watch. 2006. *Civil society perspectives on TB policy in Bangladesh, Brazil, Nigeria, Tanzania, and Thailand*. New York: Open Society Institute.

Puthanakit T., V. Saphonn, J. Ananworanich, P. Kosalaraksa, R. Hansudewechakul, U. Vibol...PREDICT Study Group. 2012. Early versus deferred antiretroviral therapy for children older than 1 year infected with HIV (PREDICT): A multicenter randomized open-label trial. *The Lancet Infectious Diseases*, 12(12): 933–941.

Raviglione, Mario C., Lee B. Reichman and Earl S. Hershfield. 2006. *Reichman and Hershfield's tuberculosis: A comprehensive, international approach*. 3rd edition. New York: Informa Healthcare.

Reuters. 2012. Study raises hope for new drugs for resistant TB. http://www.reuters.com/article/2012/07/23/us-aids-tb-drugs-idUSBRE86M1AT20120723.

Reynolds, H.W., B. Janowitz, R. Homan and L. Johnson. 2004. Cost-effectiveness of two interventions to avert HIV-positive births. Poster presentation at the XV International AIDS Conference, Bangkok, Thailand, 11–16 July.

Safe Blood for Africa Foundation. 2013. http://www.safebloodforafrica.org/.

Schackman, B.R., K.A. Gebo, R.P. Walensky, E. Losina, T. Muccio, P.E. Sax,...K.A. Freedberg. 2006. The lifetime cost of current human immunodeficiency virus care in the United States. *Med Care*, 44(11): 990–997.

ScienceNOW. 2013. Early treatment may have cured baby's HIV infection. http://news.sciencemag.org/biology/2013/03/early-treatment-may-have-cured-babys-hiv-infection.

Sidibé, Michael, Peter Piot and Mark Dybul. 2012. AIDS is not over. *Lancet*, 380(9859): 2058–2060.

Snow, R.W. and J.A. Omumbo. 2006. Malaria. In D.T. Jamison, R.G. Feachem, M.W. Makgoba, et al. eds., *Disease and Mortality in Sub-Saharan Africa*. (pp. 1–36)

2nd edition. Washington, DC: World Bank. http://www.ncbi.nlm.nih.gov/books/NBK2286/.

Solow, Robert M. 1956. A contribution to the theory of economic growth. *Quarterly Journal of Economics*, 70(1): 65–94.

Stop TB Partnership. 2013. Tuberculosis vaccines – A strategic blueprint for the next decade. http://www.stoptb.org/wg/new_vaccines/.

Sweat, M.D., K.R. O'Reilly, G.P. Schmid, J. Denison and I. de Zoysa. 2004. Cost-effectiveness of nevirapine to prevent mother-to-child HIV transmission in eight African countries. *AIDS*, 18(12): 1661–1671.

The Lancet. 2012. Global burden of disease study 2010. http://www.thelancet.com/themed/global-burden-of-disease.

UNAIDS. 2006. *2006 Report on the global AIDS Epidemic*. Geneva: UNAIDS.

UNAIDS. 2010. *Global Report: UNAIDS report on the global AIDS epidemic 2010*. Geneva: UNAIDS.

UNAIDS. 2012. *Global report: UNAIDS report on the global AIDS epidemic 2012*. Geneva: UNAIDS.

UNAIDS 2012a. Press release of Inaugural Global Scientific Strategy Towards an HIV Cure launched ahead of the XIX International AIDS Conference in Washington, DC. http://www.unaids.org/en/resources/presscentre/pressreleaseandstatementarchive/2012/july/20120719prhivcure/.

UNAIDS. 2012b. *The roadmap: Shared responsibility and global solidarity for AIDS, TB and malaria in Africa*. Geneva: UNAIDS. http://www.inaids.org,en/media.unaids/contentassets/documents/document/2012/20120715_TheRoadmap_AU_en.pdf

UNAIDS Feature Story. 2011. First meeting of BRICS health ministers brings new leadership to global health. http://www.unaids.org/en/resources/presscentre/featurestories/2011/july/20110711bchinabrics/.

UNDP. 2013. *Human development report*. New York: Oxford University Press.

UNICEF. 2013. *The state of world's children*. New York: Oxford University Press for UNICEF.

UNICEF website. 2013a. Zambia. http://www.unicef.org/zambia/.

Vanderbilt University Medical Center. 2009. TB vaccine gets its groove back. http://www.sciencedaily.com/releases/2009/05/090519152446.htm.

Victoria, C.G, J. Bryce, O. Fontaine and R. Monasch. 2000. Reducing deaths from diarrhea through oral rehydration therapy. *Bulletin of the World Health Organization*, 78(10): 1246–1255.

Voice of America. 2009. Treating TB, HIV together decreases mortality. http://www.voanews.com/articleprintview/401302.html.

Walker, Fischer C.L., Igor Rudan, Li Liu, Harish Nair, Evropi Theodoratou, Zulfiqar A. Bhutta,... Robert E. Black. 2013. Childhood pneumonia and diarrhea: Global burden of childhood pneumonia and diarrhea. *Lancet*, 381: 1405–1416.

WHO. 1998. The importance of simple/rapid assays in HIV testing. *Weekly Epidemiological Record*, 42: 321–328.

WHO. 2008. *Community involvement in tuberculosis and prevention. Towards partnership for health: Guiding principles and recommendations based on a WHO review*. Geneva: WHO.

WHO. 2008a. *Guidelines for the programmatic management of drug-resistant tuberculosis: Emergency update 2008*. Geneva: WHO.

WHO. 2009. *WHO report 2009. Global tuberculosis control: Epidemiology, strategy and financing*. Geneva: WHO.

WHO. 2010. *Guidelines for treatment of tuberculosis*. 4th edition. Geneva: WHO.

WHO. 2010a. WHO tuberculosis fact sheet no. 104, November 2010.

WHO. 2011. *Global tuberculosis control 2011*. Geneva: WHO.

WHO. 2011a. *World malaria report 2011*. Geneva: WHO.

WHO. 2012. *World malaria report 2012*. Geneva: WHO.

WHO. 2013. Global health observatory data repository. http://apps.who.int/gho/data/view.main.

WHO. 2013a. *Global update on HIV treatment: Results, impacts and opportunities*. Geneva: WHO.

WHO. 2013b. WHO tuberculosis fact sheet no. 104, October 2013.

WHO. 2013c. *Global tuberculosis report*. Geneva: WHO.

WHO. 2013d. *Countdown to 2015: Global tuberculosis report 2013: Supplement*. Geneva: WHO.

WHO. 2013e. *World malaria report 2013*. Geneva: WHO.

WHO. 2013f. Diarrheal disease fact sheet. April 2013.

WHO. 2014. TB diagnostics and laboratory strengthening. http://www.who.int/tb/laboratory/en/.

WHO. 2014a. Green Light Committee Initiative. http://www.who.int/tb/challenges/mdr/greenlightcommittee/en/.

WHO, UNICEF, UNDP and the World Bank. 2011. *Roll back malaria progress & impact series: A decade of partnership and results*. Number 7. Sept 2011. http://www.rollbackmalaria.org/multimedia/progress-and-impact-series.html.

Williams, B.G and C. Dye. 2003. Antiretroviral drugs for tuberculosis control in the era of HIV/AIDS. *Science*, 301(5639): 1535–1537.

World Bank. 2005. *The Africa action plan – Planning for the "Decade of Africa"*. Washington, DC: World Bank. http://go.worldbank.org/E2QNH2SY91.

World Bank. 2010. *Southern Africa: HIV/AIDS and Tuberculosis plan of action, 2010–2011 for Botswana, Lesotho, Namibia, South Africa, and Swaziland*. Washington, DC: World Bank.

World Bank. 2013. *World development indicators*. http://data.worldbank.org/data-catalog/world-development-indicators.

World Bank. 2013a. *Global monitoring report*. Washington, DC: World Bank.

Yakob, Laith, Rebecca Dunning and Guiyun Yan. 2011. Indoor residual spray and insecticide-treated bed nets for malaria control: Theoretical synergisms and antagonisms. *Journal of the Royal Society Interface*, 8(59): 799–806.

Index